Sunset

Alaska
TRAVEL GUIDE

By the Editors of Sunset Books
and Sunset Magazine

Sunset Publishing Corporation ■ **Menlo Park, California**

Research & Text:
Barbara J. Braasch

Coordinating Editor:
Suzanne Normand Mathison

Design:
Cynthia Hanson
Kathy Avanzino Barone

Maps:
Ted Martine
John Parsons, Eureka Cartography

Illustrations:
Sally Shimizu

Calligraphy:
Donna Prime

Our thanks . . .

to the many people and organizations who assisted in the preparation of this travel guide. Special appreciation goes to Don Dickey and members of the Alaska State Division of Tourism, Bob Giersdorf, Gert Seekins, and the Nome Convention and Visitors Bureau for their valuable assistance. And for her careful editing of the manuscript, we thank Fran Feldman.

Cover: Spectacular Mendenhall Glacier outside of Juneau attracts hikers, backpackers, and campers. Its easy accessibility has earned it the title of Alaska's "drive-in" glacier. Photographed by Ed Cooper.

Photographers

Sally Bishop: 34 bottom, 39 top. **Ben Davidson:** 26 top, 34 top. **Robert Ewell:** 83 top. **Exploration Cruise Lines:** 10 bottom, 94. **Mark E. Gibson:** 10 top, 15 bottom, 78 left, 83 bottom, 102. **Jeff Gnass:** 2, 63 top, 75. **George Herben:** 42 bottom. **Dave G. Houser:** 31, 39 bottom. **R. E. Johnson/ AlaskaPhoto:** 23. **G. C. Kelley:** 18. **Mark Kelley/AlaskaPhoto:** 15 top. **William S. Kimball:** 91 bottom. **Pat & Tom Lee/AlaskaPhoto:** 7. **Rick McIntyre:** 58 bottom. **Lael Morgan:** 91 top. **Don Normark:** 26 bottom. **Willis Peterson:** 58 top. **Ron Sanford:** 42 top, 47, 50 top, 63 bottom, 99. **Nancy Simmerman:** 50 bottom, 78 right, 86. **Harald Sund:** 55.

Editor, Sunset Books:
    Elizabeth L. Hogan

Second Printing January 1994 (Updated)

Embellished with relics from the area's colorful past, historic buildings at Crow Creek Mine, near Anchorage, invite visitors to stop, shop, and pan for gold.

Contents

Special Features

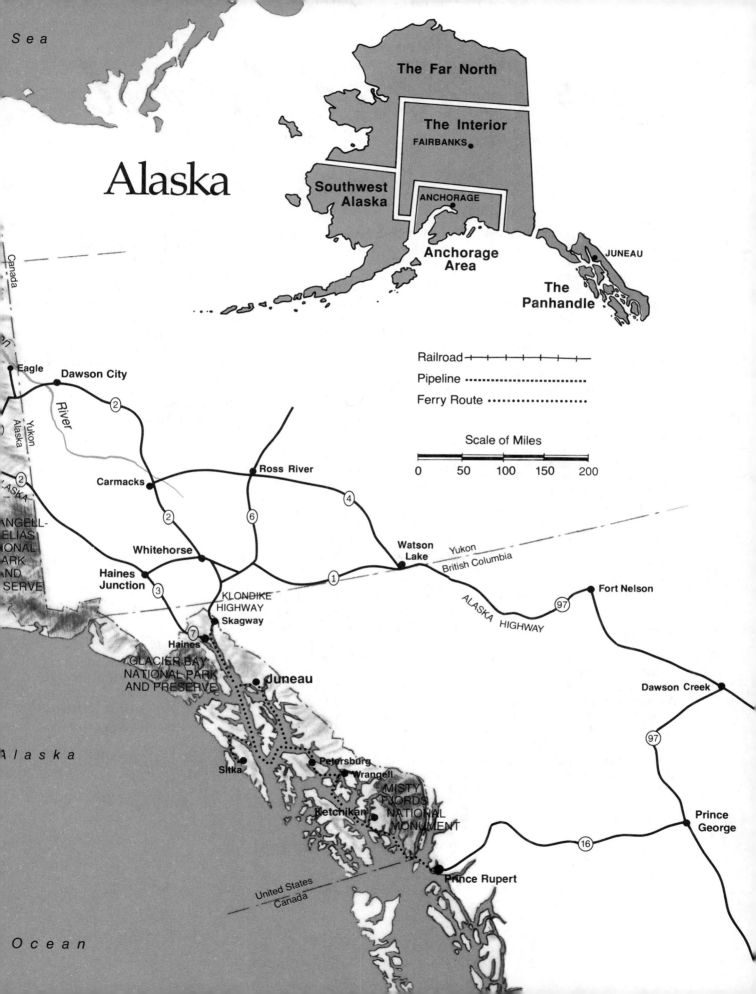

Sea

Alaska

The Far North

The Interior

FAIRBANKS

Southwest
Alaska

ANCHORAGE

Anchorage
Area

JUNEAU

The
Panhandle

Railroad
Pipeline
Ferry Route

Scale of Miles

0   50   100   150   200

Canada

Eagle

Dawson City

River

②

Yukon
Alaska

②

Ross River

Carmacks

④

ANGELL-
ELIAS
IONAL
ARK
ND
SERVE

②

⑥

Whitehorse

Watson
Lake

Yukon

British Columbia

Haines
Junction

③

①

Fort Nelson

⑨⑦

ALASKA HIGHWAY

KLONDIKE
HIGHWAY

Skagway

⑦

Haines

Dawson Creek

GLACIER BAY
NATIONAL PARK
AND PRESERVE

Juneau

⑨⑦

Alaska

Sitka

Petersburg

Wrangell

MISTY
FJORDS
NATIONAL
MONUMENT

Prince
George

Ketchikan

⑯

United States
Canada

Prince Rupert

Ocean

A Great Land

A land of superlatives, Alaska boasts some very impressive statistics. Among its scenic splendors are 19 mountains higher than 14,000 feet, including Mt. McKinley, the highest peak in North America; 5,000 glaciers, one larger than all of Switzerland; 3 million freshwater lakes, one qualifying as America's second largest; 3,000 rivers, 10 of them longer than 300 miles; and a farming community where it's not uncommon to find cabbages weighing more than 70 pounds.

The 49th state extends across four time zones and 586,400 square miles. It's roughly as large as California, Arizona, Nevada, Oregon, and Washington put together, with land enough left over to form South Carolina.

Yet this vast area is thinly populated. Over half of the state's 570,000 residents live in one metropolitan area, Anchorage. Three-quarters of the remainder reside in half a dozen other cities. The rest are scattered around the state in some 250 tiny villages.

Native people

The earliest Alaskans probably migrated from Asia over a then-existing land bridge between Asia and North America. Some early settlers may have sledded over the frozen Bering Strait or paddled skin boats across the water in summertime.

Today's native population numbers about 64,000, divided into three major groups—Eskimos, Indians, and Aleuts. Eskimos, the largest group, cluster around the Arctic coastline.

Indians migrated into the Interior, following the caribou; though the Athabascans still live in the Interior, the Tlingit, Haida, and Tsimshian Indians eventually settled in southeastern Alaska. Adept seafarers, the Aleuts settled along the islands named for them and in other areas of southwestern Alaska.

Geography on a large scale

Alaska comes from the Aleut word *Alyeska*, meaning "great land." And great it is. No matter where or how you travel, the geological book of nature is there to read.

Mountains sculptured during the Ice Age still wear frozen caps, and glacial fingers poke down into deep canyons. The Panhandle's famed Inside Passage was carved out as a result of ice cutting and melting. Meandering rivers—the Yukon, Kuskokwim, Copper, Taku, Stikine, and others—sliced tremendous valleys along their courses. Mountain ranges loom as colossal, ragged wrinkles on the landscape.

At times, molten magma breaks out from beneath the earth's crust, forming volcanoes and spewing wide lava flows. The 1964 earthquake, North America's most powerful, rearranged the landscape for hundreds of miles.

Geographically, you'll discover five distinct Alaskas: the Panhandle (southeastern Alaska), the Gulf area, the western region, the Interior, and the Arctic. Separated from British Columbia by the crest of the Coastal Range, the Panhandle dangles down from Haines and Skagway in the north to Ketchikan in the south.

The Gulf area includes the region northwest of Haines, around the Gulf of Alaska. Western Alaska takes in the Alaska Peninsula and the Aleutian and Pribilof islands.

Interior Alaska, located mainly north of the Alaska Range, sprawls from the Canadian border to the Bering Sea, taking in the headwaters of the Copper, Nenana, Kuskokwim, and Tanana rivers. Arctic Alaska, which reaches north of the Yukon River and west to the shores of the Arctic Ocean, encompasses endless tundra, treeless hills, and the jagged Brooks Range south of the Arctic slope.

Mighty Mt. McKinley, North America's highest peak, first looms into view at Stony Hill, 61 miles from the entrance on the road into Denali National Park and Preserve; free shuttle buses carry passengers deep into the wilderness.

A Frontier Vacationland

Civilization has encroached slowly on Alaska's vast expanse. Because towns are few and far between, much of the large state retains its pristine quality.

Visitors to the 49th state may feel as if they're stepping back in history about a hundred years. The terrain and climate have preserved some of the frontier conditions that have long since vanished in the Lower 48. In some places, you'll still find boardwalks, buildings with false fronts, and unpaved streets.

Though Anchorage appears to be quite cosmopolitan, its modern veneer is actually very thin. And Fairbanks may remind you of a sprawling boomtown, grown too rapidly for careful planning.

Today, oil and gas exploration in the Arctic and around Cook Inlet has replaced the more glamorous gold and fur trade of the late 19th century. The fishing and lumber industries still hold their own, despite an ongoing battle between advocates of commercial development and people who would prefer to see the state preserved as one large wilderness park.

Tourism, Alaska's third largest industry, was once the chief force working to preserve native culture: the natives maintained their customs because they could sell their products to tourists. Now, however, there's renewed interest among the natives in their traditions. Native languages and ancient crafts are being taught by village elders to younger generations. Authentic dances, songs, games, carvings, and blanket tosses are very much in evidence.

Tourists today can savor Alaska's past while remaining firmly rooted in the present. You no longer have to be a rugged pioneer to visit. Modern transportation puts nearly all of this vast land within reach, and accommodations and dining can be as good as anywhere else in the United States. Everyone—from avid angler and backpacker to art collector and photographer—finds something of interest.

Among the state's greatest assets are the Alaskan residents. Friendly and outgoing, they tend to work as hard as they play. You'll find them courteous, helpful, and eager to talk about their land.

Something-for-everyone weather

Because of the state's vast size, ocean currents, and mountain ranges, variety rules Alaska's weather. Contrary to popular belief, it's not a land of endless ice and snow.

You'll discover grand rain forests, hillsides carpeted with wildflowers, rich agricultural areas, and even a desert in the Arctic.

Generally, the coastal and Aleutian areas have a wet maritime climate, punctuated by surprisingly clear days. Mountains wear heavy snow capes year-round. Warm summers and cold winters with low precipitation mark the Interior. In the Arctic, precipitation is also low; winters are windy and cold, and summers range from cool to warm and sunny.

When to visit Alaska

Alaska's diversity makes it possible to plan a vacation at any time of year, but the most popular tourist season is from May to mid-October. Cruise ships navigate the waters of the Inside Passage only during this period; ferries operate all year but increase the number of sailings in summer.

Late spring and early autumn are ideal travel months in most of the state; normally, the weather is favorable and the scenery especially colorful.

June, July, and August are peak tourist months. Lodges, restaurants, and sightseeing excursions swing into full operation. It's usually warm (hot in the Interior), with short nights and long summer days.

State symbols

Alaska has one of the most simple and prophetic flags in the Union—eight gold stars (the Big Dipper and the North Star) on a field of blue.

The beautiful flag was designed by Benny Benson, who as a seventh-grade schoolboy won a contest in 1926 to design a flag for what was then a territory.

Explaining his design, Benson said, "The blue field is for the Alaska sky and the forget-me-not, an Alaska flower. The North Star is for the future state of Alaska, the most northerly of the Union. The dipper is for the Great Bear—symbolizing strength."

When Alaska became a state in 1959, Benson led a parade to celebrate the event, proudly carrying the flag he had designed 33 years earlier.

The forget-me-not, mentioned in Benson's speech, is now the state flower. The little blue flowers are found throughout much of the state.

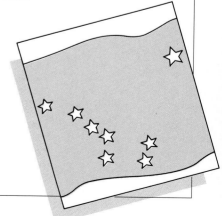

An Alaskan vocabulary

As colorful as Alaska's history is the language of the state's residents. Some words are holdovers from frontier days; others are freshly coined to fit this unique land.

Alaskan horses: Folklore calls the summer pests, mosquitoes, "large enough to saddle."

Black gold: Vast oil discoveries. North Slope oil flows through the state in an 800-mile-long pipeline.

Breakup: Spring event when ice-choked rivers start flowing. The main celebration is at Nenana.

Bush: Almost anywhere in Alaska that is not accessible by road.

Bush pilots: Alaska's "bird men." They fly to all of the state's remote spots and provide one of the best ways to get into the backcountry.

Cabin fever: Frustration resulting from the inability to get outside the house because of inclement weather, ended only by summer's long daylight hours.

Cache: Miniature cabin built on stilts to keep food out of the reach of animals. It resembles a tall doghouse.

Calve: The breaking off of great pieces of tidewater glaciers, producing large ice floes.

Cheechako: Newcomer to Alaska.

Chill factor: Wind's effect on temperature (30°F with a wind speed of 30 mph results in an actual temperature of −2°F).

Eskimo ice cream: Seal oil that has been whipped to a creamy texture and is mixed with berries and snow.

Hooligan: Smelt caught by dip netting. These tiny, oily fish are also called candlefish because they can be burned for light.

Iceworms: Tiny black worms that live on glaciers. Allergic to sunlight, they emerge from the ice only when skies are overcast. The town of Cordova honors the little creatures with a lively festival in February.

Kuspuk: Eskimo woman's parka. The back is cut loosely enough to carry a baby piggyback.

Lower 48: Continental United States.

Midnight sun: When the sun remains above the horizon at midnight.

Muktuk: Raw or cooked whale blubber and skin, considered a delicacy by Eskimos.

No-see-ums: Swarms of tiny gnats, most annoying in the bush or near still water.

Oogruk: Eskimo name for the bearded seal, whose skin is valued for the slippers called mukluks.

Outside: Anywhere other than Alaska.

Pay dirt: Mining term referring to placer gold.

Permafrost: Permanently frozen ground, usually covered by a thin layer of tundra.

Potlatch: Indian social celebration where the host provides lavish gifts for his guests to demonstrate his wealth. The occasion is often combined with a memorial totemraising.

Sitka slippers: Rubber boots worn by residents of damp southeastern Alaska.

Sourdough: One who has weathered a winter. The term originated with the prospectors, who took along their sourdough starter when they headed north.

Squaw candy: Strips of smoked salmon or other types of fish dried long enough to be chewy. It's enjoyed by natives and tourists alike.

Sundogs: Bright spots on the sun caused by tiny ice crystals.

Taiga: Russian word meaning "land of little sticks," an apt name for the spruce forests in the Interior.

Termination dust: First snowfall, marking the beginning of winter.

Ulu: Eskimo woman's fan-shaped knife used for skinning meat. Sold in stores throughout the state, ulus make useful souvenirs.

Umiak: Traditional, skin-covered boat used by Aleuts and Eskimos. The light wooden frame makes it easy to pull over ice.

Milepost in busy downtown Anchorage gives the distance to major cities around the globe; sod-roofed visitor center provides information on local and state attractions.

Sitka's traditionally attired New Archangel Russian Dancers perform colorful Cossack numbers for visitors. Most performances take place inside the city's waterfront Centennial Building.

...a vacationland

For ski enthusiasts, dog sled fans, and snowshoe trekkers, an Alaska winter vacation fills the bill. Juneau, Fairbanks, and Arctic Valley offer schussable terrain, but Alyeska Resort, near Anchorage, is the state's premier ski area. Four double chairlifts and one quad whisk visitors up vertical slopes for panoramic views of scenic Turnagain Arm and helicopters ferry skiers to remote mountains.

Sled dog races, ski competitions, and winter festivals, especially Anchorage's Fur Rendezvous in February, provide additional attractions for wintertime visitors.

What to wear, where

Casual, informal attire is the rule throughout Alaska. The emphasis is on sportswear, though you'll probably want one dressier outfit if you plan to visit night spots in the larger cities.

In summer, take a raincoat and a light wrap for cool evenings; you'll want lightweight clothing for visits to places in the warm Interior region. Comfortable walking shoes are a must for any area. Colorful parkas are provided on Arctic excursions (boots in Barrow, if needed), but you may want to bring along your own gloves and warm hat.

Cruise ship passengers will probably want to pack suits and ties or cocktail dresses for special shipboard occasions. Deck shoes aid in walking slippery gangways.

Wintertime visitors should be prepared for snow and cold temperatures.

A sampling of accommodations

From deluxe hotel rooms and cozy bed-and-breakfast inns to wilderness lodges, campgrounds, and youth hostels, Alaska provides a wide variety of lodging choices.

Hotels. Hotels in Alaska range from modern high rises to old-time cabins and roadhouses dating from dog-mushing days. Most of the latter have been modernized with electric lights and indoor plumbing.

Since tour operators book a great deal of the lodging space along popular sightseeing routes during summer, you'll have to reserve well in advance if you're traveling independently. Facilities engaged on tours, though usually comfortable, generally do not qualify as deluxe, except for several hotels in Anchorage.

Backcountry lodges. Wilderness lodges and fishing camps, tucked away in spots generally accessible only by air or water, allow visitors to sample Alaska's backcountry. Rooms are comfortable but rustic; food, served family style, may be included in the room rate. (For a listing of such lodges, see page 110.)

Camping. Alaska might well be considered one large campground. The 16-million-acre Tongass National Forest in southeastern Alaska and the 6-million-acre Chugach National Forest in southcentral Alaska offer extensive recreational possibilities. (See page 64 for camping bargains in those areas.)

Not surprisingly, Alaska's state park system is America's largest. It boasts almost 1½ million acres of land and water, and offers extensive hiking and backpacking possibilities, vantage points from which to photograph moose and grizzly bears, and crystal-clear waters for sailing among jewel-like islands.

Most public campgrounds in the state provide picnic tables and shelters, outdoor toilets, well water, fire pits, and firewood. (You may want to carry your own water and stove for emergency use.) Campgrounds usually designate trailer and recreational vehicle spaces; hookups may not be available in public campgrounds, however.

Privately owned campgrounds operate in or near most towns and along major routes. Many sites offer individual hookups, as well as rest rooms and showers. (For a listing of both public and private campgrounds, see page 116.)

In undeveloped areas, permits may be required to build camp fires; check locally for information. Always be sure your fire is out before you leave— Alaska's foliage and organic duff (ground cover) are very flammable, and fire-fighting equipment may be several hundred miles away.

Mosquitos, deer flies, and a small biting fly (called no-see-um because you usually don't) are the camper's worst enemies during summer. If you camp in swampy areas or get into brush, protect yourself with a head covering, gloves, and insect repellent. Tents with built-in insect netting are a wise choice for Alaska.

For information on reservations and fees for public campgrounds, contact Alaska State Parks (P.O. Box 107001, Anchorage, AK 99510; 907/762-2261) or Alaska Public Lands Information Center (605 W. Fourth Avenue, #105, Anchorage, AK 99501; 907/271-2737).

A good investment is what you could call the $7.2 million paid to Russia by the United States for Alaska's 365,000,000 acres. The cost comes out to about $12.30 per square mile.

Basic information

Though geographically Alaska stretches across four time zones, legislators in 1983 established two zones for the entire state: Alaska Time (one hour behind Pacific Time) for the majority of the state and Hawaii-Aleutian Time (2 hours later) for the westernmost Aleutian Islands. Canada's Yukon is on Pacific Time.

All Alaska uses the 907 area code. The Yukon area code is 403.

Planning Your Trip

Because of Alaska's diversity and great size, you'll want to plan your trip carefully so you'll have enough time for touring the areas you want to see and for the activities that interest you.

If you have only a week or two, you might want to consider a package tour that includes attractions in several regions and visits to such major cities as Juneau, Anchorage, and Fairbanks.

If you're adventurous and want to spend time discovering Alaska at your own pace, it's easy to travel independently with sufficient advance planning. Start by writing to local convention and visitors bureaus and chambers of commerce for the regions you want to visit (addresses are on page 119). Alaska Division of Tourism, Dept. 201, P.O. Box 110801, Juneau, AK 99811, is a valuable source of free information. See page 108 for more ideas.

Plan your trip in advance and make early reservations; six months ahead is not too early for peak travel periods.

Getting There

Depending on your time, you can travel to Alaska by air, sea, rail, highway, or a combination of routes. Each method has its advantages.

Air travel is the fastest and most frequent mode of transportation; cruise ship or ferry is leisurely and relaxing. Highway touring, either in your own car, by camper, or by motorcoach, allows for frequent stops and the opportunity to see more of the scenery.

Many tour companies combine these travel options, often adding a stretch on the Alaska Railroad or White Pass & Yukon. Some tours are escorted; others simply offer transportation and accommodations for visitors who wish to travel more independently. Your travel agent can tell you what's available and compare tour prices, itineraries, and optional excursions.

By air. You can fly nonstop to Anchorage, Juneau, and Ketchikan from Seattle and other cities in the Lower 48.

Connecting flights from Seattle reach all Inside Passage cities, while the state's northern reaches are accessible through Anchorage and Fairbanks.

Anchorage is Alaska's main air destination from points around the globe. Passengers on major carriers flying the Polar Route between Europe and the Far East, or the Great Circle Route between the East Coast and the Far East, may include stopovers in the state's largest city.

Air travel within Alaska is usually by jet or turboprop. Air taxis and charter services provide easy access to small communities and more remote locales, using propeller-driven craft that land on wheels, floats, or skis.

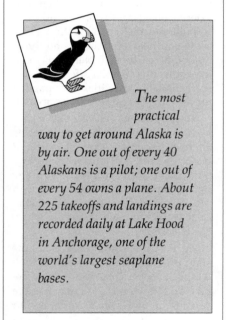

The most practical way to get around Alaska is by air. One out of every 40 Alaskans is a pilot; one out of every 54 owns a plane. About 225 takeoffs and landings are recorded daily at Lake Hood in Anchorage, one of the world's largest seaplane bases.

By sea. Possibilities in water travel range from small private boats to convenient state ferries and luxurious cruise ships that head up the Inside Passage.

The Alaska Marine Highway System (P.O. Box 25535, Juneau, AK 99802; phone 800/642-0066) provides low-cost, year-round ferry service to southeast, southcentral, and southwest Alaska.

Ferries carry both passengers and vehicles; larger vessels have food, lounges, and cabins.

In summer, Inside Passage runs have Forest Service interpreters aboard to provide information on attractions, history, and culture. Local communities often offer tours to coincide with ferry stopovers.

British Columbia Ferries (1112 Fort Street, Victoria, B.C., Canada, V8V4V2) provides service between Port Hardy on Vancouver Island and Prince Rupert, B.C., where Alaska-bound passengers can connect with state ferries.

During the summer, cruise ships sail the Inside Passage through the Panhandle. Many cruise into Glacier Bay National Park and Preserve, while others cross the Gulf of Alaska to visit ports in the southcentral area. On some ships passengers cruise round-trip; other ships offer one-way transportation that allows visitors to explore other parts of the state on their own.

By rail. There is no direct rail service between Alaska and the Lower 48, but the White Pass & Yukon Railroad connects Skagway with British Columbia. The Alaska Railroad runs 350 miles between Fairbanks and Anchorage (with a stop at Denali National Park and Preserve). They also offer service from Anchorage to Whittier (to connect with ships) and to Seward.

By motor coach. During the summer, regularly scheduled motor coach lines and independent motor coaches provide service from Seattle to Alaska and the Yukon. Other service is available from Haines and Skagway to Whitehorse, Tok, Dawson City, Fairbanks, Valdez, and Anchorage.

Driving the highways

All of Alaska's highways have names as well as numbers. Often, just the name is used when referring to the route. The primary road system con-

Festivals & festivities

The toss of a blanket, the crack of a whip, the tug of an ear, the slap of a snowshoe—Alaska's lively festivals celebrate rich Indian, Aleut, and Eskimo traditions combined with touches of its gold-mining past. More recent residents have contributed midnight baseball games, loggers' competitions, and art shows.

Alaska visitors will find something on the calendar every month; one of the most colorful celebrations is the Fur Rendezvous in February.

The following listing includes only a sampling of the entertainment available. Other events are mentioned throughout the book. Since dates change, it's advisable to check with the chambers of commerce in individual towns. For a complete listing, write to the Alaska State Division of Tourism, P.O. Box E-101, Juneau, AK 99811.

January

Russian Christmas, Kodiak. One of the most colorful celebrations of Alaska's past.

Dalton Trail Sled Dog Race, Haines.

Seward Polar Bear Festival, Seward.

Annual Winter Carnival, Willow (east of Anchorage). Last weekend in January, first weekend in February.

February

Iceworm Festival, Cordova. Whimsical celebration of glacier worms.

Fur Rendezvous, Anchorage. Alaska's largest winter celebration, with sled dog races, fur auctions, Eskimo dances, blanket tossing, snowshoe baseball, and a parade.

Anchor Point Snow Rondi, Anchor Point (southwest of Anchorage).

Annual Yukon Quest International Sled Dog Race, Whitehorse, Yukon Territory, to Fairbanks.

March

Winter Carnivals, Chatanika, Mayo, and Carmacks, Yukon.

Annual Folk Fest, Ketchikan.

Ice Golf Classic, Nome.

Iditarod Trail Sled Dog Race, from Anchorage to Nome.

Ice Festival, Fairbanks.

April

Copper Day, Cordova. Held the second Saturday of the month.

Alaska Folk Festival, Juneau.

Annual Tok Trot, Tok.

Big Breakup, Nenana, late April or early May. Marks winter's end.

May

Little Norway Festival, Petersburg. Celebrates the first halibut boat landings, Armed Forces Day, and Norwegian Independence Day.

Kodiak Crab Festival, Kodiak.

Buffalo Wallow, Delta Junction.

Salmon Derbies, Petersburg, Ketchikan, Sitka, Haines, Valdez, and Wrangell.

June

Summer Music Festival, Sitka.

Tanana River Classic, Fairbanks.

Colony Days Celebration, Palmer.

Midnight Sun Hot Air Balloon Classic, Anchorage.

Logging Championships, all Alaska.

Halibut Derby, Valdez.

July

Fourth of July Celebrations, most towns. Parades and fireworks.

Moose Dropping Festival, Talkeetna.

World Eskimo-Indian Olympics, Fairbanks.

Yukon Gold-panning Championship, Dawson City.

August

Tanana Valley Fair, Fairbanks.

Discovery Days, Dawson City.

Alaska State Fair, Palmer. Includes more than 5,000 exhibits of agriculture and homemaking.

Cry of the Wild Ram, Kodiak. Drama of early Russian America.

Silver Salmon Derby, Seward.

September

Klondike International Outhouse Race, Dawson City.

State Rodeo, Anchorage.

Equinox Marathon, Fairbanks.

October

Alaska Day, state holiday.

Quyana Alaska Native Dance Festival, Anchorage.

November

Athabascan Fiddling Festival, Fairbanks.

Christmas Comes to Kenai, Kenai.

December

Christmas Tree Lighting Ceremony, Wrangell.

Christmas Fleet Parade, Kodiak.

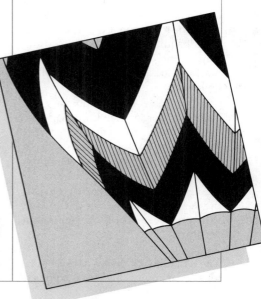

sists of these highways: Alaska, Tok Cutoff, Richardson, Glenn, George Parks (Anchorage-Fairbanks), Seward, Sterling, Klondike (connecting Skagway with Whitehorse), and Haines. All the roads are paved, with the exception of certain sections of the Haines Highway.

The three routes on which motorists can enter Alaska are the Haines, Klondike, and Alaska highways. For mile-by-mile information on facilities and attractions along all of Alaska's highways, pick up a copy of *The Milepost*, published by the Alaska Northwest Books, P.O. Box 3007. Bothell, WA 98041.

The Haines Highway. This 150-mile highway runs from Haines, where you disembark from an Inside Passage ferry, through a corner of the Yukon, and then back into Alaska to Haines Junction. Along its scenic wilderness route, it offers magnificent mountain views to delight the photographer.

Much of the road follows the old Dalton Trail to the Klondike, climbing steeply from coastal timber country to Chilkoot Pass and high meadows above the timberline. In autumn, winter, or early spring, be sure to ask about current highway conditions before leaving Haines.

Near Haines is a 2-mile detour that takes you through the old Chilkat Indian village of Klukwan. Scattered along the road are a few places to stay. At Mosquito Lake, 27 miles from Haines, there's a public campground, reached via a 2½-mile side road off the highway.

Forty miles from Haines is the Canadian border (see Canadian customs, at right). You'll find no facilities or accommodations at the border. In the Yukon, the road becomes Yukon Highway 4.

At Haines Junction, turn left to join the Alaska Highway or right to visit Whitehorse, capital of the Yukon Territory.

The Klondike Highway. This 99-mile-long year-round highway connects Skagway with the Alaska Highway just south of Whitehorse. With its spectacular scenery, this relatively new road (built in 1978) is a favorite with travelers heading for Dawson City.

Good views of the White Pass & Yukon Railroad tracks are available at several points en route. In summer, the train carries passengers to the top of the pass, where they may elect to proceed on to Whitehorse by bus.

Looking for igloos? You'll have to go to Canada to find one made from ice and snow. Alaska's Eskimos made their igloos from sod, driftwood, and whalebone.

Canadian customs is at Fraser, 22 miles north of Skagway. Carcross, a former stopping place for miners on their way to the Klondike, is the largest community along the road. At Lake Bennett you can enjoy a picnic or fish (with a license) for trout, pike, grayling, or whitefish.

The Alaska Highway. Driving the Alaska Highway is not quite the adventure it once was. Even though it's not a hazardous journey anymore, it is a long one—1,475 miles between Dawson Creek, B.C., and Fairbanks, Alaska. The route passes through mountains, over mighty rivers, through long stretches of virgin wilderness, and past fishing streams and trading posts.

The drive can easily be made in 5 to 7 days each way. If you allow 3 or 4 weeks for the round-trip, though, you'll have more time to enjoy the scenery. The highway remains open all year, except for times when the weather forces a temporary closing.

You'll find little traffic except in the height of summer.

Mid-July to mid-September is probably the most pleasant time to drive the highway; there's less traffic, the days are cooler, and the hillsides are ablaze with the golden splashes of aspen and birch. You might run into seasonal rains and perhaps some snow in the higher elevations. Late in the season, be sure to carry tire chains, a tow rope, and a shovel.

Winter travel on the Alaska Highway is not recommended, and travel during the spring thaw (March and April) should be avoided. Washouts, detours, and road construction are common obstacles.

Canadian customs. When you cross the border into Canada, you'll go through customs. Citizens of the U.S. do not need to show passports, but will need to prove citizenship by passport or original or certified copy of birth certificate. Proof of residence (driver's license or voter registration card) may also be required. Naturalized citizens should carry naturalization papers; resident aliens must have their Alien Registration Receipt Card.

Minors under 18 years of age who are traveling without their parents will also need a notarized letter of consent signed by both parents or guardians for travel into Canada.

Necessary vehicle permits are issued at the border at no charge. Bring your driver's license and vehicle registration form. Be sure you have the required Canadian vehicle liability form from your insurance company.

The following duty-free articles may be taken into Canada: personal belongings (including radios, cameras, and reasonable food supplies), sporting goods (such as hunting rifles), and up to 50 cigars, 1 carton of cigarettes, 14 ounces of tobacco, and 40 ounces of alcoholic beverages per adult.

Take all the medical prescriptions you will need for your stay. You will be unable to get refills.

Returning U.S. residents may bring back merchandise up to the value of $400 free of U.S. duty and tax, provided they have remained in Canada for at least 48 hours.

Floatplane lands at a backcountry lake to pick up an angler. Alaska's bush pilots provide air taxi service to remote fishing and hunting sites all over the state.

Ferry passengers welcome the sun on a trip along southeastern Alaska's marine highway. Picturesque Panhandle ports can be reached only by water or air.

Traveling Inside Alaska

From early reliance on travel by boat or dog team, the transportation picture within Alaska has changed rapidly over the past several decades, thanks to the airplane and automobile.

Construction of the Alaska Highway from Dawson Creek, B.C., to Fairbanks in 1942–43 gave Alaska a land link with the continental road system and stimulated additional road building inside the state.

Bus lines and railroad routes now lace Alaska, and the state ferry system in the Panhandle provides a "marine highway" to ports in that part of the state. Jet airplanes serve the principal cities and towns, and competent bush pilots—Alaska's "bird men"—reach even the most remote villages. In almost any town in the state, you can charter a plane to fly you practically anywhere.

Airlines. Regularly scheduled air service connects cities, towns, and villages throughout the state. Jet flights from Seattle reach southeast cities; Arctic destinations are accessed through Fairbanks and Anchorage. Anchorage also serves as a hub for air travel to remote southwest communities.

Buses. Though buses operate within the state, there's no direct service from the Lower 48 unless you join a motor coach tour. Scheduled service is available between Skagway and Whitehorse, Whitehorse and Dawson City, Whitehorse and Fairbanks, Anchorage and Fairbanks via Denali, Anchorage and Seward, Anchorage and Valdez, Valdez and Haines via Columbia Glacier, and Anchorage and Haines.

Rail. Train travel plays an important role for tourists visiting the state. At a time when the popularity of passenger rail travel is on the decline in the Lower 48, it holds a special attraction in Alaska.

The Alaska Railroad connects Seward, Whittier, Anchorage, Denali National Park, and Fairbanks. (For more information, see below.)

Rentals. Motorists can rent cars, campers, or motor homes at various locations throughout the state. Sometimes, you can rent in one city and "drop off" in another. The supply of rental vehicles is limited, however, so be sure to reserve in advance during peak summer months. Reservations may be made through travel agents or through local representatives of all major national firms.

Riding the rails

"Rail travel the way it used to be"—that might well be the motto of the Alaska Railroad, a 470-mile system stretching from Seward on the Kenai Peninsula to Fairbanks in the Interior.

Alaska visitors have several opportunities to ride the trains: a shuttle train is one part of the transportation network linking the port city of Whittier with Anchorage, and, in summer, passenger service is offered three times a week between Seward and Anchorage.

The most popular train, however, is the Denali Express, which runs between Anchorage, Denali National Park and Preserve, and Fairbanks. It takes about 7 hours to make the run between Anchorage and the park; Denali is about 4 hours from Fairbanks.

Northbound trains depart Anchorage at 9 A.M., make a 15-minute stop at the park station around 3:45 P.M., and arrive in Fairbanks at 8 P.M. Southbound, the train leaves Fairbanks at 10:30 A.M., arrives at the park at 2:15 P.M., and pulls into Anchorage at 9:30 P.M. With a round-trip ticket, you can spend one or more days at Denali and then hop aboard another train for the return trip. (Lodging reservations are a *must* at Denali.)

The Alaska Railroad offers both a snack bar and a dining car; a domed lounge car (with open seating) gives passengers a chance to view some of the state's most spectacular scenery. The domed car is so popular that conductors urge passengers to limit their viewing time so that everyone has a chance to enjoy the experience.

Tour Alaska and Westours attach private observation cars to the train and offer comfortable reserved seating in domed lounge cars. Attendants describe points of interest along the route. Both companies provide their own dining rooms and chefs.

For more information on the Alaska Railroad, write to P.O. Box 107500, Anchorage, AK 99510. Check with your travel agent for reservations in the private cars. Both the railroad and the tour operators offer a variety of package itineraries.

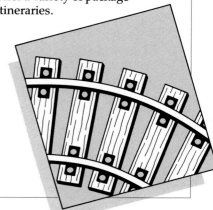

History credits no one person as the discoverer of Alaska. Before the arrival of Europeans, there had been Eskimos, Aleuts, and Indians living in some areas for 10,000 years or more.

The proximity of the Seward Peninsula to the Siberian coastline (about 56 miles) suggests that Alaska's first inhabitants came from Asia. Anthropologists believe that between 12,000 and 25,000 years ago, Mongolian tribes migrated from Asia to America by way of the Bering Strait, an isthmus that at one time connected the two continents.

Early explorers

Alaska's rich historical background contains some very exotic overtones. In the early part of the 18th century, Czar Peter the Great of Russia, who had a keen interest in geography, hired Danish Captain Vitus Bering to explore the waters to the east of Russia. Bering "discovered" the Alaska mainland in 1741.

Captain James Cook visited Alaska's coastline in 1778, and other explorers investigated Alaskan waters, leaving British, French, and Spanish names on their charts.

By 1787, the Russians had a 3-year-old settlement at Kodiak. Fur trade—especially of the highly prized sea otter—was vigorously exploited by the Russians throughout Alaska.

In 1804, Alexander Baranof, governor of Russian America, moved his headquarters from Kodiak to Sitka. This doughty little man ruled Alaska for 20 years.

At the time of the California gold rush in 1849, Sitka was known as the "Paris of the Pacific" because it displayed all the pomp and gaiety of a European court.

When Alaska became a possession of the United States, Sitka's prominence faded, and the capital of Alaska was moved to Juneau in 1906.

An American possession

Secretary of State William H. Seward negotiated the purchase of Alaska by the United States in 1867. Most Americans called the $7,200,000 purchase "Seward's Folly" and nicknamed the territory "Seward's Icebox."

Discovery of gold in the Cassiar country of British Columbia touched off a stampede from 1874 to 1876. Most of the gold seekers went in by way of Wrangell and the Stikine River.

In 1880, gold was found near what is now Juneau. Soon, the great Treadwell and Alaska-Juneau mines were flourishing. Miners would work there for a grubstake before moving on to prospect in other areas, hoping for another big strike. It was the fabulous Klondike strike of 1896–98 that finally focused world attention on the land to the north.

Between 1900 and 1910 a series of gold discoveries from Nome to Fairbanks lured still more gold seekers to Alaska. Transportation was by sea and riverboat in summer and by dog team in winter.

Alaska becomes a state

Alaska was made a U.S. territory in 1912. Its first legislature met a year later. Though Judge James Wickersham introduced the first statehood bill in Congress in 1916, it was not until January 3, 1959, that Alaska finally achieved statehood.

Meanwhile, in 1935, farmers from the drought-stricken Midwest set-

tled the Matanuska Valley, introducing agriculture into Alaska.

In 1942, during World War II, the Alaska Highway through Canada's Yukon Territory was built.

Some protection for the land claims of Alaskan natives was written into the Statehood Act. Later developments and demands for land by public and private sources caused the natives to give more thought to their ancestral hunting grounds. In 1971, the Alaska Native Claims Settlement Act gave Eskimos, Aleuts, and Indians claim to 44 million acres of land, in addition to providing more than $900 million in payments to all natives.

Recent developments

Construction began on the Trans-Alaska pipeline in 1974; oil has been flowing from Prudhoe Bay to the port city of Valdez since 1977. (For more pipeline information, see page 72.)

With the passage of the Alaska National Interest Lands Conservation Act in 1980, almost 40 percent of Alaska's land has been set aside for preservation in the form of parks, preserves, monuments, and wilderness (see page 116).

Team 12 hits the turn at the North American Sled Dog Championship Races in Fairbanks.
This exciting event shows off the dog's training and the musher's expertise.

An Outdoor Paradise

Alaska's stunning outdoors is the primary reason to visit the state. For the hiker and nature lover, a vast world of imposing scenery beckons. Uncrowded slopes await skiers; tempting lakes, streams, and rivers lure anglers; and wilderness hunters have a choice of big game—moose, mountain sheep, or the famous Alaska brown, grizzly, or black bear.

Wildlife watching

If nightlife is not Alaska's trump card, wildlife certainly is. An alert visitor can often sight moose, bear, mountain sheep, and caribou from the road. You may also see a bright-eyed fox, an occasional coyote or wolf, or perhaps a tiny pika, marmot, Dall sheep, beaver, otter, marten, mink, or hare. Visitors to the Arctic are likely to see walruses, seals, polar bears, foxes, caribou, mountain sheep, whales, otters, and many smaller animals.

Denali National Park and Preserve is Alaska's most substantial game refuge. For descriptions of the park and the wildlife there, see page 59.

Most of Alaska's summer bird life consists of migratory waterfowl that come north to nest. Bird-watchers can also find eagles and many kinds of hawks, jays, owls, spruce hens, and grouse, in addition to the ptarmigan—the state bird—and many common small birds.

The Pribilof Islands offer some of the world's greatest bird-watching opportunities. Here even an amateur ornithologist becomes an avid tracker. Here, too, you'll see the world's largest fur seal herd.

Fishing & hunting

Backcountry fishing and hunting lodges are scattered throughout the state. Most virgin wilderness areas are reached only by small plane.

Fishing. Alaska Department of Fish and Game (Public Communications Department, P.O. Box 25526, Juneau, AK 99802) provides free pamphlets on hunting and sportfishing seasons, bag and creel limits, licenses and tag fees, and tips on the best angling areas. Regional maps are available for $4 a set for areas between Anchorage and Seward, Cooper Landing and Soldotna, and Kenai/Soldotna and Homer.

Anglers find salmon in all coastal waters and in most streams. In southeastern Alaska, the ocean waters host all five Alaskan species of salmon: chum, king (also called tyce or chinook), pink, red, and silver. Starting in April, salmon show in increasing numbers. Kings range from about 10 to over 40 pounds; silver are smaller but noted for their spectacular acrobatics when hooked. Other ocean fish, including red snapper, ling cod, halibut, and rockfish, also lure anglers.

Freshwater streams and lakes and saltwater estuaries offer cutthroat, rainbow, and Dolly Varden trout, as well as Arctic char, grayling, and pike.

Central and southwestern Alaska are generally regarded as the best freshwater sportfishing regions in the state. Dedicated fly fishers will want to sample the streams that feed Iliamna Lake and Katmai National Park and Preserve on the Alaska Peninsula.

The best fishing spots for highway travelers are the freshwater lakes and streams on the Kenai Peninsula and the marine waters of Cook Inlet and Prince William Sound.

In the far northern areas, the exotic sheefish, a cross between tarpon and whitefish, are abundant. Migrating in large numbers up major river systems, they provide challenging sport for anglers. Sheefish may be taken from May through September, though July is the peak fishing time.

Hunting. Copies of the state's hunting regulations are available from the Alaska Department of Fish and Game (see at left for the address). Hunters will need licenses and tags for big game animals (available at sporting goods stores or from the Alaska Department of Fish and Game's Licensing Division). A list of guides is available for $5 from the Dept. of Commerce & Economic Development, Div. of Occupational Licensing, Box 110806, Juneau, AK 99811.

Hiking & canoeing

A few minutes' hike from any road or town puts you into Alaska's wilderness regions. Unless you're an experienced backpacker, it's not advisable to go hiking alone.

Particularly popular hiking spots are found in Denali National Park and Preserve, Wrangell–St. Elias National Park and Preserve, Chugach State Park (a portion of the Iditarod Trail), and on the Kenai Peninsula.

Those who seek areas off the beaten path can test their skills in Wrangell–St. Elias, Katmai, or Glacier Bay national parks, or in the more remote Gates of the Arctic National Park.

For vacations involving unconventional travel into wilderness areas, visitors should select knowledgeable guides. If you want to travel by water, an outfitter will take you on a canoe, kayak, or raft trip on one of Alaska's thousands of rivers and lakes.

Skiing

Downhill skiing in Alaska centers around the city of Anchorage. At nearby Alyeska Resort and Ski Area, five chairlifts whisk you up to 2,800 vertical feet of scenic slopes. You can also try Anchorage's Hilltop Ski Area, Alpenglow at Artic Valley, Eaglecrest Ski Area in Juneau, and Cleary Summit in Fairbanks.

Nordic skiers have miles of groomed and lighted trails in Anchorage. Other convenient cross-country sites include Chugach State Park, Hatcher Pass Recreation Area, and Turnagain Pass. Near Fairbanks, you can ski at Chena Hot Springs. Or try the terrain at Tongass National Forest and Eaglecrest Ski Area in the Panhandle.

Many of Alaska's special crafts tell a story about life in the "Great Land." Gold nugget jewelry takes you back to the gold rush of 1898. The art of working with ivory and soapstone has been handed down over countless years. Delicate baskets, ornamental beading, and forbidding masks speak of an ancient heritage.

The state provides a bounty of natural treasures: furs, skins, and bones from its wild creatures; fresh, frozen, or canned seafood, including salmon and king crab; and a wealth of berries, preserved for take-home tasting.

One of the rarest gifts is an item made from *qiviut* (ki-vee-ute), the underwool of the musk ox. Every spring, musk oxen lose their soft underhair. After it's plucked from the animal, it's sent to a spinning mill, returning as yarn. Native villagers knit the qiviut into soft scarves, stoles, caps, tunics, and sweaters, each with its own distinctive pattern. Qiviut is a rare treasure—and you pay high prices for items made from it.

Wood carving has undergone a renaissance. Natives are again carving authentic totem poles, masks, panels, and screens. But beware: learn about totem designs or you may take home a cheap wood whittling. Authentic Alaskan native art usually carries a Silver Hand emblem, guaranteeing that the articles you buy are made in Alaska by Alaskan natives who are at least one-quarter Eskimo, Aleut, or Indian.

Museums and native art co-ops display the best craft selections. Regardless of where you shop, look around carefully before you buy.

Below is a listing of basic materials used by Alaskan craftspeople. You'll find good design examples throughout the state.

Basketry

Eskimo, Aleut, and Indian cultures each have distinctive baskets. Tlingit, Haida, and Tsimshian Indians make baskets from cedar and spruce bark and from spruce roots. Techniques differ: thin strips of cedar are peeled from the tree and woven; spruce must first be steamed and split into long fibers. For either wood, the tighter the weave and the more intricate the work, the more expensive the piece.

Athabascan Indians weave thin strips of birch bark into large, tough baskets used for cooking. The Aleuts use rye grass to form small intricately woven baskets.

In the Arctic, you may see a few examples of the baleen basket, made from the hard material that hangs from the upper jaw of the bowhead whale. These are museum pieces.

Beadwork

The craft of beadworking got its start in Alaska when European explorers started trading glass beads with the Indians. Before that time, beads were carved from willows or seeds.

Traditional beadwork was overlaid on leather; contemporary work is often done on a felt background. The most common designs, probably also inspired by the traders, include flowers, leaves, and berries.

Though some beadwork is available throughout Alaska, you'll find the most intricate examples in southeastern Alaska.

Skin, fur & bone

As a result of the rigors of severe weather and the scarcity of materials, Eskimos perfected the art of utilizing animal fur and skin for clothing. Today, however, parkas, mukluks, and gloves made from animal skins, once so common, are very difficult to find. Hats and coats, though less expensive than in the Lower 48, are still costly. Most furriers are found in Anchorage.

The artistic use of bone is another example of the native's waste-not ingenuity. Gigantic whalebones are used for making drying racks and skin boats; vertebrae form interesting mask designs, and discs may be used as bases for ivory carvings.

Clothing

The Eskimo woman's summer wrap is a colorful paisley parka, usually handmade. You can occasionally find one for sale in city stores or in shops in the Arctic.

One store in Anchorage has some distinctive parkas in a "California weight" that make excellent reminders of your northern visit.

Gold

Gold nugget jewelry is a popular Alaskan souvenir. Before you buy, look for a label guaranteeing that the nugget is genuine.

Gold nugget jewelry is found throughout Alaska. Prices are probably best in places such as Skagway, Dawson City, Fairbanks, and Nome. In Nome, you can pan for your own gold, though it's unlikely you'll find enough to fashion a gold piece.

Jade & coral

Jade, the state gem, is found in several locations north of the Arctic Circle. Two of the largest jade deposits are located near the Kobuk River and at Jade Mountain.

Though the stone comes in many colors—green, black, brown, red, yellow, and white—most of the articles sold in Alaska are made from beautiful clear green stones with black flecks.

Jade is seldom cut in Alaska. After mining, most of it goes to Japan where it's made into jewelry or cut for larger items and then returned to the state.

You'll see a number of jade items for sale, including clock faces, bookends, and tabletops. Jade is the state gem.

Alaskan coral, generally retrieved from the icy waters around Kodiak, is processed in Hawaii and returned to Alaska for gem setting. Much of the polished coral ripples and shimmers like tiger's eye.

Ivory

Though Eskimos traditionally carved ivory for implements and dolls, most of today's carving is intended for sale. Engraving, always done by hand in the past, is often done by power tools these days.

Generally, the ivory pieces you'll find in shops come from walrus teeth and tusks. Highly prized fossil ivory was taken from mastodon and ancient walrus unearthed from perpetually frozen ground.

Walrus may be taken only by Alaskan natives living along the coast of the Arctic and North Pacific oceans, though beach ivory can be kept by anyone. Native Alaskans, however, are the only ones who can create or sell ivory handicrafts.

As ivory becomes increasingly rare, prices go up. You'll find bracelets, pendants, earrings, and cribbage boards in many shops throughout Alaska. Some very fine ivory pieces are found in Ketchikan, Juneau, Sitka, and Skagway.

Nome has several stores with many unique pieces.

Billikens, smiling ivory figures with pointed heads, make popular souvenirs.

Masks

All of Alaska's natives used masks in their ceremonial dances and in medicine men's healing rites. And some Indian masks were used as aids in storytelling. Made from skin and wood, the masks represented animals or supernatural or legendary characters.

Eskimos still use masks when performing their dances; you'll see them at Kotzebue and Barrow. Most of today's mask-making takes place in western and southwestern Alaska.

Painting

Painting is a relative newcomer to the Alaskan scene. Natives working in this medium often paint stark and powerful scenes of life a century ago. Other artists find the overwhelming views a source of inspiration.

One artist makes detailed sketches of weeds, flowers, and berries; another works in ink from an octopus. Homer and nearby Halibut Cove are artists' colonies. Look for art also in Anchorage and Juneau.

Soapstone

Soapstone, oddly enough, is usually imported from outside Alaska and then crafted by natives. Smooth form and detail distinguish fine pieces.

Green serpentine, the most popular and easily shaped, is distrib-

uted by the government each summer to outlying village artists to be carved into salable pieces. Finely carved soapstone objects are sold in most arts and crafts stores.

Woodworking

Carved wooden totems, magnificent and renowned forms of Indian sculpture, tell stories using symbolic animals, birds, and fish.

In early times, animals represented certain families in a village. Heraldic totem poles identified owners of abodes and the social status of chiefs and heads of houses.

Other totems memorialized deceased chiefs or served as mortuary poles, honoring the dead. Or they commemorated a potlatch (social get-together).

Wooden masks represent totem animals or supernatural or legendary characters. At one time, masks were used in ceremonial dances and in healing rites.

If you look carefully, you may find carvings on instruments used for hunting, fishing, or cooking.

The best places to see fine examples of totem carving are in Ketchikan, Haines, Juneau, and Sitka.

The Panhandle

Alaska's Panhandle, a narrow lacework of islands and peninsulas that hangs like a ribbon from Alaska's southeastern corner, stretches 400 miles down the seacoast at the base of the towering Coastal Range. On the other side of the mountains lies Canada.

Huge, ice-age glaciers scraped and sculptured this land, carving deep canyons that lead to the sea. Remnants of these ice rivers cling to mountaintops and poke bluish white fingers down their sides.

Densely forested slopes drop sharply toward the shore. A few settlements, dwarfed by their vertical backdrops, cling to narrow strips of flat land two or three blocks wide and stretch out for miles. Juneau, dubbed "The Longest City in the World," extends along the shore for 40 miles; Ketchikan stretches for 20 miles. Skagway, the northernmost port town in the Panhandle, appears wedged among towering peaks.

Considered by many Alaska's most scenically beautiful region, the Panhandle is easy to visit—less than 2 hours by jet or 3 days by ferry or cruise ship from the Pacific Northwest.

Where to stay. Accommodations range from modern city hotels to rustic cabins on secluded bays. In some hotels you may feel you're paying a bit steeply for a room that wouldn't measure up to deluxe standards in the Lower 48. But, on the other hand, you can also reserve a cottage for the modest price of $20 a night (see page 64).

Climate. Warmed by ocean currents and shielded from the ocean by offshore islands, the Panhandle rarely suffers from extremes in temperature. Winter temperatures seldom drop below 10°F, and summer temperatures average between 60° and 70°.

You can expect rain any month of the year, usually daily from autumn to spring. Ketchikan boasts of an annual average rainfall of 13 feet; Juneau records 90 inches a year. Skagway, though, receives a moderate 27 inches of rainfall.

The Inside Passage

You can't travel through southeastern Alaska by car or motor coach, since no highways link its communities. Ships and planes provide the only means of transportation from city to city.

Alaska Airlines provides year-round service to the Panhandle; check with travel agents for other carriers. Jets fly to Ketchikan, Wrangell, Petersburg, Sitka, Juneau, and Yakutat, with summer service to Gustavus, gateway to Glacier Bay National Park and Preserve. Air taxis connect smaller communities.

The water route is the classic one, however. Ever since the Tlingit Indians hollowed out their first canoes centuries ago, the Inside Passage has been southeastern Alaska's chief highway. For over 200 years it was the main artery of commerce and exploration for both Russian traders and American explorers.

Now, for many adventurous visitors, the marine highway serves as an introduction to the state. Modern ferries and sleek cruise ships of all sizes ply the 1,000-mile sheltered waterway maze. All types of boats can be chartered in port cities.

Whether you travel by cruise liner or ferry, the southeastern corner of Alaska is best seen from the deck of a ship. An ever-changing panorama of cloud-shrouded islands, jagged mountains, spectacular fjords, and crevassed glaciers passes before you.

Wildlife is abundant. Small pods of killer whales surface occasionally, porpoises ride the pressure waves off the bow, and a variety of birds—including the rare bald eagle—soars gracefully overhead.

The towns in the Panhandle are among the oldest in the state. Some date from Indian days; others were settled by Russian traders; still others were born because of fishing, logging, or the search for gold. Artless in layout, the towns have streets that wander about like drunken miners. Buildings are wedged in where there is space.

Snow-capped Mt. Edgecumbe, an extinct volcano, acts as a backdrop for Sitka's harbor and skyline. Once a Russian fur-trading center, the city still contains many reminders of its past.

The Panhandle

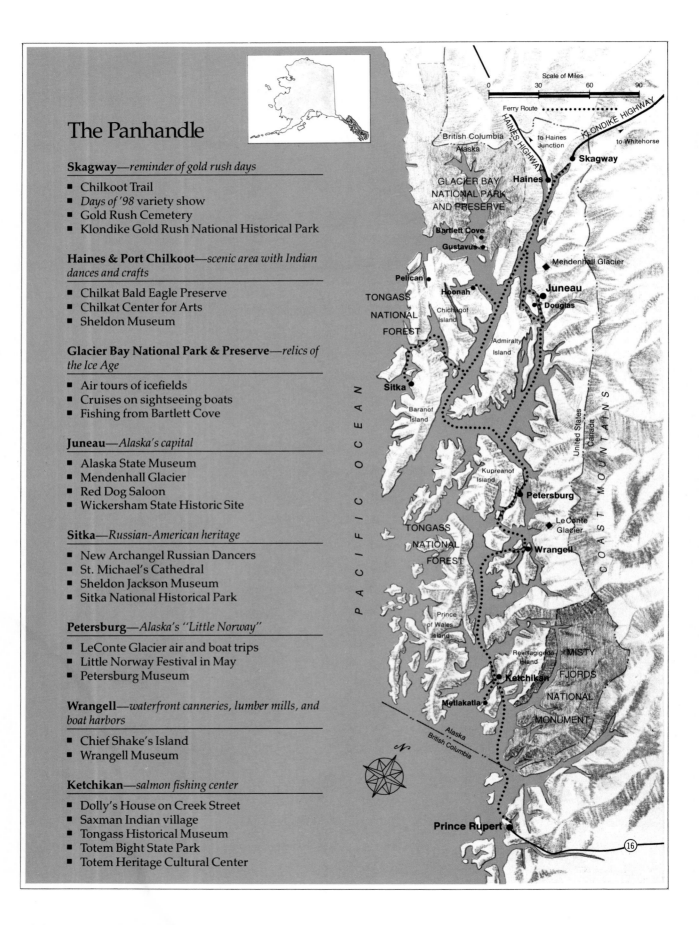

Skagway—*reminder of gold rush days*

- Chilkoot Trail
- *Days of '98* variety show
- Gold Rush Cemetery
- Klondike Gold Rush National Historical Park

Haines & Port Chilkoot—*scenic area with Indian dances and crafts*

- Chilkat Bald Eagle Preserve
- Chilkat Center for Arts
- Sheldon Museum

Glacier Bay National Park & Preserve—*relics of the Ice Age*

- Air tours of icefields
- Cruises on sightseeing boats
- Fishing from Bartlett Cove

Juneau—*Alaska's capital*

- Alaska State Museum
- Mendenhall Glacier
- Red Dog Saloon
- Wickersham State Historic Site

Sitka—*Russian-American heritage*

- New Archangel Russian Dancers
- St. Michael's Cathedral
- Sheldon Jackson Museum
- Sitka National Historical Park

Petersburg—*Alaska's "Little Norway"*

- LeConte Glacier air and boat trips
- Little Norway Festival in May
- Petersburg Museum

Wrangell—*waterfront canneries, lumber mills, and boat harbors*

- Chief Shake's Island
- Wrangell Museum

Ketchikan—*salmon fishing center*

- Dolly's House on Creek Street
- Saxman Indian village
- Tongass Historical Museum
- Totem Bight State Park
- Totem Heritage Cultural Center

Ketchikan

Busy, bustling Ketchikan calls itself the gateway to Alaska. It is, indeed, often a visitor's first stop in Alaska.

Surrounded by water, the town on Revillagigedo Island appears to cling to the edge of a dark green velvet mantle flowing from the shoulders of 3,000-foot Deer Mountain just before it trails into the Tongass Narrows.

Much of the city's business district hangs suspended above water on pilings driven into the bottom of the narrows; many homes are perched on cliffs reached by wooden staircases or narrow, winding streets.

Its good fishing waters have earned Ketchikan another title—"Salmon Capital of the World." Many sportfishing enthusiasts come here to try their luck in these prime waters. On a boat tour of the waterfront you can see some of the town's fish-processing plants.

Another claim that you would think Ketchikan residents would try to soft-pedal is that it has the highest annual rainfall of anywhere in Alaska. Instead, residents stage a lottery to guess annual precipitation amounts and display a logo showing the Ketchikan Rainbird with an umbrella held high. When there is no rain, residents call themselves sun-shocked.

For many years, Ketchikan and Juneau vied for the title of Alaska's third largest city. Depending on where you were, you'd hear one or the other claim being supported. Today, with a population of 14,600, Ketchikan ranks fourth in the state.

Ships dock in the city's watery front yard. Amphibious aircraft land and take off from the waterfront like huge geese, providing an important transportation link with outlying villages and fishing camps. If you arrive at the airport across the narrows, your bus or taxi ride into town will include a short crossing on the local shuttle ferry.

Lodging ranges from the modern Westmark Cape Fox Lodge above town to the historic Ingersoll Hotel and includes several motor lodges and B&Bs.

Anglers usually head out to wilderness retreats like the deluxe Waterfall Resort, a floatplane ride away. Campers and picnickers have a choice of several Forest Service sites not far from downtown (see page 64).

Shopping in Ketchikan is much like it is anywhere in the Panhandle. Good buys include Indian woven cedar baskets, soapstone and ivory carvings, and gold nugget jewelry. If you're looking for a replica of a totem pole, you'll find one in almost every store.

Tour information is available from the Information Center at the downtown dock, 131 Front Street. An excellent pamphlet highlights major points of interest for a self-guided walking tour. Bus tours cover a wider variety of area attractions.

Totem displays

Silent storytellers of the past, totem poles are gentle reminders of two almost forgotten Indian peoples—the Tlingits and the Haidas. You'll find several good displays of totems around Ketchikan.

Totem Bight State Park, 10 miles north of town, contains a number of poles, as well as a replica of a Tlingit ceremonial. Saxman Native Village, 3 miles south of town, welcomes visitors with a large collection of poles, local carvers at work, and native dancers.

In town, the Totem Heritage Center preserves and exhibits original, unrestored totem poles and carved house posts brought in from long-abandoned Indian villages. Trained guides take visitors through the cedar museum, designed to resemble a tribal house. Totems stand in a fire pit beneath a glass-covered smoke hole that casts natural light on the carvings.

Traditionally, totems were carved to honor a clan, a chief, or an important event. Figures and crests on the poles usually don't tell just one story but act as symbolic reminders of important events in the clan's history.

The center (601 Deermount Street) opens daily in summer, Tuesday through Friday the rest of the year.

Reminders of the past

The Tongass Historical Museum and the Ketchikan Library are housed in the Centennial Building. Erected to commemorate the 100-year anniversary of the purchase of Alaska from Russia, the building contains Russian relics, old photos of Ketchikan, and interesting Tlingit, Haida, and Tsimshian arts and crafts.

Alaskans shivered and shook during the 1964 Good Friday earthquake. On today's Richter scale, the March 27 quake would register 9.2, 80 times more energetic than San Francisco's 1906 tremor.

Don't miss Creek Street, once the town's notorious red light district. Running along Ketchikan Creek, the district is a collection of wooden shops and galleries connected by boardwalks resting on pilings.

Dolly's House, located at 24 Creek St., is the home of one of the last of the madams. Restored as an historical museum, it's open to visitors for a small fee. Dolly's clothes still hang in the closet, and her jewelry spills across the dressing table. All of the houses were closed in 1953, but Dolly Arthur continued to live in her house until she was in her seventies.

Protected against the elements, walkers explore the area around Waterfall Resort, once a cannery and now an attractive wilderness lodge near Ketchikan.

Carved and painted Indian ceremonial longhouse, along with a collection of totems, can be seen in Ketchikan's Totem Bight Park, located in an area that was once a favorite Tlingit Indian campsite.

Excursions from Ketchikan

Regularly scheduled air service and charter flights from Ketchikan take visitors to the area's beautiful mountains, waterways, and other secluded sites. One spectacular destination is Misty Fjords National Monument, which lies about 50 miles east of Ketchikan on the mainland. The Tsimshian community of Metlakatla is on Annette Island south of Ketchikan. Waterfall Resort and other wilderness retreats are located on Prince of Wales Island, only a half-hour flight to the west.

Misty Fjords National Monument

Over 2 million acres of pristine rivers and streams, gleaming icefields, forested mountains, tumbling waterfalls, and glacial lakes are contained in Misty Fjords National Monument. No roads lead into this wild land; the monument is accessible only by boat or plane.

Some cruise ships visit the monument as part of the trip through the Inside Passage. One-hour floatplane tours depart from Ketchikan. The plane skims sheer granite walls, dips into glacier-carved valleys, and sets down on one of the mountaintop lakes. A full-day combined cruise-and-air tour offers an even greater in-depth sightseeing experience.

Misty Fjords' rocky slopes are home to foraging mountain goats; dense forests shelter abundant wildlife— bears, deer, moose, wolves, martins, and fox. Otters, sea lions, harbor seals, whales, and porpoises frolic in the water. Bald eagles soar overhead and nest in trees near rivers and shorelines.

Metlakatla

On Annette Island, about 15 miles south of Ketchikan, you'll find Alaska's only Tsimshian Indian community. Metlakatla's Alaskan history began over 100 years ago as the result of a religious dispute, which forced William Duncan, a lay minister, to lead about 800 Indians north from British Columbia to establish the new town.

Duncan Cottage, where Father Duncan lived until his death in 1918, is now a museum displaying fascinating memorabilia from the town's early days. A monument honoring the original settlers stands in front of the house. The museum is open daily on weekdays and by appointment on weekends.

Though this fact was unknown to early miners, Alaska is the only state in the nation where platinum is found. More than 500,000 ounces of the rare and valuable metal have been extracted by placer mining.

Visitors will also want to see the tribal longhouse near the waterfront. The totem pole nearby was carved by one of today's villagers.

Most residents of the community fish for a living and sell their catches to the island's cannery. Though fish traps were outlawed in Alaska in 1959, Metlakatla natives are still allowed to use them.

Prince of Wales Island

Prince of Wales Island, the nation's third largest (30 miles wide and 130 miles long), is home to some of Alaska's best fishing lodges. It's also an unhurried place where you'll have an opportunity to become acquainted with local residents—loggers, hunters, and anglers—and to spot some of the island's abundant wildlife, including brown bears, minks, Sitka black-tailed deer, and bald eagles.

Forty U.S. Forest Service cabins (see page 64) are sprinkled around the forested island. Other accommodations include wilderness lodges and bed-and-breakfast inns.

Klawock, a Tlingit Indian village, is the usual destination for visitors not heading to the deluxe Waterfall Resort. It has the only airfield on the island and two lodges (Fireweed Resort and Prince of Wales Lodge). Though rental fishing boats are available at Klawock Lake, there are no facilities for overnight camping.

In town, visitors can enjoy a fine display of Tlingit totem poles or a guided tour of the local state fish hatchery. Seasonal salmon and steelhead fishing is good on the Klawock River, and a number of charter boats are available for day-long trips to other fishing holes and out-of-the-way places.

Craig, about 6 miles south of Klawock on Highway 20, is the island's largest town and the economic center for the coast's fishing fleet.

Hydaburg, the center of Haida culture in Alaska, lies still farther south. Visitors to the town's totem park, located next to the school complex, will quickly notice the distinct differences in the artistic styles of the Tlingit and Haida cultures.

Waterfall Resort, on the island's west coast, started life as a salmon cannery. Today, after a multimillion-dollar renovation, it has become a premier wilderness resort.

Fishing is still its principal reason for existence. During the season, anglers can fish for steelhead trout, halibut, red snapper, Dungeness crab, and chinook, coho, pink, and red salmon.

Wrangell & Petersburg

Lightly touched by the tourist trade because they're not on many cruise ship itineraries, both Wrangell and Petersburg can be reached by ferry. Both are worth a visit.

Friendly Wrangell

Wrangell, the state's third oldest city, lies 80 miles northwest of Ketchikan. It sits between lush green forest and blue waters, hugging the rim of a jewel-like harbor not far from the mouth of the Stikine River.

Lumber mills, shrimp and salmon canneries, cold-storage plants, and boat shops dominate the waterfront. Shops, bars, and stores line the town's one main street, and houses dot the hillside without much regard for planned routes.

Wrangell has flown the flag of three nations. The townsite on the northern tip of Wrangell Island was originally inhabited by Tlingit Indians, who used the nearby Stikine River as a trade route to the Interior.

The value of the Stikine (meaning "great river") was also recognized by the Russians, who needed the river to bring furs out of the Interior. Today, large oil tanks stand on the site of an old trading post the Russians built in 1834 near the mouth of the river.

In 1839, when the Russians leased the land to British traders also operating in the area, the Russian Redoubt Saint Dionysius became the British Fort Stikine. After the United States purchased Alaska, the town's name changed—for its third and final time—to Wrangell (for Baron von Wrangell of the Russian-American Company).

Two gold rushes touched this settlement, the first in 1874–1876 with the discovery in the Cassiar, and the second in 1897–1900, when miners stampeded through Wrangell on their way to the Klondike.

Alaska's first Protestant (Presbyterian) church was established here in 1879, the same year that famed naturalist John Muir visited the area.

Accommodations in town include Hardings Old Sourdough Lodge (boarding house–style lodging with meals), Roadhouse Lodge (with a dining room and lounge), Stikine Inn, Thunderbird Hotel, and Clarke Bed and Breakfast.

The town's small restaurants feature fresh seafood. Wrangell's hospitality is still on a very personal basis, with residents extending a warm welcome to visitors.

Attractions in this compact little town are located conveniently close together. Near the harbor, on Chief Shake's Island, stands the Bear Tribal House, one of the stops on any sightseeing tour. Chief Shake VII, the last of a long line of Tlingit chiefs, dedicated the reconstructed ceremonial house at a potlatch in 1940. Inside the tribal house are displays of carvings, tools, and other artifacts.

Other points of interest include the Wrangell Museum (housed in the town's first schoolhouse), one of the state's largest lumber mills, and a salmon-processing plant.

At Petroglyph Beach you can hunt for the 40 or more carved stone markers scattered along the stretch of beach. Other petroglyphs can be found on the lawn of the library and in the museum. Along the Stikine River you can dig for garnets; inquire at the museum for permits and information.

Excursions take visitors flightseeing over the 443,000-acre Stikine LeConte Wilderness between Wrangell and Petersburg or to LeConte Glacier, the southernmost of Alaska's tidewater glaciers.

Friendly Wrangell residents usually greet ships. Indian women spread their wares—beadwork, moccasins, shell jewelry, and other items—on the dock, and children sell wildflowers and garnets. Gift shops along Front Street feature Alaskan designs and locally crafted jewelry, ceramics, and art work.

The city hosts a salmon derby each summer and a winter festival every February.

Petersburg, "Little Norway"

Located on Mitkof Island, some 40 miles northwest of Wrangell, Petersburg appears to be a bit of old Scandinavia in the middle of Alaska. Founded in 1891 by Norwegian immigrant Peter Buschmann, Petersburg has retained an appearance and friendliness that have earned it the designation "Little Norway." Its brightly painted stores and houses and its colorful gardens set it apart from other southeastern Alaska communities.

Fishing is the backbone of the town's economy; the town is the home port of the state's largest halibut fishing fleet. Salmon and shrimp canneries, cold-storage plants, and docks line the waterfront along 21-mile Wrangell Narrows, a picturesque waterway.

Accommodations include the renovated Scandia House hotel, Beachcomber Inn, Tides Inn, and several cheerful bed-and-breakfast inns. Restaurants feature the tiny pink shrimp harvested nearby.

Several campgrounds are located near downtown. Ohmer Creek Forest Service Campground is 21 miles southeast of town on the Mitkof Highway.

Attractions in and around Petersburg include charter boat or air trips to fishing waters and hunting grounds nearby or a day-long cruise to active LeConte Glacier, which spits icebergs into a small bay. The colorful buildings lining Hammer's Slough are a photographer's delight. During spawning season, you can watch salmon climb Falls Creek Fish Ladder.

In few Alaskan communities is a walking tour quite as rewarding. Along the waterfront you can view fish being processed. The Clausen Memorial Museum houses the world-record 126½-pound king salmon. Here, too, are displays of the town's early life.

On the weekend closest to May 17, Petersburg holds a festival to celebrate Norway's Independence Day.

Juneau

Perched on a narrow shelf between massive Mt. Juneau and the deep waters of the Gastineau Channel sits Juneau, Alaska's capital and home to some 30,000 people. The town is, necessarily, very long and narrow, with streets that twist and turn up the steep hillsides. Often, wooden staircases take up where streets leave off.

At first glance, Juneau's newer high rises give the town a modern appearance. But as you wander along downtown streets, take a look at some of the older buildings and glance up to the weathered hillside houses. It's easy to see that much of Juneau's original flavor remains.

Recent renovations in downtown Juneau have added to the town's atmosphere. Careful restorations have rejuvenated several old downtown buildings. Bright-colored flowers dangle from lampposts and burst out of planters, and lines in the sidewalks recall the days when planked walkways bordered dirt streets. Banners in Marine Park, where many cruise ships dock, depict local wildlife, fishing scenes, and the nearby Mendenhall Glacier.

Campers and hikers should make the Forest Service Information Center in Centennial Hall (101 Egan Drive) their first stop for maps, cabin reservations, and trail guides.

A look back in history

Like so many Alaskan towns, Juneau owes its origins to gold. When Joe Juneau and Richard Harris discovered nuggets "as large as peas or beans" in what is now called Gold Creek, a town was born. The miners who rushed to the camp first called it Harrisburg and then Rockwell, before finally settling on the name Juneau.

In 1906, the capital, which was then in Sitka, was moved to Juneau. The former mining camp attracted new industries. Over the next 40 years, three mining companies took more than $158 million in gold from the

creeks and valleys around the city. The mines closed in 1944, victims of floods, fires, cave-ins, and, in some cases, depletions.

The Alaska-Juneau Gold Mining Company mill, which burned in 1964, is now just a skeleton on the mountainside behind the city. It looks like a huge monument to those colorful mining days.

Across the channel is Douglas Island, site of the Treadwell Gold Mine, among others. Today, a bridge connects the island and the small town of Douglas with Juneau.

Federal and state government payrolls, along with some fishing and lumbering, now form the basis of the local economy. In 1976, voters approved a measure to relocate the capital from Juneau to Willow (between Anchorage and Fairbanks), a terrible blow to Juneau and all of southeastern Alaska. But when voters refused to approve funding for the move in 1982, the measure died.

Food & lodging

Accommodations in Juneau are the most extensive in the Panhandle. Your choice includes modern chain motels, downtown hotels like the elegant Baranof and newer Westmark Juneau, and countryside B&Bs like Pearson's Pond and Blueberry Lodge.

On the Mendenhall Loop Road, a large campground offers facilities for trailers and a spectacular view of Mendenhall Glacier. A smaller campground lies at Mile 15.8 on the Glacier Highway in the Auke Bay region.

Meals range from standard fare in moderately priced coffee shops to more expensive dinners in intimate restaurants with fine Inside Passage views. Several outdoor salmon bakes (the price usually includes transportation to the site, food, and entertainment) are available as well.

Downtown attractions

Downtown Juneau is best seen on a walking tour. You can pick up a free guide and informative brochures from the Davis Log Cabin Visitor Center, 134 Third St. Total walking time is approximately 1½ hours.

You can also explore Juneau's attractions by horse and carriage, classic car, chauffeured limousine, or motor

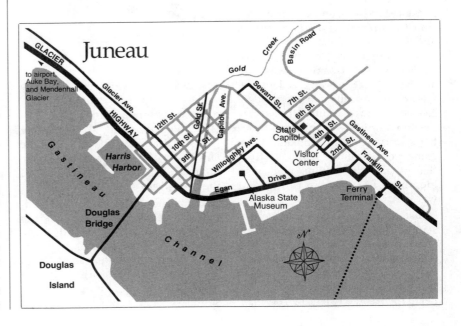

...Juneau

coach. If your sightseeing company doesn't include a stop at Gastineau Salmon Hatchery (26197 Channel Drive), you may want to tour it on your own. Most of southeast Alaska's salmon are hatched here annually. Aquariums display adult salmon and other varieties of Alaskan sea life. Guided tours are available; there is a small admission charge.

State offices. Tours of the State Capitol on Fourth Street are offered daily during the summer. The building, dating from the 1930s, houses the state's legislative body, some administrative offices, and the governor's office. In the nearby State Office Building are the offices of most of the state agencies. In its grand court, you'll find the century-old Old Witch Totem and a restored 1928 Kimball theater organ (recitals are offered on Friday from noon to 1 P.M.).

Stroll up to the Governor's Mansion on Calhoun Street. The large white Virginia-style house was built and furnished in 1913 at a cost of $40,000. Free guided tours are offered on Monday, Wednesday, and Friday, but you'll need to arrange a tour in advance; call the governor's office at 465-3500 for information.

Alaska State Museum. Within a stroll from the downtown shopping district and the state buildings is one of Alaska's most highly regarded museums. A visit to the Alaska State Museum, at 395 Whittier St., is an excellent preview of the incredible diversity you'll see as you travel around the state— Eskimo carvings and implements, totemic carvings and Chilkat Indian blankets, moosehide garments from the Athabascan culture, gold rush memorabilia, Russian relics, and wildlife displays.

Just inside the front door of the museum is one of its most dramatic displays, a towering eagle-nesting tree that was moved intact into the museum. On its branches perch some very realistic-looking birds, and beneath them stand two brown bears.

The museum is open daily; a small admission fee is charged.

Juneau-Douglas City Museum. This small museum at 4th and Main streets focuses on Juneau's mining history with historic maps of area sites, mining tools, and artifacts. One map illustrates different mining levels at the old Perseverance Gold Mine. Other exhibits feature native art and local history. The museum (open daily in summer) welcomes donations.

Wickersham State Historic Site. Judge James Wickersham purchased the house at 213 Seventh St. as a retirement home. Wickersham, a colorful character in Alaskan history, came to Alaska in 1900 to establish the first court and government in the Interior.

Juneau, the state's capital, covers so much territory (3,108 square miles) that it ranks as the largest city in North and South America. In fact, only Kiruna, Sweden, is larger in area.

A delegate to Congress for many years, he helped form the first territorial legislature and introduced legislation establishing Mt. McKinley National Park (now called Denali), the University of Alaska, and the Alaska Railroad. In 1916, he also introduced the first Alaska statehood bill.

The hillside Victorian, once a landmark for sea captains, is now a museum devoted to Alaska's early days. The judge's original furniture, diaries, and rare collections remain, as do his collections of Russian artifacts and native art. The house is open daily in summer; donations are requested.

St. Nicholas Russian Orthodox Church. The cross of historic St. Nicholas Church, at 326 Fifth St., is visible for several blocks. One of the most photographed churches in the Panhandle, it's also the oldest Russian Orthodox church in the area. Now an historical landmark, it was built in 1894 and restored to its original state in the late 1970s.

On a tour of the church (offered once a day) you'll see icons and other relics that date from as far back as the 18th century. Visitors are welcome at Sunday services (10 A.M. to noon). Note that there are no pews in the church; worshipers stand throughout the service.

Entertainment. Dance hall girls, a "shoot-out," and stories of gold mining days are the main features of the summer offering *The Lady Lou Revue*. Performances are presented daily at 8 P.M. from mid-May to late September in the Wharf Mall at Egan Drive and Main Street. The show attracts visitors, so get tickets in advance.

The ever-popular Red Dog Saloon, on S. Franklin, maintains its old-time dance hall aura with a sawdust-covered floor, honky-tonk piano, and community songfests. Go early to be sure to get a seat for the rollicking evening entertainment.

Last Chance Basin. At the site of a once-flourishing gold mine (today the location of a nightly salmon bake during the summer), you'll get a chance to pan for gold and examine old mining relics.

Shopping. Juneau shops carry handicrafts from all over the state: Eskimo walrus ivory carvings (jewelry and cribbage and chess sets), whimsical little billikens (good luck charms from walrus tusks and the teeth of sperm whales), Haida and Tlingit crafts, and paintings by noted Alaskan artists. Several stores along Franklin Street specialize in gold nugget jewelry.

Some shops in the city are dedicated to Russian, Scandinavian, or Irish wares. Don't overlook the local bookstores, where you'll find numerous titles on Alaskan history and lore.

Attractive Franklin Street, one of Juneau's main thoroughfares, stretches north from the ferry and cruise ship docks. A busy shopping street, it's also the location of the city's visitor center.

Characteristic cross and onion-shaped dome distinguish Juneau's St. Nicholas, the Panhandle's oldest Russian Orthodox church.

Excursions from Juneau

Side trips from Juneau offer visitors surprising delights. Though roads don't extend very far, Alaskans think nothing of taking off by boat or plane for a few hours, a day, or a weekend.

Right at their back door trails lead into the surrounding countryside; the trail that climbs 4,000-foot Mt. Roberts begins at the stairway at the end of Sixth Street. If you'd rather not risk meeting a bear on your own, the Juneau Parks and Recreation Department offers organized hikes on Wednesday and Saturday; call 586-5226 for a schedule.

The most popular tourist excursion from Juneau is to nearby Mendenhall Glacier, one of the Panhandle's most accessible ice floes. Juneau is also a good jumping-off spot for trips to other, less-visited areas, such as Admiralty and Chichagof islands.

Mendenhall Glacier

Mendenhall Glacier, Juneau's "drive-in" glacier, draws large crowds the year around. Sightseeing buses from town operate throughout the year. Included in the 2½-hour trip is a stop at the Chapel-by-the-Lake overlooking Auke Lake, probably one of Alaska's most photographed scenes. Nearby lies the Juneau campus of the state university.

Mendenhall Glacier is situated just 13 miles from downtown Juneau. The 12-mile-long river of ice, which melts when it reaches its own lake, was born in the 1,500-mile icefield that looms high over the city. At its face the glacier is a wall of ice over 100 feet high and nearly 1½ miles wide.

Formed during the Little Ice Age some 3,000 years ago, the glacier has been retreating since the 1800s; in 1916, it extended several miles farther down the valley. The visitor center now stands on the spot where the face was in 1940.

Mountain goats are often seen on Mt. Bullard, to the right of the glacier. Streep Creek, near the visitor center, offers a convenient point from which to view spawning sockeye, chum, and coho salmon between mid-July and late August.

Hiking trails. Trails on the glacier's east side offer spectacular views of the face and of two gushing waterfalls. From the West Glacier Trail, which starts near the campground, visitors get the best view into the glacier's steep crevasses and can hear the crunching and grinding of the never-silent ice.

Glacier walking. A helicopter flight from Juneau's airport gives you a chance to examine the Juneau Icefield. In addition to sightseeing, the helicopter tour includes time for a walk—on the glacier. Outfitted with special nonskid boots, visitors are taken on a short stroll. Guides explain glacial action and offer close-up views of deep ice crevasses.

Float trips. Half-day guided float trips in rubber rafts start at the face of the glacier and head downstream past the forests and mountains of the Mendenhall River Valley. Trips combine a few small rapids with longer stretches of calm water.

Outdoor adventures near Juneau

Juneau's ski area is Eaglecrest, located on Douglas Island 12 miles from downtown. Both cross-country and downhill skiing are offered during the winter. In summer, the area draws hikers; bring along a picnic lunch.

You won't want to miss the Shrine of St. Terese, hidden in the trees on a tiny causeway-connected island along Favorite Channel, 23 miles north of Juneau. Following the stations of the cross to a large crucifix at the top of the island gives you a magnificent view of the Chilkat Range, many miles to the northwest.

Some of the area's most magnificent wilderness regions lie only a short floatplane or boat ride away from Juneau.

Admiralty Island. The island, 15 miles west of Juneau, is comprised of more than a million acres of rain forest. Now a national monument, the island also boasts the continent's highest concentration of both bald eagles and brown bears.

Admiralty is also a canoeist's paradise. The Cross-Admiralty Canoe Trail takes boaters on a 25-mile route through wilderness, on lakes and streams, and across portages.

Angoon, the island's only settlement, is home to about 500 Tlingits. Accommodations include two motels in town, a wilderness lodge on Thayer Lake, and Forest Service cabins (see page 64).

For information on the island, write to the Forest Service Information Center, 101 Egan Dr., Juneau, AK 99801.

Chichagof Island. You can reach this island from Juneau on a 3-hour ferry trip from Auke Bay or on a 20-minute charter flight. The Indian village of Hoonah, in the northeastern corner of Chichagof, is the largest Tlingit settlement in the Panhandle.

A small museum at the Hoonah Indian Association Cultural Center is open daily on weekdays year-round, on weekends by appointment. A comfortable lodge offers fishing charters and year-round service to Glacier Bay.

Boat cruises. Explore Tracy Arm, a spectacular fjord close to Juneau that is home to two tidewater glaciers and a myriad of wildlife, on a dinner cruise aboard the MV *Glacier Express*. The 49-passenger boat leaves Juneau daily (except Tuesday and Thursday) for the 5½-hour run.

The ship also offers cruises to Glacier Bay. For information, check with Juneau's visitor center or contact Catamaran Cruiselines, 1620 Metropolitan Park Bldg., Seattle, WA 98101.

A look at glaciers

In spite of Alaska's reputation as a land of ice and snow, only 3 percent of the state is encased in ice, and that small percentage offers unique and rewarding vistas for travelers.

Though the percentage of ice is small, the land locked beneath perennial ice covers over 28,000 square miles and includes more than half the world's glaciers. Malaspina Glacier, near Yakutat, is larger than all of Switzerland.

The phenomenon of frozen and compacted water is located conveniently for visitors to the southcentral and southeastern parts of the state. It takes water to make ice, and the maritime climate of southern Alaska provides it in abundance. Extraordinary snowfall, at times exceeding 400 inches annually, provides the seed. In contrast, Alaska's Interior and its northern reaches are relatively arid.

Growth of a glacier

Whenever annual snowfall exceeds melt rate, a buildup occurs. However, this buildup does not necessarily lead to the formation of a glacier. Key ingredients seem to be time and pressure.

Over the years, the weight of snow and ice cause lower ice layers to metamorphose into a crystal formation unique to glacial ice. The plastic, or flexible, nature of these crystals enables the mass of ice to flow slowly downhill.

Alaska has more than 100,000 glaciers, ranging from tiny alpine patches to huge valley icefields.

Large glaciers do a lot of earth moving as they flow, literally creating landscapes. Glaciers are responsible for the spectacular U-shaped valleys of the western Sierras (such as Yosemite), the sharp-peaked ridges of the northern Cascades in Washington, and the dramatic fjords of Scandinavia and Alaska.

A glacial advance thousands of years ago helped grind down an ancient mountain range in eastern Canada, creating that area's great plains.

Glacial features

When you're flying over a glacier, there are some basic features to look for. The most pronounced are *moraines*.

Moraines consist of rock and dirt picked up by the glacier as it slides downhill. Lateral and medial moraines are seen as dark bands running the length of the glacier, like dark lines on a white highway. Terminal moraines, rock and debris bulldozed by the glacier, are found at the glacier's toe.

Crevasse fields are also apparent. A crevasse is a major fracture in the glacier's surface. A large field of these fractures indicates that the glacier is undergoing some stress, probably riding over a hill or into a "fall" below.

Ogives, rarer and more subtle than moraines or crevasses, are wave patterns generally formed at the base of the glacier as it slowly surges over extreme declinations in its bed.

What you'll see

Visitors to Alaska will see four types of glaciers: *alpine* glaciers high on the mountain slopes, *valley* glaciers that extend along the slopes of coastal mountain ranges or the Alaska Range, *piedmont* glaciers that flow onto a plain along the southcentral coast, and *tidewater* glaciers in Prince William Sound and throughout the Panhandle.

Tidewater glaciers provide one of nature's most dramatic spectacles. These glaciers can be approached relatively closely by boat, offering visitors a good view.

The faces of some of these glaciers can reach 600 feet. Enormous pieces of ice, some thousands of years old, calve into the sea with thundering reports. The falling ice sends up great waves, and resulting icebergs take on beautifully sculpted shapes.

Visiting a glacier

Scheduled excursions are offered to Columbia Glacier in Prince William Sound, North America's largest tidewater glacier. One of 20 in the sound, the glacier is retreating and iceberg production is extremely active.

Other boat trips give you views of LeConte Glacier near Petersburg, Twin Sawyer Glaciers in Tracy Arm, and Margerie Glacier and other awesome ice masses in Glacier Bay National Park and Preserve.

On a helicopter tour from Juneau, passengers have a chance to walk on Mendenhall Glacier.

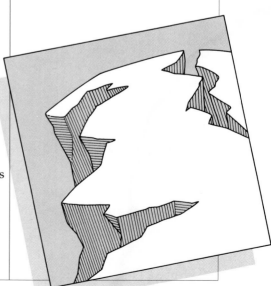

Icy landscape around Glacier Bay National Park and Preserve can be explored by scheduled excursion boat or on your own. At the head of the bay's east arm, passengers going ashore unload their gear.

Luxuriant rain forest surrounds Glacier Bay Lodge on Bartlett Cove. The lodge, the only hostelry in the park, is reached by catamaran from Juneau or by plane from Juneau, Skagway, or Haines.

Glacier Bay

About 90 miles northwest of Juneau in the Fairweather Range of the St. Elias Mountains is one of Alaska's most dramatic sites—Glacier Bay National Park and Preserve. More than 20 tremendous glaciers and many equally impressive smaller ones spread across an area of over 3 million acres.

Glacial majesty

Glacier Bay was completely covered by ice just 200 years ago. When George Vancouver explored the area in 1794, the bay was a small body of water in a barely indented glacier that extended for more than 100 miles. By the time naturalist John Muir traveled to the area in 1879, the ice had retreated 48 miles, and, by 1916, Grand Pacific Glacier, at the head of Tarr Inlet, was 65 miles from the mouth of the bay.

Several of the tidewater glaciers offer a spectacular show of geologic forces in action. As water undermines the face of the ice, great blocks up to 200 feet high break loose and crash into the sea, creating huge waves and filling the narrow inlets with massive icebergs.

The Johns Hopkins Glacier calves such volumes of ice that it's seldom possible to get closer than 2 miles to the glacier. On Tarr Inlet, Grand Pacific and Margerie glaciers are presently also very active, though both are more accessible.

Park geology

Two mountain ranges feed the ponderous rivers of ice. The Takhinsha Range, largely unexplored, feeds Muir Glacier and others on the east arm of the bay. Glaciers on the west arm originate in the lofty Fairweather Range, which culminates in 15,300-foot Mt. Fairweather. The Grand Pacific Glacier, originating in Canada between the two ranges, is a product of both mountain systems.

Glacier Bay is an ideal laboratory for the study of plant succession. The rapidly growing vegetation that springs up where glaciers have retreated gives scientists an opportunity to watch the birth of a wilderness.

At the face of the glacier, no trees or bushes are visible. Yet closer inspection reveals bits of moss, spikes of dwarf fireweed, and tiny trees sprouting among the rocks and gravel.

A little farther away, you'll see the yellow blooms of *dryas*, the first of the plants that will eventually cover the glacier-torn earth. Areas that emerged from the ice in the early 1900s are now covered with thick stands of alders, willows, moss, and grasses.

On the land that reappeared almost a century ago, cottonwood and alder shelter small spruce. Taller trees often play host to nests of bald eagles.

The lush green rain forest at Bartlett Cove (the center of park activity) was under ice less than 200 years ago. Spruce trees, covered with moss, soar to 120 feet or more. Today, however, even those giants are slowly being replaced by hemlocks.

Getting there

Glacier Bay is reached only by air or boat. Access to the Gustavus Airport is by scheduled Alaska Airlines jets or by air taxi from Skagway, Haines, or Juneau.

Alaska Sightseeing/Cruise West offers an intimate look at Glacier Bay on three-day, two-night packages from downtown Juneau. A highlight is the full day of cruising on both arms of the bay.

Many cruise ships include a day in Glacier Bay as part of their Inside Passage itinerary. From port towns in the Panhandle, tour packages that include air or boat fare, lodging, and an excursion into the bay can be arranged.

Where to stay

Park headquarters are in the Glacier Bay Lodge at Bartlett Cove. The 55-room, well-designed lodge is one of Alaska's most handsome backcountry chalets. Views from the dining room and bar are spectacular.

A huge stone fireplace attracts evening gatherings; from the lodge's wraparound terrace, you can watch the long summer sunsets.

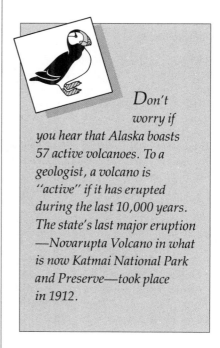

Don't worry if you hear that Alaska boasts 57 active volcanoes. To a geologist, a volcano is "active" if it has erupted during the last 10,000 years. The state's last major eruption —Novarupta Volcano in what is now Katmai National Park and Preserve—took place in 1912.

The lodge is open from Memorial Day through mid-September. For information and reservations, write to Glacier Bay Lodge, Glacier Bay Tours & Cruises, 520 Pike St., No. 1610, Seattle, WA 98101 or call (800) 451-5952.

Lodging choices in the village of Gustavus, just outside the park, include the respected Glacier Bay Country Inn and Gustavus Inn as well as smaller B&Bs and a variety of rustic cabins.

Camping

Miles of beaches make camping in Glacier Bay a delight. You'll need to bring all your own equipment and food if you don't plan to eat at the lodge.

... Glacier Bay

The campground at Bartlett Cove (no reservations or fees required) provides bearproof food caches, fire pits, and firewood. There's no place at the campground to store extra gear while you're in the backcountry.

For further information, write to the Superintendent, Glacier Bay National Park and Preserve, Gustavus, AK 99826.

What to do

The highlight of any visit to Glacier Bay is a close look at the star performers—the glaciers themselves. The closest one is 43 miles from Bartlett Cove.

Boat trips. An excursion boat leaves the lodge each morning during the season for a day-long trip up the west arm of the bay. Aboard, park naturalists explain glacial activity.

Glacier Bay Tours & Cruises, the park concessionaire, offers a variety of cruising, kayaking, and sportfishing adventures. They also cruise to Point Adolphus for whale watching and to nearby islands. Charter vessels from Gustavus and Juneau explore the bay, Elfin Cove, and other sites.

Because all the excursions are very popular, you'll need to reserve well ahead. Make reservations through the Glacier Bay Lodge (see page 35).

Boating on your own. Boating in the park is subject to special regulations in order to protect the humpback whales that frequent the area. You'll need a permit to venture up the bay from Bartlett Cove; check with rangers for current information. Fuel and water are available at the cove.

Wildlife viewing. Often, visitors will spot mountain goats, whales, or hair seals sleeping on icebergs. Large flocks of waterfowl—loons, cormorants, geese, common eiders and other ducks, various gulls and shorebirds, murres, guillemots, and puffins— wheel over coves and inlets. Ravens, grouse, and eagles inhabit the shoreline.

In summer, bears are attracted to streams by the huge numbers of spawning salmon. At Bear Track Cove, the lumbering animals have worn trails along the stream bank.

Fishing. Sportfishing outings are part of the daily activity at Glacier Bay Lodge. Charter boats, available at Bartlett Cove, take anglers out for halibut, salmon, and Dolly Varden and cutthroat trout, all plentiful in this area. You'll need a state fishing license.

Hiking and backpacking. A number of hiking trails cut through Bartlett Cove's luxuriant rain forests; in summer, park rangers conduct hikes from the lodge.

The park's extensive shoreline, island-dotted inlets, and alpine meadowland offer plenty of camping and hiking opportunities. Topographic maps and a hiker's guide are sold at the lodge. Rangers can offer tips on terrain to avoid as campsites because of tides, icefalls, and such.

Firewood is not available in the upper bay. Don't burn any wood you find: it predates the last Ice Age and is protected. White gas is sold in Gustavus and at Glacier Bay Lodge.

Campers often use the daily cruise boat as transportation between the lodge and the upper bay.

Whale watching

Among the world's largest creatures are the whales, those awesome denizens of the deep. Nearly fifteen species of these great mammals summer in Alaskan waters, providing visitors with some spectacular viewing opportunities.

Whale life

Whales usually live in family groups called pods. Research shows that they "talk" to each other, producing noises ranging from shrieks to low growling sounds that travel for miles in the water.

Whales are divided by feeding habits into two groups. *Baleen* whales consume krill, shrimp, and other small fish; *toothed* whales feed on fish, sea lions, seals, porpoises, and even other whales.

Species of baleen whales in Alaska's oceans include the blue, bowhead, northern right, humpback, sei, minke, gray, and fin, or finback. Among the toothed whales found here are the sperm, narwhal, beluga, pilot, beaked, and killer.

Where to view whales

Summer visitors who travel the Inside Passage by ship usually see whales somewhere along their journey. Glacier Bay waters boast two of the great species, the minke and humpback, and the smaller killer whale. They often put on quite a show in Bartlett Cove, but the greatest concentration is usually found in the waters outside the bay.

Other premier whale sightings are made in Prince William Sound and in the waters of Cook Inlet. Minkes, which range as far north as the Bering and Chukchi seas, are sometimes viewed around Gull Island in Kachemak Bay.

Alaska's native people

Most people who travel to the Far North know little about the native people who inhabit this region. Some even believe that Eskimos live in igloos made from ice.

Actually, Alaska's native people —the Eskimos, Indians, and Aleuts—are as diverse as the state's geographic regions; even tribes sharing a common culture may speak different languages. But almost everyone speaks English— and wears blue jeans.

By the time Vitus Bering "discovered" Alaska in 1741, Eskimos, Indians, and Aleuts were distributed throughout the region in well-defined areas, with little mixing of ethnic groups.

Most anthropologists believe that these people migrated, in successive waves over thousands of years, across the Bering Strait from Asia.

Indians

Abundant natural food and a moderate climate permitted the three Indian tribes who settled in the Panhandle to lead a fairly comfortable life.

Tsimshians. Latecomers to Alaska, the Tsimshians, originally from British Columbia, migrated in 1887 to Annette Island. Around 1,000 Tsimshians now live in the village of Metlakatla. Like most other southeastern residents, they make their living primarily from fishing.

Haidas. In the 1700s many Haida Indians immigrated to Alaska from Canada; today, about 700 or 800 live in the Panhandle. The village of Hydaburg on Prince of Wales Island is their largest community. Their culture and language are similar to that of the more numerous Tlingits, but a deep enmity existed for years between the two tribes.

Tlingits. Between 10,000 and 12,000 Tlingit Indians live in the southeastern part of the state. The Tlingits, too, came from Canada originally, but they were already settled in the Panhandle at the time of the first European contact. Their folklore contains many stories of how they crossed the mountains and glaciers on their way to the sea.

Like the Haidas, the Tlingits belong to a totemic culture, with totem poles providing a history of the main events in the life of a clan or family.

The ceremonial blanket of the Tlingits, perfected by the Chilkats of Klukwan, is one of the most beautiful products of these gifted people. In great demand, it was advantageously used by the Tlingits in their dealings with the less sophisticated Indians of the Interior.

Athabascans. Before the arrival of white people in the Interior, the Athabascan Indians were nomadic, following the moose and caribou. With no permanent villages, they developed no agriculture.

Alaska's Athabascans are closely related to the Navajos, Apaches, and Hopi Indians of the Lower 48. It's believed that the Alaskan branch of the family was driven north by the warlike Crees some 700 or 800 years ago.

Aleuts

Traditionally, the Aleuts have lived on the Alaska Peninsula and along the Aleutian Islands. Almost every island was inhabited when the Russians first explored the Aleutians.

Skilled seafarers, the Aleuts ventured far from shore in pursuit of otters, sea lions, and whales. The Aleut women of Attu Island were noted for their fine basketry.

During World War II, the Aleuts were removed from Attu Island; most resettled on Atka Island. Today, a few permanent settlements (including two on the Pribilof Islands) and 2,000 Aleuts remain.

Inupiat Eskimos

Since their arrival on this continent, Alaska's Inupiats have lived in villages along the Bering Sea and Arctic Ocean, on the coast of the Gulf of Alaska, and on Kodiak Island.

Russians first came upon the Eskimos in the middle of the 19th century. Living in permanent villages, the Eskimos hunted and foraged for salmon, berries, shorebirds, and caribou. In boats made of driftwood covered with skin, they ventured out in search of seals, walruses, and huge bowhead whales.

A sociable people, the Eskimos enjoy dances, festivals, and other social activities. Though the Arctic boasts few roads, even the most remote village keeps in touch by means of telephone, telegraph, and shortwave radio.

Eskimos, numbering 40,000, account for over half the state's native population.

Haines & Skagway

Haines and Skagway, two nearby cities tucked into the northeastern corner of the Panhandle, serve as gateways into the state's Interior. Both towns are serviced by regularly scheduled airlines and ferries. Though the two ports aren't connected by road, they're only a few minutes apart by plane or an hour's ride by ferry.

Haines & Port Chilkoot

Situated on the upper reaches of beautiful Lynn Canal and surrounded by towering, snow-clad peaks, the side-by-side communities of Haines and Port Chilkoot have preserved much of their original appearance.

Haines, a former fur-trading post, became Haines Mission (Presbyterian) in 1881. The canneries and the U.S. Army followed the church to the small community.

In 1903, Fort William H. Seward was built at nearby Port Chilkoot (now incorporated into Haines). Between 1922 and 1939, Fort Seward was the only army post in Alaska. Following World War II, the fort was sold to a group of war veterans.

Though officers' quarters are now private homes and a hotel has taken over the commanding officer's quarters, the fort remains remarkably military in appearance. Self-guided tours of the fort, now a national historical site, are popular.

Unlike towns in the lower Panhandle, Haines is a transportation hub, reached by land, sea, and air. Some cruise ships stop here, and ferries discharge both passengers and vehicles for the trek up the splendid Haines Highway.

Prevailing industries are commercial fishing and lumbering. It's possible to see Japanese freighters being loaded with timber at the dock.

The history of the Haines area is the history of the Chilkat and Tlingit Indians. Klukwan, 19 miles north of town, was the main village of the Chilkat people. At one time, it had 65 houses and about 600 residents; today only a few houses remain.

The area's early warlike and wily Indian traders dominated commerce with the Athabascans in the Interior. Their reign ended with the invasion first of fur traders and later of gold seekers following the Indian route (now called the Dalton Trail) to the Klondike.

Only 15,000 miles of roads penetrate Alaska's vast land. Except for Skagway and Haines, communities in the Panhandle are linked only by a watery "highway."

Accomplished in arts and crafts, the Chilkats were working with copper when the first white men arrived. The tribe excelled in the production of colorful goat hair blankets, still used in Tlingit ceremonies.

Lodging in Haines is limited to a handful of motels and bed-and-breakfast inns and the turn-of-the-century Halsingland Hotel in Port Chilkoot. Housed in quarters forming one side of the old fort's parade ground, the spacious hotel offers good food in its restaurant and a salmon bake nightly in season.

Campgrounds in the Haines area include three state-operated facilities: Portage Cove Wayside, ½ mile past Fort Seward on Beach Road, offering walk-in and bicycle camping only; Chilkoot Lake Wayside, 5 miles beyond the ferry terminal on Lutak Road, a scenic, well-maintained facility offering a boat launch and fishing; and Chilkat State Park, about 7 miles out Mud Bay Road, with trailer sites, picnic tables, fire pits, and spectacular views of Rainbow and Davidson glaciers.

Highlights of the area include the arts and crafts, music, and dances of the Chilkat tribe. A revival of interest in the tribe's ancient culture was stimulated by Alaska Indian Arts, Inc., a nonprofit organization. Replicas of an authentic Indian tribal house, totems, and other artifacts of Indian life have been assembled at Port Chilkoot.

At the Chilkat Center for Arts, a relocated and renovated cannery, the Chilkat Dancers, dressed in full regalia, perform the colorful dances of the Northwest Coast Indians on Monday, Wednesday, and Saturday evenings. Special performances take place when cruise ships and ferries are in port.

In the crafts workshop of Fort Seward's former Hospital Building, you can watch native artists carve totems, create blankets, and fashion silver jewelry. Haines craftspeople have produced totem poles for clients all over the world, including the world's tallest totem pole (132½ feet) for Japan's Osaka World's Fair in 1970.

Have a glass of Russian tea and peer into the past at the Sheldon Museum and Cultural Center in downtown Haines. The collection of a long-time resident provides an entrée into the days of the gold rush, when shotgun-toting Jack Dalton drove cattle and packhorses into the Interior to supply Yukon mining camps.

Other activities around town include a visit to the 49,000-acre Alaska Chilkat Bald Eagle Preserve. From October to January, Haines hosts around 3,500 bald eagles that follow the migrating salmon up the Chilkat River. It's an awesome sight to see cottonwood trees laden with eagles. Even in

Authentically garbed Chilkat Dancers reenact ancient Indian stories in performances at the Chilkat Center for Arts in Haines.

Drivers of the Skagway Street Car Company's city tour pose outside the Arctic Brotherhood Hall, a turn-of-the-century meeting place for the miners' first fraternal organization.

To the Klondike by trail & rail

When George Washington Carmack and his two Indian companions, Skookum Jim and Tagish Charlie, discovered gold in a tributary of the Klondike River in August, 1896, they had no idea it would set off one of the greatest gold rushes in history.

Thousands of stampeders poured into the newly created Alaskan shanty towns of Dyea and Skagway, the jumping-off points for the 600-mile trek to the goldfields. Hardships lay ahead on both trails—the Chilkoot out of Dyea and the White Pass out of Skagway.

The Chilkoot was toughest on men because they had to carry all their gear; pack animals could not traverse the steep slopes. Though animals did travel the White Pass Trail, more than 3,000 of them died en route, many at a place called Dead Horse Gulch.

Once over the passes, the gold seekers built boats to float the remaining 560 miles on the Yukon River to the Klondike.

Today, the Klondike Highway parallels the White Pass Trail and the railroad that was so laboriously built over the mountains. But many hikers still prefer to follow in the footsteps of those early gold prospectors. They climb the famous trail from Dyea over Chilkoot Pass and then descend to the headwaters of the Yukon River in British Columbia.

Hiking the Chilkoot Trail

Not since the winter of 1897–98, when thousands of fortune seekers poured over this and nearby White Pass on their way to the goldfields, have so many made the crossing on foot.

The resurgence of activity along the 33-mile trail began when it became part of the Klondike Gold Rush National Historical Park. Though still a difficult hike requiring 3 to 5 days, the route has been marked and cleared to the summit, bridges have been built across streams, and shelters have been erected for hikers.

Over the pass. The trail begins 9 miles northwest of Skagway, near the townsite of Dyea, and follows the Taiya River to its source near Chilkoot Pass, crossing the stream several times.

Don't be misled by those famous—and intimidating—photographs of heavily burdened miners struggling up steep slopes toward the summit of 3,739-foot Chilkoot Pass. The going is easy over most of the trail, and you gain only a thousand feet over the first 13 miles.

But then you begin to climb in earnest, gaining 2,700 feet in the 3 miles to the summit. The final ¼ mile is practically an all-fours ascent over talus—but, once at the top, hikers are rewarded with broad, majestic views of glacial peaks. Wildlife is abundant; you may see brown bear, mountain goat, moose, ptarmigan, or porcupine.

Once over the pass, the trail descends on the Canadian side into dry, open country studded with dwarf spruce and pine, and past several pristine lakes and ponds to Lake Bennett. Hikers often leave the trail to walk the tracks of the old railroad to the Klondike Highway, where they look for a ride into Carcross.

White Pass & Yukon Railroad

Though you can't get all the way from Skagway to Whitehorse today on this steam train, it's an exciting ride over the mountains following the trail of the '98ers.

Building a railroad through the rugged St. Elias Mountains, which separate the Yukon from the sea, was quite a challenge. On hand to meet the challenge was Michael J. Heney, known as the "Irish Prince."

In Skagway, Heney met with Sir Thomas Tancrede, who represented an English group willing to finance a railway. After an all-night discussion, the two agreed to construct a route through the toughest railroad country in North America.

Materials arrived at Skagway on May 27, 1898, and soon ribbons of steel pointed north toward White Pass. By July, a passenger train operated on 4 miles of track, the first train to run in Alaska and the most northerly railway on the continent at that time.

Burrowing under Tunnel Mountain presented almost insurmountable difficulties. The tunnel had to penetrate a perpendicular barrier of rock that juts out of the mountainside like a giant flying buttress. Machinery and equipment to build the 250-foot tunnel had to be hoisted manually up the sides of sheer cliffs.

A short distance from the summit of the pass, a deep canyon is spanned by a steel cantilever bridge, 215 feet above the creek bed. Below lies Dead Horse Gulch.

Track reached the 2,900-foot-high pass in February, 1899; by July, construction extended as far as Lake Bennett in British Columbia.

While workers blasted and hacked their way through the pass from the south, construction started from Whitehorse toward Carcross. The two groups met at Carcross on July 29, 1900, and celebrated the construction of one of the most difficult railroads ever built.

summer, a number of the giant birds are visible at the preserve, about 19 miles north of Haines.

In order not to disturb the eagles, visitors to the site are requested to stay off the river flats where they feed and to observe them only at a distance. There are no facilities at the site except for portable toilets and trash containers at one turnout.

Summer tourists can investigate the Haines area more thoroughly. The variety of activities offered includes bus tours, guided hikes, canoe rentals, fishing boat charters, river rafting, and flightseeing. In winter, the Chilkat River Valley attracts snowshoers, skiers, and snowmobilers.

The Haines Highway, which originates in Haines, heads north to meet the Alaska Highway at Haines Junction, 159 miles away. (For more information on the road, see page 14.)

A small Indian cemetery lies 3½ miles from town near the airport. Starting at about Mile 9, you'll see bald eagles for the next 12 miles. The Indian village of Klukwan is 19 miles from Haines. At Mile 27, you can turn off to Mosquito Lake.

Skagway

Wedged in between mountain ranges at the northern end of Lynn Canal, Skagway resembles a movie back lot for a forthcoming Western. Its board sidewalks, false-front buildings, and costumed residents make you feel that you're stepping back in time to the days of the gold rush.

There is little rush and push in Skagway today; the town really only comes to life with the arrival of a cruise ship. The 20,000 residents it had during its heyday have dwindled to a mere 800 today. But those who are left take time to be friendly, and Skagway offers a revealing look into Alaska's past.

Skagway's history dates from the summer of 1896 when George Washington Carmack and his pals, Skookum Jim and Tagish Charlie, uncovered a

bonanza of placer gold in a tributary of the Klondike River. When word of the strike got out, prospectors swarmed to Seattle docks looking for passage north.

Captain William Moore got to Skagway first and staked out land for a wharf at the mouth of the Skagway River; his cabin has been restored and is on view at 5th and Spring streets.

The rush really got underway in the summer of 1897. A tent-and-clapboard city of 10,000 quickly sprang up as prospectors prepared to assault the mountain passes.

Skagway was the starting point for two main trails to the goldfields—one that led through Dyea and onto the famous Trail of '98 over Chilkoot Pass, and the other the White Pass Trail, a route that was later followed by both the White Pass & Yukon Railroad, which connected Skagway and Whitehorse, and the Klondike Highway.

Skagway (the name comes, aptly, from the Tlingit word for "windy place") boomed, albeit turbulently, under the gang rule of "Soapy" Smith, until Soapy and a vigilante, Frank Reid, shot it out after a public meeting held to rid the town of lawless Mr. Smith. *Days of '98* performances, timed for cruise ship and ferry arrivals, depict the life and times of the infamous Soapy.

At Gold Rush Cemetery, north of town, you can see their graves. Many other graves testify to the lost hopes of those attempting to make their fortune. A waterfall named after Reid, the town hero, is just a short hike beyond the cemetery.

Klondike Gold Rush National Historical Park preserves much of this history. Its boundaries include most of downtown Skagway and the routes over the passes. The park even reaches south to Seattle to include Pioneer Square, the jumping-off spot for the gold rush.

The park's visitor center, located in the old rail depot at 2nd and Broadway, offers tours (daily at 11 A.M. and 3 P.M.) and talks on Skagway history. A half-hour film about the gold rush, narrated by Hal Holbrook, is shown several times a day.

The Trail of '98 Museum, upstairs in Skagway's city hall building (7th and Spring streets), is housed in Alaska's first granite building. Originally a Methodist college dating from 1899, the museum contains many relics of those golden days. Many of the old court records are on display, along with some of the old courtroom furnishings.

Accommodations in Skagway include small motels, bed-and-breakfast inns, a restored and renovated gold rush–era hotel, and a newer hotel with turn-of-the-century decor. The hotels have restaurants; you'll find others on Broadway and on side streets.

Campgrounds are available at the City RV Park by the small boat harbor, Hanousek Park at 14th and Broadway, Hoover's RV Park at 4th and State, and a small park at the Dyea-Chilkoot trail head, ½ mile south of the Chilkoot Trail on Dyea Road.

Activities around town feature sightseeing by horse and buggy, touring cars, or bus, as well as "The Skagway Story," a 2-hour tour of the area and a half-hour film on the White Pass & Yukon Railroad in the historic Arctic Brotherhood Hall.

Skagway and Haines are only 13 miles apart by ferry or plane, but 360 miles by car. Frequent flights link the two towns. But, if you have the time, the drive via the Klondike, Alaska, and Haines highways is very scenic. It's often possible to rent a car in one town and return it to the other, but do expect a drop-off charge. To make a full loop, take the ferry back to Skagway from Haines; there's normally space on this short run.

White Pass & Yukon Railroad, built in 1898 to carry prospectors and supplies to the Klondike gold fields, still carries passengers over the mountains on a spectacular round-trip excursion past cascading waterfalls and over awesome gorges. From mid-May to mid-September, two trains daily depart the downtown station for the 3-hour run. Tickets cost $72 (half-price children 3 to 12), but the trip is worth it.

Just one gulp away—a brown bear perches precariously at the waterfall's edge to catch dinner, a spawning salmon that has fought its way up the Brooks River in Katmai National Park and Preserve.

Abandoned now, Kennecott Copper Mine's barn-red buildings sprawl down the hillside in Alaska's Wrangell–St. Elias National Park and Preserve. Hiking is the only way to reach the site.

Statistics only hint at the size and grandeur of Alaska, the largest state in the Union. It boasts the nation's highest mountains and longest scenic rivers, as well as more than half its coastline and most of its dwindling wildlife.

In contrast to the Lower 48, Alaska's lands appear virtually unmarked, affected only by seasons, weather, the descent of a glacier down a mountain valley, or the migration of a caribou herd across the tundra.

In 1980, Congress guaranteed that much of this primeval wilderness would remain intact. With the passage of the Alaska National Interest Lands Conservation Act, almost one-third of Alaskan lands were preserved in national parks, preserves, monuments, forests, and other wilderness areas.

Protecting the wilderness

Because the land is relatively unproductive and fragile, parks and refuges must be larger than they are in the Lower 48. One grizzly bear, for example, needs 100 square miles just to feed itself and rear its young.

Under the new law, acreage was added to Denali National Park, and Katmai and Glacier Bay were expanded and upgraded to park status to preserve entire ecosystems.

Also protected were such scenic splendors as Gates of the Arctic, a vast area encompassing the north and south slopes of the Brooks Range; the spectacular Lake Clark region, where the Alaska and Aleutian ranges meet; Kobuk Sand Dunes in Kobuk Valley National Park, containing Alaska's surprising desert lands; Aniakchak Caldera, a spectacle of volcanism; and Wrangell–St. Elias, a collection of the continent's greatest peaks and glaciers.

The Tongass and Chugach national forests (the country's largest national forestlands) increased in acreage. Wildlife refuges were established for millions of birds, sea lions, seals, otters, walruses, whales, and polar bears. And over 20 of the state's 3,000 rivers were classified as "wild and scenic" to restrict future development and incompatible use.

A controversial issue

The sweeping lands act was bitterly debated for years. Everyone agreed that some portion of the wilderness should be preserved. The question was, how much?

When Secretary of State, William H. Seward engineered the purchase of Alaska from Russia in 1867, most people thought of this region as an icebox. They never dreamed of its varied landscapes: lush rain forests, towering mountain ranges, rolling tundra plains, long stretches of braided rivers, and islands and lakes too numerous to name.

Underneath the beauty, though, lay vast untapped resources of precious oil, gas, and minerals. Virtually unlimited forests attracted lumbering interests. And the natives, realizing the economic potential of future commercial use, wanted a share of the profits.

Though the resulting Alaska Native Claims Settlement Act of 1971 gave the Eskimos, Aleuts, and Indians claim to 44 million acres, it added, almost as an afterthought, an amendment setting aside land for possible national parks, forests, wildlife refuges, and scenic and wild rivers.

Thus, the controversy began between conservatives and developers. The urge to preserve Alaska's untouched wilderness clashed head-on with economic pressures.

The bill that eventually passed both houses of Congress contained some expected modifications. Normally, national parks do not permit logging, hunting, or other resource exploitation within their boundaries; motorized access is also restricted.

However, because many of these new parklands were already occupied or used traditionally by Alaska's natives, the law allows them to continue their subsistence hunting, fishing, and food-gathering activities. Natives may also use boats, aircraft, and snowmobiles as long as it is customary for their subsistence. Sport hunting in national preserves is permitted for everyone.

A park roster

Though detailed information on many of the state's national parks, preserves, and monuments is given throughout this book, you can receive additional material by writing directly to the parks.

A listing of addresses for Alaska's national parklands can be found on page 116. Some parks are difficult to reach and may lack facilities.

Sitka

One of the Panhandle's most scenic and historic cities, Sitka gives every visitor an especially warm welcome. When you see the town, you'll understand why Russian emissary Alexander Baranof decided to build his castle here—and why the Tlingits had already claimed the spot.

The town occupies one of the state's most ideal settings, looking out over the blue waters of Sitka Sound to the perfect symmetry of Mt. Edgecumbe, an extinct volcano that might be a twin to Japan's Mt. Fuji. Boat trips give you a close look at the many forested islands clustered in the harbor. The town's major sights are within easy walking distance of the harbor.

A Russian history

Until the Russians arrived in the late 1700s, seeking to extend their empire to the south and west, Sitka was the home of the Tlingit Indians. In 1804, Alexander Baranof, governor of the Russian colonies, selected the site for his new capital. Two years later, while Baranof was away, the Tlingit Indians rebelled, killing most of the Russian inhabitants and destroying their property. Baranof returned with an armada and retook the region, but only after a fierce battle.

Sitka went on to become the heart of a fur-trading empire that reached as far south as Fort Ross in northern California. Russian colonists built factories, ships, schools, hospitals, and a fine governor's home.

Known as the "Paris of the Pacific," the town was a center of trade, industry, and culture in the new world and at one time was the largest community on the Pacific coast. In the Tlingit Indian language, Sitka means "in this place." The place carried the name Fort Archangel Michael for 68 years.

When rising costs made the Alaskan colony a burden, Russia decided to sell. Alaska was transferred to the United States on October 18, 1867, in tearful ceremonies held on Castle Hill,

a huge, boxlike rock (behind the post office) where Baranof's home stood. Though the residence is no longer standing, the site commands an impressive view of the town.

Pieces of living history, the Panhandle's carved totem poles make bold statements about the lives of the people for whom they were erected. Poles stand as long as nature permits, usually around 60 years.

Following the transfer, a period of lawlessness and decline ensued, accompanied by numerous Indian uprisings and riots. In 1884, Alaska was established as a civil and judicial district, with its capital at Sitka. In 1906, the seat of government was moved to Juneau.

Commercial fishing and a pulp mill once provided the basis of the economy, but today, Sitka is a naval town. The government operates a hospital and boarding school here for natives.

Highlights

Sitka's attractions are many—and varied. It's unfortunate that so few cruise ships visit this port, and that those who do stop are on such a tight schedule. The only visitor complaint seems to be that it would be nice to have more time here.

Russian heritage. Many vestiges of Sitka's early days are still evident. On

a stroll around town you'll see a reconstructed Russian blockhouse; nearby lies an early-day Russian Orthodox cemetery. The earliest burials date back to the mid-1800s.

The Byzantine dome of St. Michael's Cathedral is visible from almost everywhere in town. Built between 1844 and 1848 and often described as the finest example of Russian architecture in the United States, the cathedral was carefully reconstructed through a community effort after a fire destroyed the original structure in 1966. Even the bronze bells in the spire were recast from the originals that had melted during the fire. Most of the vestments, marriage crowns, and beautifully detailed icons were saved and are now on display. Visiting hours are from 11 A.M. to 3 P.M. on Monday through Saturday, and from noon to 3 P.M. on Sunday; donations are requested.

The Russian Bishop's House, at the corner of Lincoln and Monastery streets, also dates from the 1840s. The restored house, now a part of Sitka National Historical Park (see below), is open daily during the summer and by appointment in winter. Bishop Ivan Veniaminov, later known as St. Innocent, was its first resident. Inside you'll find several restored rooms and displays of Russian artifacts, as well as the bishop's quarters and the Chapel of the Annunciation.

Sitka National Historical Park. In addition to the bishop's house, Sitka National Historical Park also includes a larger section, with a visitor center, about a mile southeast of downtown. The park was established in 1910 to commemorate the Battle of Sitka, a battle between the Indians and the Russians that took place on the point of land where the Indian River flows into Sitka Sound. All that remains of the fort is its outline, marked by posts, but the surroundings are largely unchanged.

In the visitor center, you'll find excellent exhibits and information that will help you make the most out of your visit. It's also your opportunity to watch Alaskan native craftspeople at work. The building itself, constructed in Indian longhouse style, makes use of house poles from potlatches.

The 54-acre park, which commemorates the last stand of the Tlingits, protects and preserves remnants of their culture. Footpaths meander among dense stands of hemlock, spruce, and alder.

Elder citizens have been respected and cared for in Alaska since 1913, when the first Pioneers' Home was established in Sitka to offer a residence to "indigent prospectors" and long-time residents.

Within the forestland stand a number of totems, some almost 60 feet tall. None of them came from Sitka originally; instead, they were brought here in 1905 from villages throughout southeastern Alaska for the Louisiana Purchase Exposition of 1904. Many of the poles are copies of the now-deteriorating originals.

Sheldon Jackson Museum. At the entrance to the Sheldon Jackson College campus, between the Sitka National Historical Park and the center of town, you can enjoy a rich collection of Russian, Eskimo, and Indian relics plus an elaborate display of native art.

In addition to founding Protestant missions and schools in Alaska, Dr. Jackson started the first public school system and introduced domestic reindeer to the region. He amassed his collection of Indian art, now regarded as the state's largest, on his travels throughout Alaska.

Pioneers' Home. For an education on life in early-day Alaska, visitors are welcome at the Pioneers' Home in downtown Sitka. The oldest of five such institutions, it's a state-supported retirement home for long-time Alaskans.

Residents produce arts and crafts for sale. The crafts room (in the basement) is open year-round from 8 A.M. to 4 P.M. The home's entrance is off Lincoln and Katlian streets. ''The Prospector,'' a large statue in front, symbolizes the pioneer spirit.

Centennial Building. The main attraction of any visit to Sitka is played out on the stage of the waterfront Centennial Building, where visitors are welcomed by the New Archangel Russian Dancers. Colorfully clad performers offer some of the Russian ethnic folk dances that recall Sitka's glittering past. (Performances take place when ships are in port.)

The Sitka Historical Society operates a small museum in the building. Exhibits focus on the purchase of Alaska, the natives, and the industries of the area.

Shopping. Sitka's compact downtown contains a variety of small shops that make the port one of Alaska's best for shopping. The Russian-American Company in the Bayview Trading Company (across from the harbor) sells fine Russian handicrafts plus Indian and Eskimo art. At The Observatory (202 Katlian St.) you can pick up antiquarian maps, prints, and books. Made in Alaska (237 Lincoln St.) offers handcrafted gifts, many made by local Sitkans. Also, don't overlook the gift store at the park for historical books on native cultures.

Where to stay

The Westmark Shee Atika hotel (98 rooms with mountain or harbor views, restaurant, and lounge) is the first choice for many Sitka overnighters. Other lodging options include The Potlatch motel (30 rooms) or one of the number of bed-and-breakfast inns around town. Mountain View Bed & Breakfast is a popular choice.

The U.S. Forest Service maintains a campground at Starrigavan Creek, 7 miles from downtown Sitka, at the end of the town's road system.

Getting around

Sitka is easily reached by scheduled and charter flights and by ferry. The picturesque fort is also on the itinerary of a few cruise ships.

A 3-hour sightseeing tour offers visits to the historical park, Sheldon Jackson Museum, St. Michael's Cathedral, and Centennial Building. On certain days the tour also includes a performance by the Russian dancers and a trip to Old Sitka.

Harbor and fishing tours are provided by several companies. Check with the Sitka Convention and Visitors Bureau (330 Harbor Dr.) for further information.

Climate & clothing

Those heavy-duty rubber boots are called Sitka slippers for good reason. Like other Panhandle towns, Sitka enjoys a temperate and moist maritime climate.

Dress casually and comfortably for a visit, and take along a rainproof coat.

Special festivities

Sitka's big celebration is the Alaska Day Festival in mid-October. Festivities include a costume parade, re-enactment of the Transfer from Russia ceremony, Tlingit dances, and Baranof's Ball.

Every June some of the world's finest musicians gather for the acclaimed Sitka Summer Music Festival. Chamber music performances are offered Tuesday and Friday evenings from the glass-walled stage of the Centennial Building. Musicians are housed at Sheldon Jackson College. For further information on the performances, write to the Sitka Summer Music Festival, P.O. Box 907, Sitka, AK 99835.

The Interior

Broad river valleys, muskeg flats, and old, worn-down mountains characterize the part of Alaska commonly referred to as "the Interior."

The Russians and British penetrated this region, which lies north of the Coastal Range and east of the Alaska Range, between 1834 and 1847 through waterways in summer and along dog trails in winter. In 1883 and 1885, some years after the United States purchased Alaska, U.S. Army Lt. Frederick Schwatka and Lt. Henry T. Allen journeyed into this wild area. Allen went in by the Copper River, where he reported the discovery of great ore deposits.

Discovery of gold in Fortymile River in 1886 lured prospectors and miners a decade before the more fabled Klondike rush. When another discovery was made in 1895 in Birch Creek near Circle, that town's population swelled to 500. The boom was short-lived, however; the Dawson rush a year later drew most of the miners away from this region.

Fairbanks, Alaska's second largest city and the hub of the Interior, calls itself the Golden Heart of Alaska. And so it was until the late 1930s, when gold became scarcer and dwindled in value.

Some 30 years later, Fairbanks became the center of another rush—this time for "black gold." As a point of departure for the North Slope oil fields, the city once again experienced a boom. Even gold made a slight comeback. You can still see working mines around town and inspect a giant dredge.

Visiting the Interior

Fairbanks, the center of inland Alaska, is reached by air, rail, or highway. Many visitors on their way to Fairbanks traverse the Interior on the Alaska Highway. Others rent cars in Anchorage or Fairbanks to explore the region at their own pace.

Where to stay. Fairbanks has several dozen lodging places, including hotels, motels, bed-and-breakfast inns, and a youth hostel. About a dozen public and private campgrounds are located in and around town. Some offer hookups.

Most hotels have their own restaurants and lounges. Other eating places and clubs are scattered throughout the city.

You'll find all the services you need here—dry cleaners, laundromats, supermarkets, and department stores. Prices in Fairbanks are fairly high for all services.

Denali National Park and Preserve, slightly over 100 miles away, offers a variety of accommodations in and around the park. In summer, make reservations well in advance.

Accommodations in the other small towns scattered around the Interior are limited.

Weather. The Interior rewards the visitor with the state's warmest summer weather—and its coldest winter climes (temperatures can plummet to −60°F). In summer, temperatures in Fairbanks often climb as high as 90°F; occasional thunderstorms darken the usually sunny skies. Winds are very light (you'll wish they were stronger during peak mosquito season). Daylight hours are long—about 21 hours—and it never really gets dark in June and July.

Alaska Railroad operates year-round over 470 miles of track between Seward and Fairbanks. Here, a train crosses Riley Creek Bridge between Anchorage and Denali National Park and Preserve.

The Interior

Circle—*location of historic hot spring*

Dawson City, Y.T.—*Klondike miners' goal*
- August Discovery Day celebration
- Diamond Tooth Gertie's cancan show
- Palace Grand Theatre "mellerdrammers"
- Robert Service and Jack London cabins
- Yukon River rafting

Fairbanks—*gold and oil boomtown*
- Alaskaland's collection of history
- *Discovery* stern-wheeler cruises
- Pipeline visit
- University of Alaska museum

Denali National Park & Preserve—*wildlife preserve*
- Backcountry hiking and camping
- Park bus tours
- Views of mighty Mt. McKinley

Nenana—*scene of Ice Classic, including lottery on ice "breakup" on the Tanana River*

Whitehorse, Y.T.—*riverboat center*
- *Frantic Follies* variety show
- *Klondike* stern-wheeler museum
- MacBride Museum
- Riverboat cruises

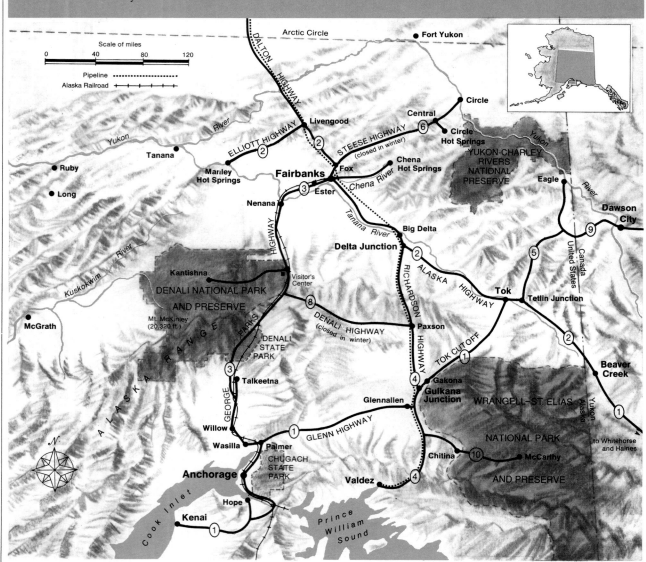

The Alaska Highway

The Alaska Highway begins officially in Dawson Creek, British Columbia, a booming, bustling town in the rich agricultural and oil country of the Peace River. Many motorists like to have their pictures taken at the popular "Mile 0" post that marks the start of the 1,475-mile road.

Most of the Alaska Highway is in Canada. Basically, it's a good, asphalt-paved road, with a surface that ranges from poor to excellent. The original mileposts are no longer an accurate indication of driving distance; newer Canadian posts show kilometers, but even they are incorrect as the highway is constantly being shortened and straightened.

You'll travel about 300 miles from Dawson Creek to Fort Nelson, another boom town near the site of an early Hudson's Bay trading post. From there it's an additional 618 miles to Whitehorse. (When you arrive at Morley River, you'll be about halfway to Fairbanks.)

Today, the longest stretch without services is 100 miles. For information on side trips along the way, turn to page 52.

Whitehorse, Yukon

Whitehorse is the governmental and trading center for the Yukon Territory. Once the focal point of navigation on the Yukon River, the city has preserved one of the fleet of 250 riverboats that plied local waters during the days of the gold rush. The S.S. *Klondike*, an old stern-wheel steamer converted into a museum, is beached on the river bank. Board the craft, now a national historic site, for a tour.

Around town. Free historical walking tours are offered three times daily during the summer. Meet at the Donnenworth House, 3126 3rd Ave.

Be sure to visit the MacBride Museum with its fine collection of artifacts from the Yukon's past. Inside the sod-roofed building you'll see relics

and photographs from the gold rush and riverboat era. Outside are displays of railway and mining equipment, as well as Sam McGee's cabin.

Another place in Whitehorse where history comes alive is the Old Log Church Museum. Built in 1900 as an Anglican church, it numbered among its parishioners the famous Yukoner Robert W. Service. It was for a church concert in 1904 that the well-known poet composed the ballad *The Shooting of Dan McGrew.* Service never recited it there, however, because the parishioners felt it was too risqué.

Service wrote numerous poems of the Yukon; in 1908, when he moved to Dawson, they were published in a collection called *Songs of a Sourdough.*

Born in England, poet Robert Service arrived in the Klondike at the time of the gold rush, an adventure that he chronicled in such memorable ballads as **The Cremation of Sam McGee.**

If you're staying overnight in Whitehorse, you may want to take in the long-running *Frantic Follies* vaudeville show. The performance features readings from Service's poetry.

Tours take visitors through the city to historic Lake Laberge, or upstream to the hydroelectric dam at Schwatka Lake. The water backed up by the dam forms the lake that tamed the infamous Whitehorse Rapids, where author Jack London earned a small fortune piloting riverboats.

On the east side of the dam is one of the world's longest all-wooden fish ladders. In August, when salmon run upstream to spawn, visitors can view the fish through a window at the side of the ladder.

Side trips from Whitehorse

You can drive to Alaska's southeast communities of Skagway and Haines over connecting highways. Today the White Pass & Yukon Railroad, which used to connect Whitehorse and Skagway, only operates as far as the summit of White Pass. But the Information Center at 302 Steele Street presents a free slide show on the railroad, Robert Service, and other town history.

The MV *Schwatka* offers 2-hour river cruises through Miles Canyon. A suspension bridge across the 125-foot-deep canyon can be reached by a side road from the Alaska Highway.

To Dawson City

North of Whitehorse, a mostly asphalt-surfaced road heads north to Dawson City, a delightful historical remnant of the romantic Klondike days. Now an historical complex, the town is being restored. Many old shrines have received a face-lift, and it's business as usual at some long-established firms. From Dawson City, you rejoin the Alaska Highway at Tetlin Junction, Alaska.

Dawson City offers plenty for the visitor to see and do. On a get-acquainted stroll up and down the old wooden sidewalks, you'll mingle with the spirits of Coatless Curley, Hamgrease Jimmy, Diamond Tooth Gertie, and Nellie the Pig.

At the Visitor Reception Centre, Front and King Streets, you can find out about city sightseeing tours, Yukon River excursions, Klondike River float trips, and evening entertainment. The center (open daily in summer) presents a slide show and films on sternwheelers and area mining.

Working alone with traditional methods, a carpenter skillfully peels logs to complete a building deep in the state's Interior.

October snowfall at Haines Junction on the Alaska Highway whitens the ground and trees and gently blankets the tiny church of Our Lady of the Way, made from an old Quonset hut.

...Highway

Parks Canada Center offers free guided walking tours of downtown Dawson's historic sites departing from the visitor center and St. Paul's Cathedral, 1st and Church streets.

Dawson City is the only city in Canada licensed for gambling. (For additional information on Dawson, see page 52.)

Whitehorse to Tok

North of Whitehorse, you travel through scenic country past log structures built by early prospectors. About 76 miles from Whitehorse is Aishihik Road (open in summer only). Seventeen miles down this road (not recommended for trailers or large recreational vehicles) is Otter Falls. Just beyond the falls is Aishihik Lake, where you'll find picnic sites, a campground, and a boat-launching ramp.

Haines Junction. At Haines Junction, headquarters for the Kluane National Park, the Alaska Highway meets up with State 3. Just north of Haines Junction, you skirt resplendent Kluane Lake.

Haines Junction has always been an important stop along the Alaska Highway. The town offers a variety of accommodations, eating places, gas stations, and other services. From here, helicopter tours give overviews of the nearby national park.

Because Haines Junction is also an overnight stop for tour buses traveling the Alaska Highway, a small visitor information center has been opened by the Yukon government. Check here for information on a slide show about the Yukon and Alaska. Performances take place at the community center; an admission fee is charged.

Beaver Creek. At Mile 1202 (Beaver Creek) is a customary stop—the 174-room Alas/Kon Border Lodge (now a Westours hotel), with a dining room, cocktail lounge, service station, and adjoining campground with hookups. North of Beaver Creek is the U.S.–Canada border.

Tok. The paved Glenn Highway from Anchorage joins the Alaska Highway at Tok, a friendly little community with a number of places to stay, including several state campgrounds with facilities for RVs.

Tok residents raise, breed, and train dogs, making the village one of Alaska's headquarters for dog mushing, a state sport. Since Tok is also a trading center for several Athabascan Indian villages, birch baskets, beaded moccasins, boots, and necklaces are good buys here.

Tok to Delta Junction

From Tok, the Alaska Highway follows the Tanana River drainage to Delta Junction, where it converges with the Richardson Highway. Strung out along the Delta River, Delta Junction saw its fortunes rise during construction of the Alaska pipeline, which crosses the Tanana River nearby.

In 1926, a small herd of bison was brought to the Delta area. They thrived and multiplied to such an extent that the government had to establish the National Bison Range in order to contain them. Nevertheless, they're still a problem to local farmers and, occasionally, to motorists. The best view of the bison is from Mile 241.3 on the Richardson Highway.

Delta Junction's information center is at the junction of the Alaska and Richardson highways. Continue north on the Alaska Highway to reach Fairbanks; turn south on the Richardson to go to Valdez and Prince William Sound.

Big Delta State Historical Park (rest rooms and picnic tables), 9 miles north of the information center, marks the turnoff of the old trail from Fairbanks to Valdez. A self-guided walking tour takes you past some of the restored buildings, including long-operating Rika's Roadhouse, that stood at this crossroads.

The Big Delta Bridge across the Tanana River affords a good view of the suspended pipeline. At Salcha River (good fishing) and at Quartz and Harding lakes, you'll find campgrounds.

Delta Junction to Fairbanks

The 98 miles between Delta Junction and Fairbanks offers some beautiful vistas. Be alert for moose feeding in swamps along the road. Several motels and lodges offer food and accommodations.

At the Chena Lakes Area, which offers campgrounds and picnic tables, you can pull rainbow trout or silver salmon from the lake, or angle for pike, whitefish, or grayling from the Chena River.

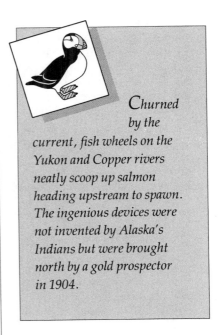

Churned by the current, fish wheels on the Yukon and Copper rivers neatly scoop up salmon heading upstream to spawn. The ingenious devices were not invented by Alaska's Indians but were brought north by a gold prospector in 1904.

Stop at the community of North Pole (14 miles south of Fairbanks) to visit Santa Claus House, shop for gifts at several stores, and postmark a letter from Santa to young friends.

Motorists who drive all of the Alaska Highway to its official end at the sod-roofed visitor center on the bank of the Chena River have earned their feeling of accomplishment. A sign proclaims that they have covered 1,523 miles (the original mileage figure) from Mile 0 at Dawson Creek, B.C. The marker also shows the distance from Fairbanks to some 75 cities around the world.

The city's visitor center (First and Cushman streets) also offers information on Fairbanks and other destinations throughout the state.

Of all Yukon Territory attractions, Canada's Klondike goldfields are the best known. Historic Dawson City evokes the romantic days of the rush that brought gold seekers to the banks of the Yukon River. Many of the original buildings still stand, intriguing visitors with their "Trail of '98" history.

The route to Dawson City, 327 miles north of Whitehorse, is via Klondike Highway 2 off the Alaska Highway. The mostly asphalt-surfaced loop route connects with the Top of the World and Taylor highways to return motorists to the Alaska Highway at Tetlin Junction.

The Klondike Highway is open year-round; the Top of the World and Taylor highways close during the winter. Accommodations, food, and gasoline are available in larger communities and at lodges and campgrounds along the loop.

Dawson City

Once a rich and bawdy gold rush town, Dawson City was, in its heyday, the largest settlement north of San Francisco and west of Winnipeg.

Yukon history is peppered with colorful characters, many of whom lived in Dawson City. Klondike Kate (whose real name was Kitty Rockwell) came to Dawson as a dance hall girl and became the toast of the Klondike. Arizona Charlie Meadows, a veteran of the Buffalo Bill show, sold whiskey to miners until he lost his bar in a flood and was forced to resort to sharpshooting to make a living.

Three of the main figures of the gold discovery—Tagish Charlie, Skookum Jim, and Kate Carmack—rest in a small cemetery 50 miles south of Whitehorse on the northern shores of Lake Bennett.

After the gold rush, Dawson City gradually became a virtual ghost town, reviving only after the road from Whitehorse was completed. Today, it's primarily a summer tourist town, though some mining continues.

In summer, you can still hear strains of honky-tonk music punctuated by the click of roulette wheels. The city relives its past in mid-August on Discovery Day, an annual fun-filled celebration.

Now a national historic site, Dawson City is being restored by Parks Canada, which presents films and slide shows in the information center at Front and King streets. You can stroll along the boardwalks past renovated residences, shops, and museums. Several mines allow you to pan for your own "color."

Other attractions include miniature stern-wheeler cruises, rafting trips on the Yukon or other rivers, "mellerdrammers" at the restored Palace Grand Theatre, gambling and cancan shows at Diamond Tooth Gertie's, touring the S.S. *Keno* (last steamer on the Yukon River), and visits to the cabins of Robert Service and Jack London. Gold rush films are shown daily in the historic Dawson City Museum.

From Dawson to the Alaska Highway

A free ferry at Dawson City carries passengers and vehicles across the Yukon River to the beginning of the Top of the World Highway. From here, it's 176 miles to the junction with the Alaska Highway.

The scenic gravel route has some steep and washboard sections and can be slippery in wet weather. If you meet an ore truck coming off a side road, pull over and let it pass—the truckers tend to speed.

Near the Alaska-Canada border is the Boundary Roadhouse (cabins, limited trailer space, gas, and home cooking). A small airstrip is maintained for the convenience of hunters.

Road to Eagle. A turnoff north onto the Taylor Highway leads to Eagle, a bush village on the banks of the Yukon. Here, Judge James Wickersham established the first U.S. Court in the Interior. You can visit the court and see the remains of Fort Egbert on a guided tour of the town, offered daily from Memorial Day to Labor Day.

Eagle is the headquarters city for Yukon-Charley Rivers National Preserve.

Back on the highway. Head southwest on the Taylor Highway to reach Tetlin Junction. The road follows the high country through a wilderness with scant population.

The main stopping place is a lodge near Fortymile River (service station, good food, and a friendly bar). Some gold mining still goes on in this district.

The Taylor Highway joins the Alaska Highway at Mile 1301, Tetlin Junction.

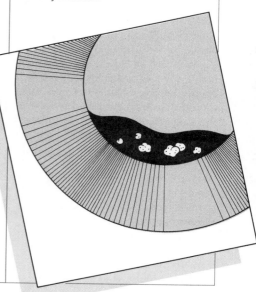

Fairbanks

A former trading post on the banks of the Chena River, Fairbanks stands in sharp contrast to its unpopulated, far-flung surroundings. A flat city, it disappoints travelers initially. From a plane, though, you can see low, rolling hills blanketed with stands of birch and white spruce. To the north and south, mountains rise majestically from the valley floor.

A service and supply point for the oil pipeline, Fairbanks grew rapidly in a somewhat disorganized fashion. The city is still one of contrasts—fancy new homes, hotels, and shopping centers rise next to creaky log cabins and buildings dating from the early 1900s.

A look back into history

Fairbanks traces its origins to 1901 when Captain E. T. Barnette, a trader and riverboat operator, was side-tracked into the Chena River on his way up the Tanana. When Felix Pedro, a prospector, told him about promising placer deposits in the area, Barnette decided to set up a trading post along the riverbank.

In 1902, Pedro discovered gold in the Tanana Valley, 16 miles from present-day Fairbanks. Word of the discovery spread quickly; by the next year a boom camp emerged, named for Charles Fairbanks of Indiana, then vice president of the United States. When Judge James Wickersham moved the U.S. Court from Eagle to Fairbanks, the future of the town was assured.

In winter, snow-covered trails from Eagle, Circle, Valdez, and other outlying towns were tramped down. With the coming of spring, riverboats from St. Michael and Dawson carried the gold seekers, and Fairbanks became a trading center.

Later, as delegate to the U.S. Congress from Alaska, Judge Wickersham was active in promoting the construction of the 470-mile railroad line from Seward to Fairbanks in order to "open up the Interior." Begun in 1914, the railroad was completed in 1923, making possible the transportation of huge machinery, such as dredges, to rework the creeks that had only been scratched by the early miners' primitive methods.

Getting there

Fairbanks, Alaska's second largest city, is easily reached from Anchorage, southeastern Alaska, and the Lower 48. Because Fairbanks is the hub of many interior air and road routes, regularly scheduled service and charter air trips depart from it to outlying towns and settlements.

Among your choices are flights to Chena Hot Springs, Circle Hot Springs, Eagle, the Arctic, and the Indian villages of Minto and Tanana; rail, bus, or car trips to Nenana; and air, rail, or auto tours to Denali National Park and Preserve.

Arrangements for hunting, boating, and fishing trips can be made through private charters.

Around town

Both at the airport and at the Visitor Information Center at First and Cushman streets, you'll find brochures, maps, and tips on what to see and how to get there. Pick up free maps for self-guided walking tours of the historic downtown and University of Alaska plus suggested driving tours. Note that sightseeing in the Interior is definitely geared for summer tourists. A car comes in handy for exploring.

City tours. Bus tours typically include downtown attractions, residential areas, visits to a gold dredge and the pipeline, and stops on the University of Alaska campus. Even if you're on your own, you'll find it informative to take a tour; later, you can revisit areas that interest you.

Information on state lands. For an especially helpful introduction to the state, visit the Alaska Public Lands Information Center at 250 Cushman St. (open daily in summer).

This office provides visitors with information on access, regulations, and availability of all of the state's parklands and refuges. A trip-planning computer gives travelers free print-outs on more than 200 recreational areas. Movies and slide shows are offered several times a day.

University of Alaska. This attractive campus is worth much more time than you get on a scheduled sightseeing excursion. In the museum you'll discover one of the state's finest collections of pioneer relics and Eskimo, Aleut, and Indian artifacts. Look, too, for notable displays of wildlife. Blue Babe, a preserved 36,000-year-old bison, is a star attraction. The museum is open daily in summer.

History buffs will want to peruse the collection of many rare, old books on Alaska's beginnings in the Elmer Rasmuson Library.

At the university's research station on Yankovich Road, musk oxen, caribou, reindeer, and moose can be viewed from platforms adjacent to the station; binoculars are recommended for observing critters in the far pastures. Tours of the musk ox, reindeer, caribou, and other Alaskan wildlife are offered at 1:30 and 3 P.M. Tuesday and Saturday in summer.

For a slide show of the aurora borealis, stop by the Geophysical Institute on Thursday at 2 P.M. The university's seismology lab and geodata center are also open to visitors.

Alaskaland. Situated near the banks of the Chena River, 44-acre Alaskaland, the state's only pioneer theme park, reveals Fairbanks's past and present. Memories of early mining days come alive on a stroll through Gold Rush Town, a village created from relocated log cabins, and Mining Village, a display of gold-mining equipment and gold panning.

Other attractions include the old stern-wheeler *Nenana*, a re-created

...Fairbanks

Eskimo village, the Pioneer Museum, and the Big Stampede Show, a pictorial history of the gold rush era. The Crooked Creek & Whiskey Island Railroad, a favorite with the children, encircles the park.

A domed building on the grounds is home for the Eskimo-Indian Olympics, held during the Golden Days celebration in July. To compete for awards a contestant must be at least one-quarter native. The only exception is the muktuk-eating contest, which is open to anyone with a hearty appetite for whale blubber.

To enjoy a little mining entertainment, stop by the turn-of-the-century Palace Theater and Saloon. Evening programs combine music with plays based on characters and incidents from the gold rush. Productions are scheduled nightly during the summer.

The Alaska Salmon Bake, in the picnic area at one corner of the Alaskaland grounds, serves salmon, halibut, ribs, fresh vegetables, and salad for lunch and dinner. If you can attend only one salmon bake while you're in Alaska, make it this one.

Shopping. Gift and curio shops carrying a wide assortment of goods line downtown streets. Furriers sell both skin and fur garments, including coats, jackets, and hats. Local craftspeople sell fine, handmade Alaskan jade and gold jewelry. Also available are prized garments knit from *qiviut*, the cashmere-soft wool of the musk ox. Made by natives from villages around the Interior and the Arctic, these garments are expensive, but they make beautiful and unusual gifts.

Side trips

The story goes that if you drink the water in the small community of Fox, about 12 miles from Fairbanks, you'll always come back for more—no matter where you live. The water tap from the artesian well is on the Elliott Highway (State 2), about half a mile on the left beyond the intersection with the Steese Highway (State 6).

To enjoy more of Alaska's water, try soaking in one of the bubbling thermal springs outside of Fairbanks. Today's visitors enjoy them as much as the miners did. For more information on the hot springs, turn to page 57.

Out at Gold Dredge No. 8, at Mile 9 on the Old Steese Highway, you'll learn why this monstrous machine from a bygone era is classified as a national historic district. Tour the dredge and try your hand at panning for gold (for

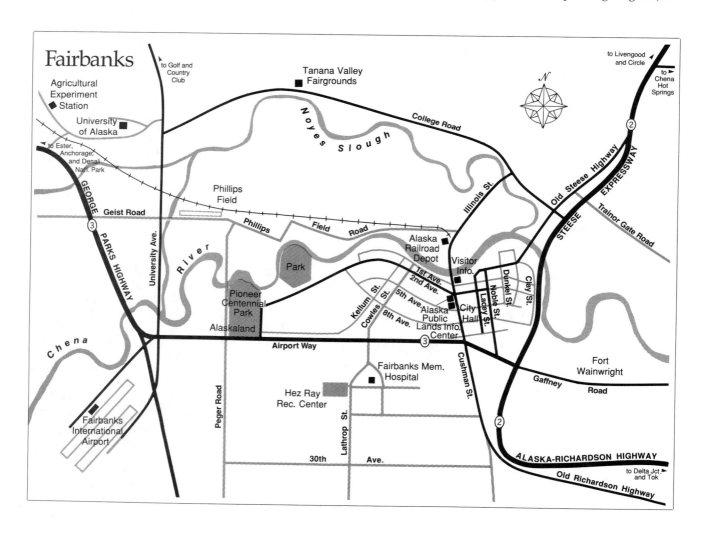

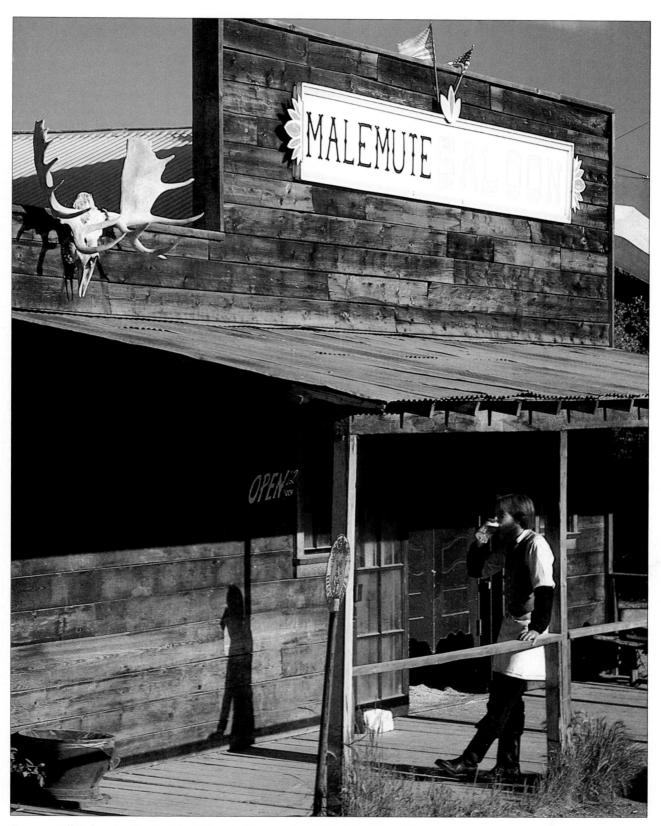

*Boys are still "whooping it up" at the Malemute Saloon as they did in Robert Service's
day. Bartender at the popular bar at Cripple Creek Resort in Ester breaks for a beer.*

a small fee). Also at the site are a restaurant, bar, gift shop, and motel.

Another national historic monument from the gold rush days, the Pump House (Mile 1.3 on the Chena Pump Road) was part of the vast system of pumps, sluiceways, ditches, and flumes constructed in 1933 by the Fairbanks Exploration Co. The renovated building is now a riverbank restaurant and lounge.

Stern-wheeler cruises

Long before roads were cut through the wilderness, stern-wheel paddleboats plied the riverways. Today you can recapture the excitement and adventure of the past by cruising aboard a stern-wheeler reproduction.

Your stern-wheeler first heads down the Chena River to the broad Tanana; there it takes you on a 30-mile round-trip into the backcountry, a 4-hour excursion. The boat stops at a re-created Indian fishing camp where you go ashore to watch a fish wheel in operation, learn how salmon are cleaned and dried, find out about the care and training of sled dogs, and study native architecture.

Sometimes moose, bear, and beaver are sighted on this unusual trip. Along the river are some attractive homes; many have small planes as well as boats tethered to their docks.

The *Discovery III*, the latest of the line, is docked just outside Fairbanks off Airport Way on Discovery Road. Ships depart twice daily, at 8:45 A.M. and 2 P.M., from late May to mid-September. The cost is moderate and the trip is often included in package tour itineraries. Contact Alaska Riverboat Discovery, 1975 Discovery Drive, Fairbanks, AK 99709 for more information.

The Malemute Saloon

"A bunch of the boys were whooping it up. . . ." So begins Robert Service's *The Shooting of Dan McGrew*. You can join them at the Malemute Saloon at Ester, just 9 miles south of Fairbanks on the George Parks Highway (State 3).

Once the center of the Cripple Creek mining district, the town was a bustling community of 15,000 in its heyday. Today, it's been declared a national historic site.

Ester is probably best known now for the saloon with the sawdust floor, as realistic an old-time Alaskan bar as you'll find. Live entertainment includes rollicking gold rush melodies and spirited recitations of Service's tales of the North.

The hotel and bunkhouse, now modernized, accept guests (20 rooms are available). The restaurant's all-you-can-eat dinner includes crab, reindeer steak, fried chicken, halibut, and biscuits with homemade blueberry jam. For information on lodging, dinner, or complimentary transportation to Ester from Fairbanks, write P.O. Box 101, Ester, AK 99725 or phone (907) 479-2500.

Two spectacular multimedia shows (separate admission fees) are presented nightly Memorial Day to Labor Day in the Firehouse Theater. The Crown of Light show features the aurora borealis.

Special events

During the summer, a number of colorful events fill the city's calendar. In June, you can watch the annual Midnight Sun Baseball game, played without artificial lights. The Golden Days celebration in July commemorates the founding of Fairbanks.

Also held in July are the World Eskimo-Indian Olympics, an unusual competition focused on strength and endurance.

Northern lights mystery

What is the origin of the northern lights, the luminous display of streams of light that arch across the arctic night sky? According to one Eskimo legend, it's the spirits of the dead playing ball with a walrus head. Natives also claim that the aurora borealis responds to certain sounds; early Eskimos tried to attract the lights by whistling or banging on metal.

Scientists have another explanation for the display. They believe that it all begins when a few charged solar particles penetrate the earth's atmospheric shield. These electrons ionize the atoms and molecules in the atmosphere, creating the aurora.

The light show starts slowly as a simple arc in the evening sky, intensifying around midnight to a more violent explosion of ricocheting and cascading flares of color. Some people even claim to hear a rustling sound during the performance. Why the energy becomes more powerful and the colors more intense is still being debated in scientific circles.

The lights are visible as many as 243 nights (not during the summer) in different areas of the state. The best observation spot is on the northern outskirts of Fairbanks. You'll need a clear sky.

The spectacle has also been preserved on tape by Alaska's Geophysical Institute; you can see (or buy) a copy at the University of Alaska Museum at Fairbanks.

Another dramatic presentation, set to music, is offered at a nightly show at Cripple Creek Resort in Ester.

The best views of the midnight sun can be found along the route to one of the state's most surprising destinations—historic mineral hot springs.

From Fairbanks, the partially paved Steese Highway leads 162 miles into the Interior to Circle. En route you can visit sites of old and new mining camps and bathe in hot springs once patronized by prospectors. Pedro Monument stands 16 miles outside of Fairbanks, at the site of the first gold discovery in Tanana Valley.

Enjoying the sun

During the summer solstice (June 20–22), when the sun is at its greatest distance north of the celestial equator, the sun slowly circles the northern horizon. If the weather is clear, you'll get your best view of the midnight sun from Eagle Summit (elevation 3,880 feet), 108 miles from Fairbanks.

The sky takes on a twilight glow as the sun dips down to the west; but instead of setting, the sun swings laterally along the horizon to a due north position at midnight, never once too low to view. The long sunset then becomes sunrise, the orb moves on to the eastern sky, and a new day begins.

From the barren crest of Eagle Summit, you have an unobstructed view across the low-lying Yukon River valley to the northern horizon. In autumn, migrating caribou cross the summit.

Beyond the summit, the road drops down into the Yukon watershed. From Mile 109, the roadway to the small town of Central (gas, food, and lodging) has been widened. You can view remnants of the town's once thriving mining past in Central's museum. The old Central House roadhouse at Mile-

post 128 replaced a structure dating from the 1890s. A branch road leads to Circle Hot Springs, 8 miles away.

Circle Hot Springs

Discovered in 1893 by a prospector trailing a wounded moose, the hot springs soon became a popular winter destination for miners.

Its hot mineral waters still attract visitors today. Hot water piped under a large garden plot gives vegetables an early start in spring, enabling them to grow to tremendous size during the short summer.

At the popular Arctic Circle Hot Springs Resort, you can try gold panning and fishing, in addition to sampling the mineral springs. Tourist facilities include a camper parking area, general store, bakery, curio shop, and airstrip.

The recently renovated lodge (more comfortable than the original tent bathhouses) offers rooms, cabins, a dining room and cocktail lounge, and an indoor swimming pool.

Circle

Until the pipeline haul road was built to Prudhoe Bay, Circle, at the end of the Steese Highway, was the northernmost point in Alaska to which it was possible to drive from an interconnecting highway system.

At Circle, you're only 50 miles south of the Arctic Circle.

Today, the once-large miners' supply center is a small community with a grocery store, gas station, motel, and trading post. On the Yukon River, a campground makes a popular summer destination for canoe enthusiasts and floatplane owners. Several other campgrounds and trail systems are

located along the highway between Fairbanks and Circle.

Other hot springs

Roads branch off from the Steese Highway to two other spas—Chena and Manley hot springs.

Chena Hot Springs takes its name from the nearby Chena River. To reach the springs, exit the Steese Highway at Mile 4.6 and follow the Chena Hot Springs Road 56½ miles. The resort offers lodging, food, a lounge, a pool, and camping spaces.

To reach Manley Hot Springs, turn off the Steese Highway onto the Elliott Highway at Fox, 11 miles north of Fairbanks. The year-round resort lies at the end of a 152-mile gravel road. The hot springs are on a hillside just before you enter town.

Once a busy trading community during mining days, Manley is now a quiet settlement with great civic pride. The town maintains a public campground and keeps up spacious lawns that give the locale a parklike look.

The Yukon River brings frequent travelers; the small town also receives quite a bit of air traffic from Fairbanks.

Aristocratic Dall sheep make their home high among the crags and slopes of Alaska's mountain ranges.

Blonde Toklat grizzly sow stands up to sniff the air and survey the terrain for possible danger to her cubs. The grizzly is one of the state's most dangerous animals.

Denali National Park

There are higher mountains in the world but few that rise as monumentally as Mt. McKinley—from a valley only 1,000 feet above sea level to an altitude of 20,320 feet. It's the park's main spectacle, even at a distance of 26 miles (the closest approach by car), and overshadows other wilderness attractions that are themselves reason enough for a visit.

Called *Denali* ("the high one") by the Indians, the mountain was named McKinley in 1896 by William L. Dickey, a prospector. But the name of the park surrounding this mighty mountain has recently been changed from Mt. McKinley National Park to Denali National Park and Preserve.

Originally created in 1917, the park, which straddles the Alaska Range south of Fairbanks, was enlarged in 1932 to nearly 2 million acres. In 1980, under the Alaska National Interest Lands Conservation Act, the boundaries were expanded. Today, the park and preserve encompass 5.6 million acres.

In summer, the frequent cloudy, rainy weather (caused by the mountain itself) prevents many visitors from ever seeing Mt. McKinley. During periods of low visibility, your only view of its top might be from a plane. Flying between Fairbanks and Anchorage, you can see its snowy summit rising above surrounding clouds.

Getting to the park

The all-weather George Parks Highway (State 3), which follows a direct route between Fairbanks and Anchorage, skirts the edge of the park. About 120 miles south of Fairbanks (237 miles north of Anchorage), it crosses the road into the park. In summer, the park can also be reached from Paxson along the gravel-surfaced Denali Highway (State 8).

Except for a stretch along the Susitna River, the Alaska Railroad travels the same route as the George Parks Highway and is a very popular park approach. For the best views, ride in one of the special vistadome cars available on the Anchorage-Denali-Fairbanks run. Trains run daily in summer. The trip takes about 7 hours from Anchorage, about 4 hours from Fairbanks.

Regularly scheduled motor coach service to the park is available from either Fairbanks or Anchorage. If you sign up for a package tour, transportation to the park is usually included.

Airlines make scheduled trips to Denali from both Fairbanks and Anchorage. You can also take flightseeing trips from the park area or from Talkeetna, Anchorage, or Fairbanks. A round-trip air tour from Anchorage takes 3 to 4 hours.

What to take

For a safe and enjoyable visit to the park, plan for variable weather. A layered look will take you from hot summer days to cooler evenings. In spring and autumn, add a warm sweater or coat underneath your rain gear. Bring sturdy walking shoes or boots.

For a day's ride on the shuttle bus or a hike in the park, take along a picnic lunch and snacks, insect repellent, binoculars with a spotting scope, and a camera with a telephoto lens.

Where to stay

Except in summer when lodging around the park is at a premium, it's not difficult to find accommodations that match the type of wilderness experience you're seeking. With advance reservations, you have a choice of everything from hotel rooms and lodges to primitive tent-cabins and railway car roomettes.

In addition to hotels, lodges, and campgrounds inside the park, motels, bed-and-breakfast inns, a hostel, and campgrounds along the George Parks Highway just outside the park offer lodging. If you're traveling on your own, it's best to consult a travel agent.

Hotels and lodges in the park. The Denali Park Hotel is the only hotel inside the east end of the park. It offers the unique choice of either conventional hotel rooms or Pullman-style railroad sleeping cars. The coffee shop is in a couple of remodeled dining cars, and the bar is actually several rejuvenated lounge cars.

Feel a breeze? It could be a chinook, *an unseasonably warm wind that can cause winter thaw,* a taku, *a sudden gale blowing off an icecap, or a* williwaw, *a gust that spills over a mountainside into an otherwise protected valley.*

Deep within the park are two lodges and an historic roadhouse. Camp Denali, a true wilderness lodge dedicated to lovers of the outdoors, has a main lodge, a dining hall, and chalet-style cabins. Each room has running water, propane lights, a hot plate, and a wood stove; showers and rest rooms are nearby. The rooms in the small North Face Lodge have private baths. Historic Kantishna Roadhouse offers cabin lodging.

Both the North Face and Kantishna include meals and transportation from the park entrance in the room cost.

Activities in this area center around Wonder Lake, where you can swim or paddle a canoe or kayak. Additional diversions include hiking and mountain climbing, fishing, berry picking, and picture taking.

Alaska's bonanza of wildlife offers visitors myriad viewing opportunities. The range of birds, sea mammals, and big game animals extends from the southeastern tip of the Panhandle to the farthest northern point of the frozen Arctic coast.

Listed below are some of the most plentiful of the state's birds and animals, and the areas they inhabit.

Birds galore

More species of birds are found in Alaska than in any other state. Even in the chilliest reaches of the Arctic, bird life abounds. The Pribilof Islands are an ornithologist's dream, playing host to some 180 species of birds.

The bald eagle, a very conspicuous bird, is found in greater numbers in Alaska than in all other states combined. The prime habitat for bald eagles is the forested coastline and offshore islands of southeastern Alaska. One of the heaviest concentrations dwells on the 678-mile coastline of Admiralty Island, where the average is almost two nests per mile. The Chilkat Valley near Haines is another favorite nesting area.

Eagles nest solitarily atop spiring snags, returning to the same nest year after year. The white headfeathers of the mature eagle gave this regal bird its name—the term bald was commonly used during the 17th and 18th centuries to signify white.

Grouse and ptarmigan come in several different kinds and species in Alaska. It takes a sharp eye to spot the well-camouflaged ptarmigan, Alaska's state bird. In summer, its subtle color blends with the brown of the tundra. As the year advances, the ptarmigan takes on the snowy white of its wintery background.

Of all the grouse in Alaska, the spruce grouse seems most at home. These birds feed on the needles of spruce trees. You'll find handsome blue grouse in southeastern Alaska and small ptarmigan in the Arctic. These birds never fail to tempt hunter and photographer alike.

Shorebirds in Alaska are another fascination for those who learn when and where to look for them. The coastal waters from Ketchikan to the Pribilof Islands abound with seafaring murres, puffins, cormorants, and gulls.

Some of the "bird cliffs" harbor thousands of nesting sea birds, incubating their eggs in the most unlikely nooks and crannies. A narrated cruise out of Homer in Kachemak Bay to Halibut Cove offers a close-up look at many species of such birds.

Inland species found in marshy river bottoms include ducks, swans, and geese. Bird life takes on an international flavor when the wheatears arrive from Asia, the golden plovers fly in from Hawaii, and the warblers wend their way north from Mexico and South America.

Even in winter you'll see a surprising variety of seasonal residents: chickadees, jays, woodpeckers, several kinds of owls, water ouzels, and the ubiquitous ravens.

Sea mammals

Seals, sea lions, whales, and porpoises are prevalent in Alaskan waters, from the far north to the southeastern coast.

Seals can be spotted from Ketchikan's waterfront and along the highway north of Juneau. You'll also see many seals sunning on ice floes in Prince William Sound and Glacier Bay.

The rare ribbon seal is found in the northwestern Bering Sea and along the coast from Point Barrow to the Aleutians. Harbor seals inhabit the area from the northern Bering Sea down through southeastern Alaska. Ringed seals are found only in the far northern reaches.

Large bearded seals, some weighing as much as 700 pounds, live in the Bering, Chukchi, and Arctic seas. They're characterized by their pronounced whiskers.

Fur seals usually spend most of their time in the open ocean, hauling themselves out on the Pribilof Islands in late spring. The Gulf of Alaska and waters to the south form the territory of the Steller sea lions, large relatives of the fur seal.

Whales and porpoises are often seen by visitors to Alaska. The most prominent of the big whales is the humpback. Difficult to identify in the water, it often obliges by jumping right out into view. Killer whales have long dorsal fins and striking white markings. The beluga whales of Cook Inlet and the Bering Sea are completely white.

Whales are often seen in Glacier Bay; a large feeding area is located just outside the bay's entrance.

Compared to whales, porpoises look surprisingly small. Harbor porpoises are gray; Dall's porpoises have white areas on their backs. You'll chance upon them anywhere from the Panhandle northward.

Sea otters, portly members of the weasel family, usually float on their backs, their heads and feet just visible above the water. These playful mammals inhabit shallow areas of the coastline.

The toothy walrus, prized by native carvers for its ivory tusks and teeth, never ventures south of the Bering Sea. It migrates north in spring to the Chukchi Sea, following closely behind the ice breakup.

Big game animals

A photographer's and hunter's paradise, Alaska has as many big game animals as the rest of the states put together. Somewhere along your trip you'll get at least a glimpse of a few of these very impressive creatures.

Bears come in several sizes and colors. Black bears are found all over the state. They're called glacier bears in the Glacier Bay area of southeastern Alaska and cinnamon bears elsewhere.

The larger brown bear is found throughout the state's southern coastal area—from the Panhandle to the Alaska Peninsula. Some of the state's largest brown bears are found on Kodiak Island.

Its near relative, the grizzly, ranges in color from light blonde to black. Visitors usually view the blonde version of the grizzly from a distance in Denali National Park.

Polar bears, the northern relatives, inhabit the Bering Sea and Arctic Ocean ice packs. These shy white creatures are protected against most hunters.

Bison were introduced to Alaska in the early 1900s. A large herd now roams the Big Delta region south of Fairbanks, sometimes wandering so close to the Alaska Highway that motorists have to be alert to avoid them.

Caribou wander in herds across the interior and northern parts of the state. Some of the likeliest places to see these nomadic creatures are in Denali National Park and Preserve and Prudhoe Bay.

Curly-horned Dall sheep can be found in all of Alaska's major mountain areas. At Sheep Mountain, a reserve along the highway northeast of Anchorage, travelers can watch the sheep scamper high up on the mountainsides. They can also be seen in Denali National Park.

Elk are barely accessible to visitors. Three large herds are on islands: Afognak and Raspberry islands near Kodiak, and Revillagigedo Island near Ketchikan.

Moose are common sights throughout most of Alaska. These large, ungainly members of the deer family wander in great numbers along the highway between Anchorage and Fairbanks. On the Kenai Peninsula, a natural wilderness area is set aside for them.

Musk oxen, native to Alaska, became extinct in the mid-1800s. Early in this century, a few of these shaggy beasts were brought from Greenland to the University of Alaska at Fairbanks. The herd was eventually established on Nunivak Island, where it thrived.

Today, approximately 1,200 musk oxen in five herds inhabit Alaska's western and northern coastlines. You can get close to a musk ox at the Anchorage Zoo.

Reindeer might be considered tamed caribou. Not really "wild" animals, they are still a curiosity to Alaska's visitors. Outside of Nome, on the Seward Peninsula, you have a chance to see an Eskimo round up his reindeer herd.

Sitka deer have a characteristic black tail. In spring and early summer, they sometimes approach southeastern roadways early in the morning or late in the evening. They're also found in the Prince William Sound area and on Kodiak Island.

Alaskan wolves are very wary. You may hear them howling, but it's doubtful that you'll see them. Denali National Park provides your best opportunity. Many wolves have followed caribou herds deep into Arctic regions.

Missing species

With all of the abundant wildlife in the state, a few species are missing. Snakes, for example, are not native to most of Alaska. Until a few little garter snakes were found in the Panhandle, it was believed there were none in the state.

Raccoons are also not Alaskan natives although some were introduced to the area a few years ago. Efforts are now being made to reduce their numbers.

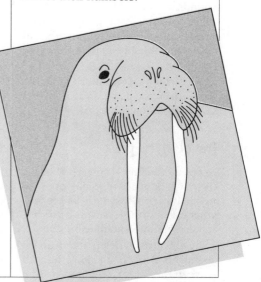

... Denali

From this location it's fun to visit the almost–ghost town of Kantishna (population 2 in winter) or pull yourself across rushing Moose Creek in a hand cable car. There's even enough gold remaining in these once-rich diggings to make gold panning worthwhile; check beforehand, though, since much of the land is privately owned.

Camping in the park. Seven campgrounds are located along the road that penetrates into the heart of the park. No hookups are available at any of the campgrounds; those that accommodate recreational vehicles have running water. Except for Riley Creek campground at the park entrance, which is open year-round (no facilities in winter, however), campgrounds are available from late May to early September.

All campsites are assigned on a first-come, first-served basis; some charge a small fee. In summer, expect a 14-day camping limit. If you plan to camp in the park, you must choose a campsite and then register in person at the Riley Creek information center (open daily in summer) for a visit beginning that day. Once the campgrounds are already full for the day, you may register for a site on the following day.

Motorists may drive to the Riley Creek and Savage River campgrounds without permits for their cars. Travel to other campgrounds is by permit only for one round-trip. All other travel must be made on the free shuttle bus.

For further information, write to Denali National Park and Preserve, P.O. Box 9, Denali Park, AK 99755.

Travel in the park

Except for the first 14 miles (to Savage River), park roads are not open to private vehicles. Instead, visitors take either a free shuttle bus or a concessionaire-operated wildlife tour bus.

Shuttle buses pick up and drop off passengers at any point along the road between the Riley Creek information center and Wonder Lake. If any wildlife wanders by, the drivers stop so passengers can take pictures. The round-trip ride to Eielson Visitor Center, the usual terminus for visitors who are simply viewing wildlife, takes about 7½ hours. Bring a lunch; no food is available here.

Six- to eight-hour guided wildlife tours depart twice a day from Denali Park Hotel (tickets and information are available inside). The price includes a box lunch. The early-morning tours are best—you'll see more wildlife, and the buses generally go farther into the park. In the afternoon, the buses may not travel far enough to offer a view of Mt. McKinley.

The classic view of Mt. McKinley is from Wonder Lake, the last stop of the shuttle buses. On calm days, the mountain's reflection in the lake doubles the grandeur of the peak, making it difficult to grasp its true scale.

From east to west, Alaska is 2,400 miles wide, the same distance as from Savannah, Georgia, to San Diego, California. There is an average of only one person to every eight miles, 40 times more room per person than in the Lower 48.

Viewing the wildife

Soon after you enter the park, the road climbs out of spruce forest into wide open country above the timberline. You'll get your first peek at Mt. McKinley from aptly named Savage River. At Stony Hill Overlook, be prepared for a spectacular view of the mountain. Though it's 37 miles away, on a clear day it looks much closer.

The drive along the park highway is like a visit to a great natural zoo, only here the animals roam free. Beyond Savage River, Dall sheep begin to appear on the mountainsides. The cliffs and crags above Igloo Creek, about 30 miles out on the park road, are often dotted with groups of sheep.

In June, caribou assemble on the tundra just before their annual migration northward. By the end of June, herds numbering in the hundreds can be seen grazing below Eielson Visitor Center.

At Sable Pass, 40 miles from the park entrance, grizzly bears are so numerous that park officials forbid you to leave the roadway. This restriction both protects visitors from bears and lessens the chance that bears might be driven away from the area to seek more private surroundings.

Moose are common throughout the park. You'll frequently see these ungainly creatures knee-deep in the lowland ponds bordering the highway, plunging their heads beneath the surface of the water in search of tender water grasses. Alaskan moose are *very* big—they're the world's largest deer.

Other wildlife you may be able to spot from the road includes porcupines, marmots, squirrels, foxes, snowshoe hares, coyotes, wolves (mostly around Polychrome Pass), and beavers. Youngsters will especially enjoy watching beavers busily at work in the early morning and late afternoon in the dozens of small, tundra-bordered lakes located about 70 miles from the park entrance.

Birds in great variety, including many species of nesting waterfowl, summer within park boundaries. Others, including the golden eagle, ptarmigan, and great horned owl, are year-round residents.

What to do in the park

Scheduled events, in addition to the wildlife tour, include campfire talks, short hikes on several trails departing from the hotel, and sled dog demonstrations by park rangers. Check the list of activities posted at the visitor center in the lobby of the Denali Park Hotel.

Indian spirit houses at Eklutna, near Anchorage, protect the treasured possessions of departed souls.

Kayaker in Prince William Sound paddles silently past a shimmering waterfall, just one of the scenic attractions in the numerous fjords that reach inland from the sound.

...*Denali*

Hiking and backpacking. Denali National Park is a true wilderness with few official trails. Despite its vast size, hiking is fairly easy since most of the park is open tundra, making it possible to select a destination and then to walk directly toward it.

Some good areas for day hikes include Savage River, Primrose Ridge, Polychrome Pass, and Wonder Lake. Before you venture out on your own, however, get an area map from the Riley Creek or Eielson visitor centers.

If you plan to stay overnight, you'll need a use permit (free of charge) that you return when the trip is completed. Permits are available at the Riley Creek information center.

Mountaineering. To do any mountaineering above 12,000 feet, you must request permission at least 2 months in advance and register at park headquarters before you set out. Special equipment and knowledge are necessary to traverse glaciers and snowfields safely.

At Talkeetna, the National Park Service maintains a ranger station that's staffed full-time from mid-April to mid-September (occasionally during the rest of the year). Rangers trained in mountaineering can provide information on climbing Mt. McKinley and other peaks in the Alaska Range.

Fishing. Surprisingly, fishing is not good in most of the park rivers because of the milky, pulverized silt they usually carry. But anglers can catch trout in Wonder Lake and Arctic grayling in a few clear mountain streams.

Photography. The park is a paradise for photographing wildlife, especially if you're equipped with a pair of binoculars and a telephoto lens.

The best shots of Mt. McKinley are from Stony Hill, Eielson Visitor Center, and Wonder Lake. Lighting is best in the early morning and late afternoon, also the times when the mountain is most likely to be free of clouds.

Other activities. Private operators in the park offer flightseeing and river rafting. Popular winter events include dog sled tours, cross-country skiing, and snowshoeing.

Wilderness lodging bargains

If you're eager to explore some of Alaska's more remote regions, you'll find inexpensive accommodations in the Tongass and Chugach national forests. Though you'll have to rough it a bit, you can rent a rustic cabin in the wilderness of either forest for only $10 a day.

More than 200 cabins are scattered throughout the forestlands. In most cases, you reach the Tongass cabins by charter boat or floatplane from the nearest town; such transportation will be the most expensive part of your vacation. Chugach cabins are primarily ''hike-in'' facilities.

Cabins, ranging from simple log structures to more elaborate A-frames, will usually accommodate four persons comfortably. Some can handle up to 12 people.

All are equipped with bunks and pit toilets. Most have plank floors; none have electricity. Visitors must provide camping gear, bedding, food, and utensils (including a cook stove and an axe for chopping firewood).

Most of the cabins are on remote lakes or isolated bays and inlets. A skiff is included as part of the equipment for all cabins situated on the water. Skiffs can accept outboard motors up to 7½ hp.

You must bring your own outboard motor and Coast Guard–approved flotation gear if you plan to boat or fish. You'll also need an Alaska fishing license.

Use permits for all sites are issued on a first-come, first-served basis. Length of stay is limited to 7 days between April 1 and October 31 and to 10 days during the rest of the year.

For cabin information, write to the Forest Service at the office nearest the area you wish to visit:

Tongass National Forest
Sitka Ranger District
P.O. Box 504
Sitka, AK 99835

Ketchikan Area
Federal Building
Ketchikan, AK 99901

Petersburg Ranger District
P.O. Box 1328
Petersburg, AK 99833

Wrangell Ranger District
P.O. Box 51
Wrangell, AK 99929

Juneau Ranger District
P.O. Box 2097
Juneau, AK 99803
(address above also serves Admiralty Island cabins)

Chugach National Forest
Anchorage Ranger District
P.O. Box 110469
Anchorage, AK 99511

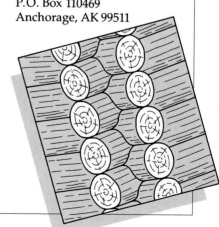

Though there are always inherent dangers in the back country, you'll probably avoid trouble if you carefully respect the ways of its inhabitants.

In Denali National Park and other wilderness areas of the state, you're treading on the home territory of the grizzly. Lumbering about this wild country, these large, powerful animals are unpredictable and dangerous.

Grizzlies defend their territory, themselves, and their young. Survival is their most compelling instinct. To reduce the chances of conflict between man and bear, you should use reasonable judgment and take all necessary precautions.

Some suggestions for avoiding a confrontation are offered below.

Keeping bears away

A grizzly should never be surprised or closely approached. Use a telephoto lens when taking photographs; keep your distance. Prevent possible encounters by keeping away from those cuddly-looking cubs. Somewhere nearby lurks about 500 pounds of mother.

Dogs are not permitted in Denali's back country. In bear country, they could be a liability. If your pet gets into a contest with a grizzly, he may run to you in fear, perhaps bringing his opponent with him.

Bears eat almost anything, so keep your campsite clean. Burn all refuse, and wash or burn cans to destroy odors. Carry out everything you carry in. In camp, seal food in plastic bags and cache them somewhere other than around your immediate camp area.

Keep your clothes free of food odor. Also avoid perfume or deodorants while hiking in the wilderness.

If you meet

Bear attacks are very rare. If you encounter a bear, never run. You can't outrun a grizzly, and your motion may excite the bear and trigger its chase instincts. Grizzlies can run up to 41 miles per hour—much faster than you could escape.

If a bear approaches, remain calm. Speak in a firm, calm voice, hold up your arms, and slowly back away, always keeping your eyes on the animal.

Above all, watch a bear's responses. If a bear stands and waves its nose in the air, it's trying to identify you. If it makes a series of woofs and grunts, it's challenging you for space. If a bear turns sideways, it's demonstrating its size. These are all invitations for you to retreat slowly backward.

Other bears

All of the precautions mentioned above for dealing with grizzlies should also be observed with the other types of bears in Alaska.

Brown bears. A near relative of the grizzly, the large brown bear is as unpredictable and can be as vicious. Brown bears are generally found in the coastal regions of the state, while the grizzly roams throughout the Interior and northern reaches.

Black bears. Smaller in stature than the grizzly and the brown bears, black bears are found throughout the state. Despite their name, the black bear's coat comes in a variety of shades from beige to black. In some regions, light-colored black bears are known as "glacier bears"; elsewhere, they are referred to as "cinnamon bears."

Polar bears. In Alaska, these shaggy white creatures almost never venture ashore from their Bering Sea and Arctic Ocean ice-packs. They are rarely seen except by intrepid Eskimos who venture out onto the ice.

Best bear-viewing sites

Riding on the shuttle and tour buses in Denali National Park and Preserve gives most visitors their first chance to spot a grizzly. It's also the best way to observe them—at a comfortable distance.

During the summer, when the salmon make their upstream spawning runs, bears line riverbanks, often wading into the water to snatch out the fish. Some of the best places to watch the action are at Brooks Lodge in Katmai National Park and Preserve and along the less-accessible McNeil River on the Alaska Peninsula.

You can view the famed Kodiak brown bears on a trip to the island from which the bears receive their name. About 2,400 of these gigantic creatures roam throughout a wildlife refuge that covers almost 80 percent of the island.

Parks Highway 3

Though George Parks Highway is the official name of Highway 3, it's better known as the Anchorage-Fairbanks Highway because it connects Alaska's two largest cities. Completed in 1971, this scenic 358-mile roadway crosses some of the grandest and most rugged land Alaska has to offer.

As it passes through the Talkeetna Mountains and the Alaska Range, over rushing streams and alongside meadows filled with wildflowers in the spring and summer, the highway rewards visitors with impressive sights, ranging from elegant stands of white birches to glimpses of the great glaciers that feed the region's rivers. Even Mt. McKinley reveals itself to motorists about 70 miles from Anchorage.

Alaska has 19 mountains over 14,000 feet high, 17 of which are the highest peaks in the United States. Mighty Mt. McKinley, an unmistakable landmark, soars to 20,320 feet; however, because the mountain is often shrouded in clouds, less than 40 percent of Alaska's visitors ever see it.

The highway is well engineered and maintained for year-round driving. Even so, motorists in winter should check road conditions by calling the Alaska Department of Transportation or the Alaska State Troopers in Anchorage or Fairbanks. In summer, the road is usually under repair because of damage caused by frost heaves.

The Alaska Railroad and the highway intersect again and again on their paths between the two cities. Both follow the courses of some of the region's major rivers. Along the route you'll see signs calling out Houston, Honolulu, and Montana Creek, all obviously named by early settlers homesick for their former homes in the Lower 48.

Driving Highway 3 from Anchorage

After passing through the fertile Matanuska Valley just outside Anchorage, you reach the pioneer town of Wasilla, the fastest-growing area in the state.

Wasilla, once a little hamlet, is now the largest community on the highway, with a population approaching 4,000.

Scattered around Wasilla, which is bordered on two sides by clear blue fishing lakes, are houses, cabins, and trailers, making the town look almost like a suburb of Anchorage. Shopping malls, lakeside resorts, and a spate of other services attract visitors to the town.

On Main Street, north of the highway, lie the Wasilla museum, library and post office, and Teeland's store. For a small admission fee, you can tour both the museum, open daily year-round, and Frontier Village, an historical park with renovated buildings from pioneer days, including Alaska's first public sauna.

For a taste of real Alaskana, stop by Teeland's Country Store. Now a national historic site, the store has served miners, railroaders, and homesteaders since 1905.

Wasilla is home to the Iditarod Trail Committee, the group that stages the sled dog race from Anchorage to Nome (see page 68 for a complete description of the race). The committee maintains a visitor center and gift shop at Mile 2.2 on Knik Road.

Outside Wasilla, the highway enters the Talkeetna Mountains. Hatcher Pass Road (also called Willow Road East) loops between Willow and Wasilla through gold-mining country. Though the mines are closed now, "color" can still be uncovered. The road is passable only during the summer.

Big Lake detour. About 52 miles from Anchorage, a side road off the highway leads to Big Lake, a favorite year-round recreation destination for the city's residents.

Popular for swimming, boating, jet skiing, fishing, and camping in the summer, the region teems with ice skaters, cross-country skiers, and sled dog racers during the winter. It's the site of a regatta and triathlon in June and a midwinter snow machine race.

Waterways connect the large lake with several smaller bodies of water, making it easy to boat for several miles. Anglers try for trout, Dolly Varden, and salmon.

Big Lake offers visitors a variety of services: marinas (boat rentals), campgrounds, picnic areas, and restaurants. Motels and lodges ring the lake.

Willow was the site selected in 1976 as the state's new capital. Land speculators quickly bought up surrounding acreage, put in streets, and were ready to build homes for dispossessed Juneau-ites, only to have their plans dashed when voters refused to approve funding for the move in 1982.

The town, on both the highway and the railroad, got its start around 1897 when gold was discovered in the area. When mining ceased in the 1940s, Willow nearly became a ghost town, recovering only when the highway was pushed through. Now the town sponsors an annual winter carnival that features dog mushing, cross-country skiing, wood-chopping contests, and other festivities.

Nancy Lake Recreation Area lies just outside Willow in the forested Susitna

Valley. Along the access road well-marked trails fork off to other nearby lakes. Campers find plenty of sites (tables, fire pits, toilets); firewood is often included.

Alaska's Interior can be plagued by a winter phenomenon known as ice fog. A curtain of tiny ice crystals formed when the air is so cold it cannot retain water vapor, it's most noticeable when pollutants are trapped with the cold air just above the ground's surface.

About 30 miles from Willow, the paved Talkeetna Spur Road leads to the colorful town of Talkeetna. Along the route, gravel roads branch off to several small lakes; a campground and picnic area are located at Christianson Lake.

Talkeetna residents fight to preserve the flavor of their town, noted for its crooked streets, log cabins, and early-day pioneer atmosphere. For information, stop at the tourist information center and gift shop located in an historic log cabin behind the "Welcome to Beautiful Downtown Talkeetna" sign.

Talkeetna's old-fashioned Main Street, the town's only paved road, is lined with log cabins, clapboard houses, and small commercial buildings. The town, which dates back to the turn of the century, was a mining and trapping settlement. The name came from an Indian word meaning "where the rivers meet"—the Talkeetna, Chilitna, and Susitna converge here. The upper reaches of the

Talkeetna and Susitna are popular with river runners and hunters. A park on the Susitna at the end of Main Street makes a fine place for a picnic. Anglers can cast their lines from sandbars in the river.

Many Mt. McKinley climbing expeditions start here. Ski-equipped aircraft depart from Talkeetna for Kahlitna Glacier, where they deposit passengers and gear for the climb up the West Buttress Route to the summit of South Peak. You can find a guide in Talkeetna, but before setting out, be sure to stop by the Talkeetna Ranger Station for information on registration. For climbs above 12,000 feet, you'll need to request permission 2 months ahead.

Trapper Creek, at the junction of the George Parks Highway and Petersville Road, is the southern gateway to Denali National Park and Preserve and the Alaska Range. The town's businesses are strung along the highway and up Petersville Road, which heads west and north about 40 miles through homesteads and gold-mining areas.

About 20 miles farther along the highway, you reach a turnout with a display board indicating the peaks you can see from the road. To the north you'll catch glimpses of glaciers sprawling down the southern slopes of the Alaska Range; Ruth, Buckskin, and Eldridge are the most conspicuous.

Byers Lake, at Mile 147, has a large camping area with picnic tables, fire pits, water, and toilets. In summer, the bearded spruce, huge cottonwood, and lush undergrowth give the area the appearance of a tropical rain forest. Hike the trail leading up to a butte above the lake for a good view of Mt. McKinley.

Hurricane Gulch is crossed by railroad and highway bridges constructed 260 feet above the water. From the highway rest area, photographers can follow a pleasant trail to the edge of the gulch for some panoramic shots.

Once across beautiful 2,343-foot Broad Pass, you reach the turnoff to the Denali Highway. From there, State

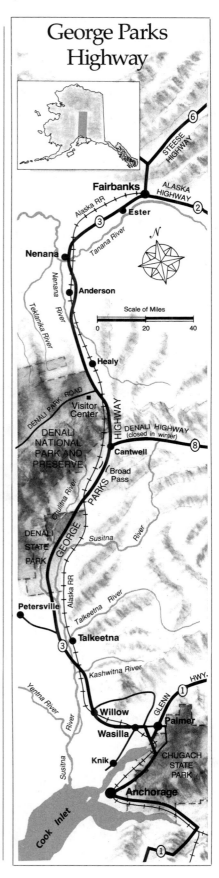

George Parks Highway

3 crosses and recrosses the Nenana River; about 10 miles from the park entrance, watch out for strong winds over the Moody Bridge–Nenana Bridge Number 4.

Denali National Park and Preserve's access road intersects with the highway at Milepost 237.3. The Alaska Railroad station also lies nearby. At the Riley Creek Visitor Center, hub of campground activities, you can sign up for campsites (see page 62) and pick up shuttle bus schedules.

In addition to the variety of accommodations strung along the highway, lodging is available within the park.

Healy, a coal town 14 miles north of the park entrance, is the site of a steam plant that furnishes electrical power to Fairbanks and the Tanana Valley. The town's rapidly growing business district is spread along the spur road off the highway.

Across the Nenana River from Healy lie several other mining settlements. Usibelli Coal Mine supplies coal to the University of Alaska, the Fairbanks area, and even South Korea. The mine began a successful reclamation project in 1971; now Dall sheep graze where once there was evidence only of strip mining.

Nenana, about 60 miles farther along the highway, is a river port settled in 1916 on the site of an old Indian village. For several years it served as the construction base for the northern portion of the Alaska Railroad, which was completed in 1923. During open-water season, river freight traffic is still important to the little town.

Stop at the picturesque log cabin visitor center for coffee and an introduction to the Big Breakup ceremony that takes place each spring when the thaw sets in on the Tanana River.

Nenana's Ice Classic, an annual event with cash prizes for the lucky winners who guess the exact minute the ice breaks up on the river, begins its festivities in late February when tripods are set up on the river. A line attached to one of the tripods stops a clock, recording the official breakup time, which usually occurs on a day in late April or early May. You can join in the fun of this icy guessing game, the largest in the world, by buying a ticket at the information center.

Though the Ice Classic is Nenana's chief claim to fame, the town boasts other assets as well. It's favorably placed at the head of one of Alaska's most scenic valleys, dominated by miles-high Mt. McKinley on the southwestern horizon. In the valley hunters find an abundance of moose, caribou, Dall sheep, black bears, and Toklat grizzlies. Visitors can watch fish wheels scooping up salmon from the waters of the Tanana River and buy fresh or smoked salmon in late summer and early fall.

Back on the highway, you'll be headed for Fairbanks, less than 60 miles away. Because the land is so flat, you'll be treated to impressive views of the city long before you arrive there.

"The Last Great Race"

You can't compare the Iditarod Trail Sled Dog Race to any other world competition. The first Saturday in March, 50 or more of the world's finest mushers, each with 12 to 20 leaping, barking dogs, depart from Anchorage at 2-minute intervals on their way to Nome. The first team to arrive collects the $50,000 first prize; the total purse is $250,000.

Teams travel over 1,100 miles of trails through deep snow, over rugged mountains, and across icy rivers and bleak tundra. The nearly 2-week trek is the ultimate test of man and dog.

The annual race is not only a challenge but also a re-creation of an historical event. The Iditarod honors the heroic dogs and drivers who relayed life-saving serum to diphtheria-stricken Nome in 1925.

The Anchorage departure is both entertaining and free. With a little planning, you can join the finishers in Nome. Teams start arriving about 12 days after the start of the race and continue for a 2-week span.

Celebrations in Nome take place from the first arrival to the last. Events include dog weight-pulling contests (all breeds compete; the best can pull close to 4,000 pounds on a sled) and other Eskimo games. You can play golf in a tournament on the frozen Bering Sea, watch snowmobile races, join a cribbage tournament, and enjoy parades, dancing, and native storytelling.

Airlines offer special low fares to Nome on their 75-minute flights from Anchorage. Lodging in Nome is extremely limited. When the Nome Nugget Inn, Polaris Hotel, bed-and-breakfast inns, and rental apartments are full, the Nome Visitors and Convention Bureau arranges accommodations with private families.

You'll need warm boots, long johns, a parka, warm gloves, and a hat. Weather conditions are usually clear and sunny. The temperature at this time of year ranges from −5°F to 30°F.

An experience of a lifetime or a grueling exercise in survival, hiking in Alaska's backcountry can be rewarding—if you're well prepared. Backpacking here requires the best in equipment and outdoor skills.

Hikers in this vast outdoor world must plan carefully for rapidly changing weather conditions. In the higher elevations, snow can be encountered at any time of the year.

The number of established trails in Alaska seems quite low, especially when compared to the Lower 48; most are clustered in the Panhandle, on the Kenai Peninsula, and around Anchorage. In the state's newer parks, the lack of trails ensures a true wilderness experience.

Experienced hikers with good topographic maps will find some of the state's best hiking is cross-country, above the tree line.

No matter where you hike, be prepared for a varied terrain. You'll find everything from unseen tussocks in the Arctic tundra to unexpected streams to ford. Patches of tangled bush and hordes of vigorous insects are low-country hazards.

Clothing choices

Footwear that fits properly and is well broken in may be the most important part of your hiking gear. Walking shoes should be light, sturdy, easy to remove, as waterproof as possible, and quick to dry. Alaska's sharp rocks and wet muskeg are best handled in hunting boots with rubber soles and leather uppers.

Most veteran hikers take along an old pair of running shoes for use in crossing streams. That keeps regular hiking boots dry and ensures safer footing in rushing water.

Clothing should have a tight weave to impede wind and mosquitos. Cotton shirts and chamois-lined pants are good choices. So are thick wool shirts and parkas. Sweaters with polypropylene fibers provide warmth, water resistance, and a thick barrier against probing insects.

Camping equipment

You'll find a good selection of camping equipment at sporting goods stores in Alaska. Outfitters and guides usually furnish equipment for escorted expeditions.

If you're staying overnight in the backcountry, the best type of shelter in what can be wet, cold weather is a good-quality mountain tent with a separate rainfly.

A gasoline or kerosene stove allows you to cook anywhere, even inside your tent during a heavy storm. It's also a valuable tool in treating hypothermia; firewood in the backcountry can be difficult to find or, when available, soaking wet.

Most of the state's streams and lakes are infested with *Giardia*, a parasite that causes a virulent form of intestinal upset known locally as "beaver fever." All water used for drinking, cooking, or brushing your teeth should be boiled for at least 5 minutes.

Dealing with bears

For some suggestions on coping with bears, a possibility on any backcountry trek, turn to page 65.

One light and nonlethal weapon you might want to consider taking with you is a can of dog-repellent spray. An obvious drawback is that the bear must be within 10 feet before the spray can be effective.

For information . . .

A variety of free hiking material is available from several sources in the state.

Information on hiking in Alaska's national parks and monuments is available from the headquarters of the National Park Service, 2525 Gambell St., Anchorage, AK 99503, or directly from the individual parks (see page 116).

For details on summer and winter hiking in Chugach State Park (everything from a 1-mile interpretive loop to a portion of the Iditarod Trail that passes over a mountain range to the coast) and other state facilities, write to State Park Information, Pouch 7001, Anchorage, AK 99510.

The U.S. Fish and Wildlife Service (1101 E. Tudor Rd., Anchorage, AK 99503) offers brochures on hiking in the state's refuges.

Alaska Public Lands Information Center (250 Cushman St., Fairbanks, AK 99701) provides trip-planning information on many types of public lands.

The USDA Forest Service Information Center (101 Egan Dr., Juneau, AK 99801) has trail guides and maps for forestland in the Juneau, Yakutat, and Admiralty Island areas.

On the Kenai Peninsula, an extensive system of hiking trails is maintained by rangers from the Chugach National Forest (P.O. Box 110469, Anchorage, AK 99511). One of the most popular routes is the 38½-mile trail over Resurrection Pass.

For information on wilderness trails in Kluane National Park in the Yukon Territory, write to the park in Haines Junction, YT Y0B 1L0. Other Yukon hiking material is available from Tourism Yukon, Box 2703, Whitehorse, YT Y1A 2C6.

Richardson Highway

The drive on the Richardson Highway (State 4) from the Interior to the coastal city of Valdez takes you into ruggedly beautiful mountains, over two passes, through the lovely Copper River Valley, and alongside an impressive glacier. Midway on the 368-mile route is a connection with the Glenn Highway to Anchorage.

The Richardson Highway, Alaska's first road, dates from the late 1800s. Originally a pack trail for gold seekers traveling in wagons, on snowshoes, or by dog sled, the trail was gradually upgraded to its present condition as a modern paved highway. Grades are so well engineered that even motorists pulling trailers have no trouble.

The Richardson Highway branches off the Alaska Highway at Delta Junction, 98 miles from Fairbanks, and ends at Valdez on Prince William Sound. For most of the way, you'll be traveling the same route as the Alaska pipeline.

From Delta Junction. At its start, the highway crosses a huge terminal moraine before dropping down to the Delta River, which pours out of the Alaska Range.

About 11 miles past Donnelly Creek State Campground, equipped with campsites, picnic tables, fire pits, and toilets, you look west to Black Rapids Glacier—dubbed the "galloping glacier" in 1936–37 when it made a sudden and dramatic advance of several miles, moving as much as 25 feet a day. The glacier is now in retreat.

Isabel Pass. Bare, rocky, ragged mountains line the road on either side as you follow the river toward Isabel Pass (3,310 feet). Near the pass, a side road leads to Fielding Lake, a popular camping and fishing spot. From the highway you'll be able to see Gulkana Glacier and Summit Lake.

At the summit of Isabel Pass stands an historical marker honoring General Wilds P. Richardson, first president of the Alaska Road Commission, for whom the highway is named.

Through the pass the road follows Summit Lake's outlet river, where you can watch salmon spawning in season. In autumn you may see caribou in this area.

Around Paxson. Paxson is the site of one of the original roadhouses built a day's stagecoach ride apart for the convenience of travelers in the early 1900s. Though some of these way stations still stand in different parts of the state, Paxson's has been replaced by a modern lodge with a similar name. The area offers good hunting and fishing.

At Paxson, the Denali Highway branches off to Denali National Park and Preserve. South of here the Richardson Highway parallels Paxson Lake, noted for good fishing. Eighteen miles south of Paxson is Sourdough Roadhouse, the oldest roadhouse in Alaska still operating in the original building. Once a stopping place for weary dog mushers and teamsters, it's noted for good food, including sourdough hotcakes.

Copper Center. At Gulkana Junction the Richardson and Glenn highways join up for 14 miles until Glennallen, where the Glenn Highway heads west toward Anchorage; the Richardson Highway continues south to Copper Center, an old settlement dating back to gold rush days. Today, the community offers lodging, private campgrounds, restaurants, stores, a gas station, and fishing charters.

Established in 1896 as a trading post, Copper Center was transformed a year later into a mining camp, thanks to the influx of thousands of gold seekers who crossed the dangerous Valdez Glacier en route to Dawson. Many fortune hunters got only as far as Copper Center, where they turned back to Valdez and waited for ships to carry them back to the Outside. By 1899, only a few hardy souls were left in the camp.

Just outside Copper Center is the original Copper Indian village and native school. The site of the first homestead in southcentral Alaska, the town also boasts the first hotel in the valley, the Copper Center Lodge, which started life in the late 1890s and was recently selected by the Centennial Commission as a site of historical importance.

A museum in the lodge's bunkhouse annex displays Russian artifacts, Athabascan baskets, and mining memorabilia.

Highway to Chitina and McCarthy. A few miles farther south is Willow Lake, mirroring on clear days the towering, glacier-frosted peaks of the Wrangell Range. Past the lake the Richardson Highway intersects the Edgerton Highway, which leads to Chitina. From Chitina, a narrow dirt road penetrates into Wrangell–St. Elias National Park and Preserve, ending at McCarthy, just before the ghost town of Kennicott.

Presently under reconstruction, the Edgerton road is "paved" partly with frost heaves and partly with gravel.

Chitina. An old town with new vitality as an entrance to the Wrangell–St. Elias National Park and Preserve, Chitina was a lusty, brawling village in the early 1900s. Founded as a camp the railroad built to haul copper concentrates from the rich Kennecott mines, Chitina survived until 1938, when both the railroad and the mines ceased operations.

Recently reborn, the town today offers a motel, several restaurants, a gas station, and a post office. Campgrounds are located beside Trout Lake in downtown Chitina, along the road to O'Brien Creek, and on the McCarthy side of the Copper River Bridge.

Travelers come to Chitina to get information from the National Park Service ranger station or, in season, to take part in the salmon run on the Copper River. It's worth a visit just to see the fish wheels and dip nets in action.

Several tour packages include trips on the Copper River past half a dozen major glaciers, several of which calve directly into the river. Wide, fast, and milky with glacial debris, the river provides a swiftly moving ride past some of North America's largest peaks.

McCarthy and Kennicott. The road from Chitina to McCarthy is a narrow, 59-mile dirt route recommended only for the adventurous summer traveler. Not suitable for large campers or trailers, the road takes 4 hours to drive and can be very slippery in wet weather. Along the way it crosses several streams. Before you head out, ask the rangers at Chitina about road conditions, as well as travel in the park.

At the end of the road, two hand-pulled cable trams are the only way to cross the Kennicott River and enter tiny McCarthy. Travelers should be strong enough to pull themselves across several hundred feet, part of which is uphill. You should never attempt to wade across the river—the strong currents and glacial water make it very dangerous.

Dependent on the nearby Kennecott Copper Mine, McCarthy flourished from the turn of the century until the mine and railway were abandoned. Today, McCarthy has a handful of residents, a few stores, a lodge (not always open), a bed-and-breakfast inn, and an air charter service.

The town of Kennicott, about 6 miles away, nestles in spectacular mountain and glacier country. Abandoned mine buildings spill down hillsides that once yielded about $175 million in copper ore. Relics of mining days are still in evidence, but visitors are asked to leave them untouched, as the town is part of a national park.

Kennicott Glacier Lodge (offering modern rooms, a restaurant, and a bar) features vacation packages that include tours of the ghost town and mine, river rafting, glacier hiking, and flightseeing. For information, write to P.O. Box 103940, Anchorage, AK 99510.

Wrangell–St. Elias National Park and Preserve. The entire southeastern corner of the Alaskan mainland is included in this 12-million-acre national park and preserve that stretches from the Gulf of Alaska to the Copper River

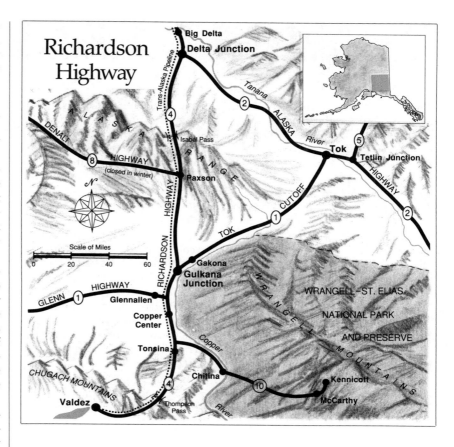

Basin. In addition to the McCarthy road, entrance to the park is by Nabesna Road out of Tok and from Yakutat.

For information on park activities, contact the Superintendent, Wrangell–St. Elias National Park and Preserve, P.O. Box 29, Glennallen, AK 99588.

Near Valdez. Back on the Richardson Highway, you come to the Tonsina Lodge, a two-story log building erected during gold rush days and one of the first buildings to have ''inside plumbing.''

After winding through the scenic Copper River Valley, with the snow-covered Wrangell Mountains forming a backdrop above old river-cut gravel terraces, the highway climbs toward Thompson Pass (2,722 feet), passing beaver dams and Worthington Glacier.

Twenty-five miles from Valdez, the road begins a rapid descent from the pass. Spectacular waterfalls cascade over magnificent rock formations; Horsetail and Bridal Veil falls are

among the best. In Keystone Canyon, you'll see an old hand-cut tunnel made during the early days when there was a plan to build a railroad here.

Valdez. Moved to its present location (4 miles away from its original site) after the devastating 1964 earthquake, Valdez (pronounced Val DEEZ) today is a thoroughly modern town. Founded by miners and packers so they could reach the goldfields of Fairbanks, the town recalls those days in its present frenzied level of activity. In fact, the supply of accommodations and facilities in town can hardly keep up with the demand for them in this terminus of the Alaska pipeline.

Even blemished by storage tanks, oil freighters, and sections of pipeline, the town's surroundings are impressive. A beautiful fjord and towering snow-capped mountains attract the eye. Valdez's small boat harbor is crowded with pleasure craft. (For more information on Valdez and nearby Prince William Sound, turn to page 80.)

Though 800 miles of 48-inch pipe may seem inconsequential in a state as vast as Alaska, the impact of the oil pipeline on Alaskan economic and social conditions has been enormous.

Almost bisecting the state, the pipeline winds from the Arctic region of Prudhoe Bay to the ice-free port of Valdez. In Valdez, the oil is stored to await passage on tankers to various ports in California and Washington.

A new gold rush

One Alaskan has declared that "pipeline construction is the most important economic phenomenon to happen to Alaska since the gold rush." A contemporary "Eureka!" was first shouted in the summer of 1968, when two major oil companies, Atlantic Richfield and British Petroleum, struck oil 8,000 to 10,000 feet below the tundra at Prudhoe Bay.

Declaring it the greatest oil strike ever made in North America, experts speculated that 9.7 billion barrels of recoverable oil and 25.4 trillion cubic feet of natural gas lay beneath the surface. Oil companies soon envisioned a pipeline carrying 1.2 million barrels a day to help quench the national thirst.

Construction of the pipeline

After major oil companies had formed the Alyeska Pipeline Service Company to build and operate the pipeline, hundreds of men and women were hired to create one of the most technologically sophisticated undertakings of this kind in history.

The pipeline is built to withstand the often cruel Alaskan climate, in which temperatures can range from 90°F to −60°F. For almost half its 800 miles, the pipeline travels above ground on thousands of vertical supports planted in sensitive permafrost. Friction generated by pumping pressure keeps the oil at about 140°F; in addition, the pipe is heavily insulated to maintain a pumpable temperature in case of stoppage.

But before any of this construction could proceed, certain legal and political problems had to be solved. One fundamental question was, "Who owns Alaska?" Native organizations claimed that neither the Alaska Purchase nor the Statehood Act established the land rights of natives living for generations in Alaska.

Until ownership could be determined, Secretary of the Interior Stuart Udall halted all transfers of land and leases. This decision united the strangest bedfellows in Alaskan history—the major oil companies and the native Alaskans.

Realizing the potential cost of any construction delay, the major oil companies resolutely lobbied on behalf of the natives. The result was the Native Claims Settlement Act of 1971. This act created 13 native-owned, profit-making corporations endowed with $1 billion in revenue and over 40 million acres of land.

Though the natives and the Alaskan government welcomed this cash inflow as a solution to many economic and social needs, environmentalists remained unappeased, fearing that the pipeline would threaten the very fragile ecosystem of Alaska.

Environmental challenges

For 4 years, construction of the pipeline was blocked by a flurry of suits against Alyeska, as environmentalists challenged the integrity of the company's plan. They pointed out that the flowing temperature of oil—140°F—could easily thaw permafrost, endangering the structural stability of the line.

Then, too, the pipeline would run through the Denali Fault, a region of potentially high earthquake activity, where in the past earthquakes have struck within 50 miles of the pipeline route. A major break could spill as much as 90,000 barrels of oil over Alaskan terrain.

Because the pipeline would also run through the Brooks Range, one of the United States' few remaining stretches of wilderness, environmentalists felt it might disrupt the migration of large caribou and other animals. And since the oil was to travel in tankers from Valdez, the threat of oil spills was ever-present.

Despite these fears, investment in the pipeline was substantial enough that construction seemed inevitable. In November, 1973, Congress, pressured by diminished domestic production, increased consumption, and, more importantly, price increases resulting from the Arab oil embargo, passed the Pipeline Authorization Act.

Making the pipeline safer

Though the oil companies were not legally required to do so, they made extensive revisions of design to respond to conservationists' concerns.

Alyeska changed its original plan of running 95 percent of the pipe underground to running 50 percent above ground, lessening the danger that the oil might thaw the permafrost. The company claims the pipeline can withstand earthquake shocks registering 8.5 on the Richter scale.

In addition, Alyeska took measures to anchor the tanker terminal at Valdez in bedrock and to surround the storage tanks with large dikes to contain spills, should they occur.

As the pipeline neared completion in the spring of 1976, yet another controversy reared up. News leaked out that, in the rush to complete construction, critically important sections of pipe were welded improperly. After a congressional investigation and a construction delay, Alyeska replaced or repaired 30 percent of the pipeline's welds.

These precautionary measures, along with inflated paychecks and other costly delays, ballooned the estimated pipeline cost of $1.5 billion to an actual cost of $9 billion.

Oil's effect on the state

Oil first flowed through the pipeline in late June, 1977. With the discovery of oil, "get rich quick" mania invaded Alaska. Economists claimed that the pipeline project would propel Alaska toward a higher economic plane.

In the years since its inauguration, the pipeline has been assessed more realistically. Certainly, it has been one of the most expensive, ambitious, and successful projects ever undertaken; moreover, it has brought great prosperity to the state.

More than 5.5 billion barrels of oil worth more than $100 billion have flowed south through its 800 miles of pipe, over 3 mountain ranges and 834 bodies of water into more than 7,000 tankers.

In the heady days of 1981, prices for North Slope crude climbed above $30 a barrel. But only a few years later, oil prices declined sharply, buffeting Alaska's economy. More than 25,000 jobs were lost in the oil slump. Some Alaskans even called it a recession.

Recently, another drilling site has been located. The oil industry believes that 3.5 billion barrels of petroleum lie beneath the inhospitable coastal plain of the Arctic National Wildlife Refuge, some 120 miles to the west of the Prudhoe Bay oil field. Again, environmentalist concerns for this wilderness, the summer home of the 180,000-strong Porcupine River caribou herd, are being balanced against the domestic need for oil and the revenue it brings.

Viewing the pipeline

You can get a good look at the pipeline on any sightseeing tour of Fairbanks. And at Valdez, the pipeline's terminus, you can watch tankers being loaded with oil. For a more panoramic view of this tribute to technology, you'll need to drive north from Fairbanks on the Dalton Highway (formerly known as the pipeline haul road).

The 416-mile highway paralleling the pipeline begins at Mile 73.1 on the Elliott Highway (State 2) and ends at Prudhoe Bay on the shores of the Arctic Ocean. Only the first 210 miles are open to public travel. To go beyond this point, you'll need to join a sightseeing excursion to Prudhoe Bay. Such tours are presently being offered by Princess Tours.

Highway cautions. Conditions on the gravel road vary from good to dusty and rough. Watch out for trucks all along the route. If possible, pull over and let them pass. Always drive with your lights on and stop only at turnouts.

Gas, food, and other services are available at Mile 56, just past the Yukon River bridge, and at the small community of Coldfoot, located at Mile 173.6. Take with

you drinking water, extra food and clothing, and emergency equipment for both you and your car.

Terrain. The countryside along the highway is very scenic and offers plenty of wildlife-viewing and other recreational opportunities. Most of the rivers winding through the region are offshoots of the Koyukuk River.

Rivers can be swollen as the snowpack melts from the Brooks Range. The best fishing is during July and August; try for grayling, pike, whitefish, or salmon in large streams. Bring mosquito repellent!

The rolling tundra is blanketed with summer wildflowers. Along the route you'll see a variety of birds. Bears, wolves, foxes, and sheep are often sighted as well.

Coldfoot. Site of a former gold-mining camp, the community got its name in 1900 when prospectors came this far up the Koyukuk River, got cold feet, and turned around. An old cemetery is a reminder of those days.

Coldfoot has a restaurant, motel, grocery, and garage. It's also the jumping-off spot for trips into the nearby Gates of the Arctic National Park and Preserve.

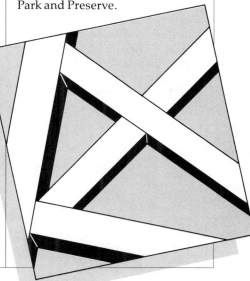

Anchorage Area

A sprawling, modern metropolis and commercial center, Anchorage surprises the first-time visitor by its familiar aspect. With its large airport, multilaned freeways, and skyscrapers, it reminds people of their homes in the Lower 48.

The city, the state's largest, traces its history back to 1915 when it was a tent camp for the railroad being built to connect the port of Seward on the Kenai Peninsula with the Interior. Various economic booms have contributed to its growth over the years. Today, more than half the state's total population lives here. Though the city was severely damaged by the 1964 Good Friday earthquake, the principal reminder of the devastation is in carefully preserved Earthquake Park.

Situated dramatically on a benchland 30 feet above high tide, Anchorage fronts on Cook Inlet; the Chugach Mountains form a backdrop. To the north, the city commands a view of the Talkeetna Mountains and the snow-capped Alaska Range.

Two muddy branches of the inlet (the Knik and Turnagain arms) surround the broad peninsula on which the city lies. Southeast of the city, both the paved Seward Highway and the Alaska Railroad skirt the north shore of Turnagain Arm, aptly named by Captain Cook, who discovered it while seeking the Northwest Passage.

It's 48 miles to Portage, where the highway and railroad swing south onto the Kenai Peninsula. To the east, the Kenai Mountains disguise the fact that this peninsula is connected to the Alaskan mainland by a strip of land barely 10 miles wide.

Highways to the Interior start in Anchorage. You follow the George Parks Highway to Denali National Park and Preserve and to Fairbanks. The Glenn Highway stretches eastward to meet the scenic Richardson Highway leading to Valdez. (A combination land-water excursion on the Glenn, Richardson, and Seward highways with a boat trip between Valdez and Whittier makes an enjoyable 2-day loop.)

Getting there

Dubbed the "Air Crossroads of the World," Anchorage is a jumping-off spot to many other parts of the state. From here it's easy to reach the Panhandle, the Arctic, the Kenai Peninsula, the Alaska Peninsula, Kodiak Island, and the Aleutian and Pribilof islands. Mt. McKinley and Fairbanks are only a short distance away by air.

International airlines fly out of a separate terminal at the Anchorage airport, scheduled interstate air carriers reach the Lower 48, and a half-dozen intra-Alaska airlines, as well as many bush pilots, maintain headquarters here.

Anchorage is also the hub for the Alaska Railroad. Trains run daily in summer (less frequently the rest of the year) from Anchorage north to Denali National Park and Fairbanks, and from Anchorage to Whittier on Turnagain Arm. Three-times-a-week passenger service connects Anchorage and Seward.

Weather

The climate in Anchorage closely resembles that of the Rocky Mountains. Annual rainfall is only 14 inches; snowfall averages 60 inches. Summers are very pleasant.

Adopt a layered look for shifts in temperature. You may want to bring a suit or dress for city dining, though casual wear is acceptable.

Anchorage, Alaska's largest city, rises dramatically between Cook Inlet and the Chugach Mountains. At high tide, water surges over Turnagain Arm's mud flats (foreground), the site of the world's second highest tidal bore.

City Life

Anchorage is a city of contrasts and contradictions. Fancy hotels and roof-top restaurants overlook salmon-spawning streams; flocks of wild birds nest in lakes that boast awesome collections of noisy floatplanes.

Around town

The city's compact, neatly laid out downtown makes it surprisingly easy to find your way around. For maps and information, make your first stop the Visitor Information Center's sod-roofed log cabin (corner of 4th and F streets). A call to 276-3200 gives you a daily recorded listing of events.

City tours provide an overview of the area's attractions, including the Captain Cook monument in Resolution Park, the University of Alaska-Anchorage, and Lake Spenard and Lake Hood (floatplane headquarters).

To stroll through downtown on your own, pick up a walking map of major attractions at the visitor center.

Visit a museum. The handsome Anchorage Museum of History and Art (121 W. 7th Ave.) houses many rare artifacts of native life and arts and crafts plus fine arts permanent and rotating collections.

Erected in 1915 by pioneer Oscar Anderson, the little frame house at 420 M St. has been restored and opened to the public as a museum. There's a small fee to visit.

Northeast of town, Ft. Richardson has a nice wildlife museum as well as a fish hatchery. Get a pass at the gatehouse off Glenn Highway.

Arts and artifacts are also on display weekdays at the National Bank of Alaska's Heritage Library and Museum (301 W. Northern Lights Blvd.).

Alaskan artifacts currently among several museum collections in St. Petersburg, Russia, will be relocated to a new native museum currently under construction at Ship Creek Landings near the Alaska Railroad Depot.

Go to a show. When the 4th Avenue Theatre opened in 1947, it marked Anchorage's transition from a frontier town to a permanent city. Today the refurbished Art Deco palace presents a gift shop and cafe as well as classic films about Alaska.

For the kids. A science discovery center, The Imaginarium (725 W. 5th Ave.) offers hands-on fun for kids. There's a small admission charge.

Sample the shops. Numerous downtown gift stores display much of the

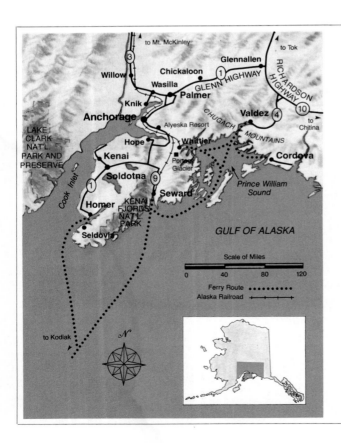

In & Around Anchorage

Anchorage—*state's largest city*

- Earthquake Park
- Museum of History and Art
- 4th Street Theatre

Around Anchorage—*farmland, glaciers, and water trips*

- Eklutna Russian spirit houses
- Matanuska Valley's giant farm produce
- Mt. Alyeska ski area
- Portage Glacier
- Prince William Sound scenic cruises

Kenai Peninsula—*outdoor vacationland*

- Canoe trails in moose range
- Homer's art colony
- Kachemak Bay boating and fishing
- Russian village of Ninilchik
- Seward's around-the-clock salmon derby

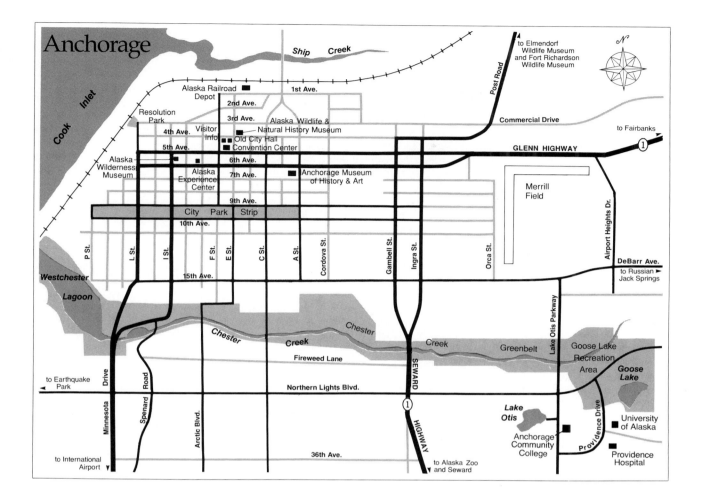

best in Alaskan arts and crafts, as well as some of the worst tourist trinkets. Buying pieces with the Silver Hand emblem ensures that the object was crafted by a native.

Interesting shops include TAHETA Art & Culture Group Co-op, 605 A St.; Alaska Native Arts & Crafts Association, 333 W. 4th Ave.; Alaska Heritage Arts, 400 D St.; and Oomingmak Musk Ox Producers Co-op, 604 H St.

Take in the zoo. The Alaska Zoo showcases Alaskan wildlife, including moose, bears, otters, musk oxen, and some of the more exotic animals. Open daily, it charges a small fee.

Pick a park. At Russian Jack Springs you can golf on a 9-hole course with artificial turf greens. This becomes a cross-country ski course in winter. An amazing variety of tropical plants, fish, and birds thrives here in the city's greenhouse.

Check the Yellow Pages for bicycle rentals and try one of the bike paths winding through Russian Jack Springs, along the Campbell Creek Greenbelt, or along the Chester Creek Greenbelt.

Watch a tidal bore. Timing is all-important here if you want to catch one of nature's best shows, Turnagain Arm's record-level changing tides. Check the newspaper for the time of low tide. Though the wall of water rushing over the mud flats makes interesting viewing, it's hazardous for boaters and windsurfers.

Staying in Anchorage

Visitors will find plenty of places to stay in town. The Anchorage Hilton, Captain Cook, and Sheraton qualify as luxury hotels. Be sure you have confirmed reservations during the summer or for the annual Fur Rendezvous in February.

Several public and private campgrounds and camper parks are situated in or near the city, and wilderness lies only minutes away. At Chugach State Park, east of Anchorage, you can watch wildlife, pick blueberries, hike, fish, ski, or go dog sledding or snowmobiling, depending on the season.

Dining is a delight. In addition to hotel dining rooms and several good seafood restaurants, Anchorage offers restaurants specializing in a variety of international cuisines.

Community nightlife centers around productions at the three-theater Alaska Center for the Performing Arts (612 W. 6th Ave.).

Past and present collide in Anchorage's compact downtown area, where buildings from early times, such as this tidy frame house, dwell side by side with more modern structures.

Above the clouds, three cross-country skiers enjoy the weak midday sun and the solitude of ski touring at Turnagain Pass near the Alyeska Resort.

Excursions from Anchorage

Cruise to the face of a sparkling blue glacier, ride a lift at the state's largest ski resort, photograph an iceberg, or tour a gold mine—all these adventures await visitors, and all are within close proximity to Anchorage.

Using the city as a base, you can easily make short trips into the surrounding countryside. Visits to Matanuska Valley, Portage Glacier, Mt. Alyeska, and Prince William Sound are included in many package excursions.

Matanuska Valley

Alaska's largest farming region, Matanuska Valley lies some 40 miles northeast of Anchorage. Nestled amidst rugged, glacially carved peaks, this lush valley was settled in the 1930s by drought-stricken Midwestern farmers. Some of the families still live in the region.

Though the growing season lasts only 4 months, long daylight hours produce record-size vegetables—turnips weighing more than 7 pounds, cabbages that tip the scales at 70 pounds, huge potatoes, and strawberries the size of plums.

Eklutna. Any trip to the Matanuska Valley should include a stop for photographs at the old Indian village of Eklutna, 26 miles from Anchorage on the Glenn Highway. Be sure to visit Old St. Nicholas Russian Orthodox Church (a prayer chapel, built in 1962, is nearby).

Don't miss the Indian burial ground with its colorful spirit houses. These brightly painted miniature houses are placed over graves to hold the spirits of the deceased and to protect their possessions. Crosses in front of the spirit houses indicate conversions to the Russian Orthodox church. Contributions go toward maintaining the property.

Palmer and environs. Alaska's only agriculturally oriented community,

Palmer is the trading center for the valley. In late August and early September, the city plays host to the Alaska State Fair. On display are over 5,000 agricultural and homemaking exhibits. Palmer is also the site of the Colony Days Celebration in June.

Pick up a walking tour map of the area's major attractions at the Palmer Visitor Center (732 S. Valley Way), which is open year-round.

You can tour the valley on a network of farm roads. The gift shop at the Musk Ox Farm on Archie Road, off the Glenn Highway, offers unique knitted garments made from the animal's underwool. Guided tours are available at the Alaska Experimental Farm on Trunk Road, off the George Parks Highway.

As Captain Cook discovered, the incoming tide in Turnagain Arm outside Anchorage can reach 39 feet in height and attain a speed of 10 mph.

Matanuska Glacier. About 60 miles east of Palmer on the Glenn Highway lies Matanuska Glacier, one of the few in Alaska that you can drive to and explore. Several trails to the glacier begin at a campground at its foot.

Independence Mine. The Hatcher Pass Road intersects with the Glenn Highway about 1½ miles beyond Palmer. Follow the gravel road for 17½ miles to reach Independence Mine State Historical Park (open Friday through Monday in summer).

Though the mine ceased operations over 30 years ago, the 271-acre site offers an interesting perspective on the development of hardrock gold mining throughout the state. Displays in the visitor center, the former manager's house, explain mine operations, and photographs show the actual work.

You can wander down to the camp mess hall and over to the restored assay office museum. From here you can examine the crumbling mill complex. Guided tours of the complex are offered weekends only for a slight fee.

You can either return to Anchorage or continue on the road across scenic Hatcher Pass (check road conditions first). From the summit it's about 30 miles to Willow on the George Parks Highway.

Alyeska Resort & Portage Glacier

A 50-mile stretch of the Seward Highway winds southeast along the Turnagain Arm of Cook Inlet. Near the point where Glacier Creek flows into the arm (37 miles south of Anchorage) are Girdwood, site of an old railroad station, and the short road to Alyeska Resort.

Alyeska Resort. Skiers challenge the slopes during winter; a major summer attraction is the 1¼-mile double chair lift. The panoramic view from the sundeck and restaurant at the top of the lift leaves you breathless. You look out over spruce-covered slopes, cliffs, and waterfalls to beautiful Girdwood Valley and the waters of Turnagain Arm. In summer, smoothly rolling alpine meadows abound with colorful wildflowers. Eight glaciers are cradled among mountain peaks.

Alyeska Resort offers a 300-room hotel, cafes, lounges, gift stores, and a ski shop with equipment rentals and a school. Glacier skiing and lighted slopes for night skiing are added seasonal attractions.

...excursions

Nearby Crow Creek Mine, site of an 1888 gold strike, lets you try your hand at panning. Eight of the mine's historic buildings have been restored. There's a fee to enter.

Portage Glacier. At the head of Turnagain Arm, on a 6-mile spur from the former town of Portage (destroyed in the 1964 earthquake), is the turnoff to Portage Glacier's Begich-Boggs Visitor Center, Portage Glacier Lodge, and three Forest Service campgrounds.

Open daily during the summer (weekends only in spring and autumn), the center offers fine views of the glacier and the iceberg-choked lake through floor-to-ceiling windows. Displays and films explain the area's history; naturalists are on hand to answer questions and provide information on Chugach National Forest.

A hiking trail leads up the valley from the center. During July and August, watch salmon spawning in nearby Portage Creek.

As recently as 1913, the glacier's face ended where the parking lot is today.

Now the glacier is in retreat; its face is presently several miles away.

Prince William Sound

Sixty miles southeast of Anchorage is lovely Prince William Sound, a saltwater bay protected by rugged cliffs, indented by glaciers, and punctuated by forested islands. Here is the home of Columbia Glacier, a mammoth mass of ice 40 miles long and over 4 miles wide, with a 150- to 250-foot-high face.

For a most rewarding excursion from Anchorage, be sure to include a sightseeing or ferry boat cruise on the sound. Make arrangements before leaving Anchorage. Access is from the port cities of Whittier or Valdez.

Getting to Whittier. No road leads to this small seaport. During the summer, the Alaska Railroad operates a daily train between Anchorage and Whittier and offers several shuttles between Portage and Whittier for both passengers and vehicles. At Whittier you can board a ferry to Valdez or Cordova.

Valdez. Valdez, the southern terminus of the 800-mile-long Alaska pipeline, is the only Prince William Sound community connecting with the state's road system, via the Richardson Highway (see page 70).

Dubbed the "Switzerland of Alaska" for its beautiful setting, Valdez was hard hit by a tidal wave following the 1964 earthquake. When the time came to rebuild the town, it was moved 4 miles to a new and better site.

The popularity of Prince William Sound and the growth of the oil industry have strained this small city's tourist facilities. During the peak summer season, you'll need advance reservations. Several attractive campgrounds in the area sport their own private waterfalls.

Puerto de Valdez, a beautiful fjord in the sound, was given its name by a Spanish explorer in 1790. A settlement sprang up in 1898 on a terminal moraine at the head of the fjord. From here, gold seekers crossed formidable glaciers and mountains to reach the Klondike goldfields.

As Fairbanks boomed in the early 1900s, Valdez became its supply port. Stores landed at Valdez were then hauled 365 miles over the Valdez Trail (now the Richardson Highway) by dog teams in winter and horses in sum-

---

Anchorage Fur Rendezvous

The Anchorage Fur Rendezvous, or "Rondy," as it's affectionately called in Alaska, began when Anchorage was a tent city and fur trappers traveled a thousand miles by dog sled to swap pelts for provisions.

Now Alaska's biggest festival, the mid-February event has been celebrated for over 50 years. Locals call it their Mardi Gras because of the colorful 100-float parade and the spirited Miners' and Trappers' Costume Ball.

Daily activities include a carnival, an assortment of exhibitions, and a bazaar selling everything from

locally produced smoked salmon and reindeer sausage to fur clothes and scrimshaw.

Weekends are busiest, with snowshoe baseball games, outhouse races (pulled on skis or sleds), hot air balloon rallies, folk dance competitions, and performances by Alaska's Indians and Eskimos.

You'll also have the opportunity to watch world-championship dog sled races. Dogs are directed only by voice commands—no reins. Brief dog sled rides are offered during Rondy.

For more information on the celebration, write to the Rondy Headquarters, P.O. Box 773, Anchorage, AK 99510; (907) 277-8615.

mer; the trail was improved later so wagons could be used.

Today, Valdez is accessible by car or bus from Anchorage and Fairbanks, by ferry from Cordova and Whittier, and by air.

Cruising the sound. Several sightseeing boats cruise Prince William Sound from both Whittier and Valdez. All-inclusive tours from Anchorage include round-trip transportation, boat cruise, and overnight accommodations.

Boats inch audaciously up toward Columbia Glacier to give passengers a look at giant slabs of ice breaking loose and thundering down into the sea.

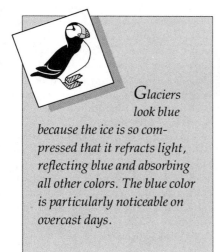

Glaciers look blue because the ice is so compressed that it refracts light, reflecting blue and absorbing all other colors. The blue color is particularly noticeable on overcast days.

En route you'll view some of the area's abundant wildlife—sea lions, harbor seals, whales, otters, and many different kinds of birds, including bald eagles.

You can also go kayaking, sailing, or fishing for a day or longer with one of the many charter companies operating out of Valdez.

The ferry MV *Bartlett* operates daily during the summer between Whittier and Valdez, with twice-a-week service to Cordova. The Whittier-Valdez segment takes a little over 6 hours.

The ferry MV *Tustumena* connects Seward on the Kenai Peninsula with Valdez and Cordova. You can drive to Seward (about 130 miles from Anchorage), board the ferry, and arrive in Valdez about 12 hours later. For information on ferry service in this area, write to the Alaska Marine Highway, P.O. Box R, Juneau, AK 99811.

Though ferries don't permit as close or as long a look at Columbia Glacier as sightseeing boats afford, they do pause so you can see and hear this active tidewater glacier.

Cordova. Because it's off the track, the small community of Cordova retains a delightful flavor of old Alaska. It's reached either by ferry from Valdez—and, in summer, from Whittier—or by air. When completed, the Copper River Highway will intersect the Richardson Highway south of Thompson Pass.

Once a lusty, brawling railroad and mining terminal, Cordova was the setting for Rex Beach's *Iron Trail*. This novel is an account of the building of the Copper River Railroad to the rich copper deposits of the Kennecott mines, which produced copper worth more than $100 million before being abandoned in 1938.

People come to Cordova for the good fishing (saltwater or freshwater) and hunting in season. The town is located near the mouth of the Copper River, scene of famed salmon runs. The Copper River Mud Flats teem with ducks, geese, and swans.

In addition to the commercial salmon industry, clam and crab canneries operate busily. Boats and planes are available for charter. In winter, skiing is a popular sport; the annual Iceworm Festival is staged here in February.

An icy performer

Prince William Sound's premier attraction and most active iceberg producer is magnificent Columbia Glacier. Its statistics are as impressive as its appearance.

Largest of some 20 glaciers in the sound, this frozen river of ice covers some 440 square miles, flowing for more than 40 miles from its source in the Chugach Mountains before dropping into the bay that bears its name.

At its terminus, the glacier is more than 6 miles across. Its face, which visitors can see on a trip across the sound, rises as high as 250 feet above sea level.

A retreating giant

Unfortunately, it's not as easy for boats to get as close to Columbia Glacier as it was in the past, when passengers could get right up to the massive ice wall and hear the thunder of its calving. The glacier has retreated over a mile since 1983 and its dramatically increased iceberg production has nearly choked the bay.

Scientists are currently studying the iceberg output, expected to increase as much as four-fold in the next 20 years, since it poses a threat to tankers transporting oil from Valdez.

What you'll see

Life at the face of the glacier is active. Harbor seals ride the bergs that rock violently with the force of the collapsing ice. Porpoises play in the waves, and gulls and bald eagles soar overhead, ready to swoop down on the great numbers of fish that feed here.

Sightseeing cruises and charter boats from Valdez, Cordova, and Whittier offer tours of Prince William Sound, including visits to the more accessible glaciers. A flight-seeing trip gives a good look at the glacier's broad expanse.

Kenai Peninsula

The Kenai Peninsula, a huge chunk of land that jabs like a fat thumb south from Anchorage into the Gulf of Alaska, is a perfect destination for sportfishing, clamming, camping, canoeing, sailing, hiking, berry picking, birding, or just getting off the beaten path.

The ruggedly beautiful, untracked interior of this peninsula is still wild enough to get lost in. But along the coast, old Russian fishing villages and newer oil towns provide a variety of tourist facilities.

To the southeast, in Kenai Fjords National Park, the ice-scoured Kenai Mountains drop straight down into deep glacial fjords. To the west, rolling tundra plains, covered with a light stand of aspen and birch, slope down to graceful ribbons of beach along Cook Inlet.

A frontier feeling lingers here. Families live scattered about in hand-hewn log cabins. You can still see evidence of the first Russian settlers who came in 1791, establishing their second permanent Alaskan colony in what is now the town of Kenai. Small homesteads and truck gardens abound along the coast in the vicinity of Kenai and Homer, Alaska's fishing and canning centers.

Even though the Kenai Peninsula is close enough to Anchorage to be sampled easily in a day, the activities here could keep you busy for an entire vacation.

Getting to the Kenai

From Anchorage, ERA Aviation, MarkAir Express, and SouthCentral Air offer scheduled service to Seward, Soldotna, Kenai, and Homer. Several air taxis also provide flights throughout the area.

Seward Bus Line operates scheduled service between Anchorage and that city; Homer Bus Line links that Kachemak Bay town with Anchorage. The state ferry system serves Seward, Homer, and Seldovia. In summer, daily Alaska Railroad trains connect Anchorage and Seward.

Rental cars, trucks, campers, and motor homes are available for the motorist from Anchorage. The Seward Highway (State 1) heads southeast from Anchorage to the turnoff to Portage Glacier and then swings southwest into the Kenai Peninsula, where it divides. State 9 heads south to Seward, and State 1, which becomes the Sterling Highway, turns west. Both roads are paved. In most towns along the route, motorists will find gas stations, stores, restaurants, and lodging.

Anchorage to Seward

After the Portage Glacier turnoff (about 50 miles from Anchorage), the Seward Highway gradually climbs through impressive forests to Turnagain Pass. In summer, open meadows along the road are brightly splashed with false azaleas, wild roses, violets, and several types of berries.

The turnoff to Hope, an historic mining community and the summer home of many Anchorage residents, is about 12 miles beyond the pass. In 1896, about 2,500 prospectors poured into Hope and nearby Sunrise in Kenai's big gold rush. Though the rush was short lived, a few mines kept producing, and a few sourdoughs drifted in to work them.

You can try your hand at panning in Resurrection Creek. Turn off the 17-mile Hope Highway onto Resurrection Pass Trail a mile before town; a small campground lies at the end of the road.

Back on State 1, it's 20 more miles to the junction with the Sterling Highway at Tern Lake, named for the Arctic terns nesting here each summer. State 9 climbs over Moose Pass and then gradually winds down to Seward through spectacular mountains dotted with good trout-fishing lakes and streams. You'll need a fishing license to cast your line.

Seward, 127 miles from Anchorage, nestles between Resurrection Bay and hulking Mt. Marathon. Lovely Seward is a thriving port, a favorite boating and fishing spot for Anchorage residents, and the gateway to the Kenai Fjords National Park.

The harbor has long been the main Alaska Railroad port. Founded in 1903 as a starting point for the Alaska Central Railroad, the town was named for William H. Seward, the U.S. secretary of state who negotiated the Alaska purchase.

In 1793, here at Resurrection Bay, Alexander Baranof launched the *Phoenix*, the first ship built in Alaska. Today, in the harbor, you'll find boats you can charter for sportfishing and touring the Kenai Fjords coastline.

Hotels, motels, and campgrounds accommodate visitors who come to see the annual endurance race up 3,000-foot Mt. Marathon on July 4 or who participate in the annual Silver Salmon Derby, an 8-day, around-the-clock event in midsummer. Pick up a walking tour brochure at the visitor center (an old railroad car) at 3rd and Jefferson streets. A museum in the basement of City Hall re-creates rooms from early settlers' homes.

Kenai Fjords National Park, 580,000 acres of coastal mountain system, encompasses the Harding Icefield (a 300-square-mile remnant of the Ice Age), an inlet-carved coastline, and an exciting variety of wildlife. A popular boat tour introduces visitors to tidewater glaciers and marine life.

In the visitor center in the small-boat harbor area you'll find information on activities and camping; or write to the Superintendent, P.O. Box 1727, Seward, AK 99664.

The Sterling Highway

From its junction with the Seward Highway, the Sterling Highway runs 135 miles to Homer. You'll pass dozens of motels, lodges, and hunting

Solitary moose, more commonly found among sheltering trees and brush, wanders through soggy tundra.

A bustling fishing, boating, and camping site, the narrow Homer Spit gravel bar juts out almost 5 miles into Kachemak Bay. Spilling down from the Kenai Mountains across the bay is the glacial wonderland of the Harding Icefield.

and fishing camps along the way. The highway starts in a rocky, mountainous region where you may be able to spot Dall sheep clambering up the face of the mountains. Look up high.

When you leave the Chugach National Forest, you're in moose country. Here, in the lowlands, thick stands of spruce, birch, and aspen hide hundreds of tiny lakes and streams that offer food and protection for these ungainly members of the deer family.

Kenai National Wildlife Refuge

Set aside by presidential order in 1941, the Kenai National Wildlife Refuge encompasses almost 2 million acres. It was established to preserve representative native wildlife species—in particular, the largest antlered animal on earth, the moose. The range also provides a habitat for brown and black bears, Dall sheep, mountain goats, caribou, and other mammals.

Spawning salmon and rainbow, Dolly Varden, and lake trout inhabit most of the waters. Many kinds of birds nest here.

The refuge is a popular recreational area, offering fishing, boating, hiking, camping, and picnicking in the summer; in winter there's ice fishing, cross-country skiing, dog sledding, snowshoeing, and snowmobiling.

Perhaps the most interesting feature of the refuge are the Kenai Canoe Trails that wind through the northern part of the refuge along rivers or lakes connected by short portages. There are two routes: Swanson Lake, 80 miles of waterways linking more than 40 lakes, and Swan Lake, a 60-mile route connecting 30 lakes.

Canoe rentals and shuttle service to the head of the trail system are available from the bridge over Moose River near Soldotna. Guided tours and fishing charters are also offered. A trip could take anywhere from 1 to 5 days. For information on canoeing, contact the Refuge Manager, P.O. Box 2139, Soldotna, AK 99669.

En route to Homer

From the Kenai National Wildlife Refuge the highway passes a number of intriguing towns and villages. Each is worth a stop or a short visit.

Soldotna, about 55 miles west of the junction of state highways 1 and 9, is itself a junction point. Turn right to reach Kenai or stay on the Sterling Highway 78 miles to get to Homer, an artists' colony.

Soldotna is a center for Kenai River sportfishing (claimed to be the best in the world) and a bedroom community for the Cook Inlet oil industry. It has every facility you're likely to need, including two shopping centers. For a list of fishing guides, write to the Chamber of Commerce, P.O. Box 236, Soldotna, AK 99669.

A "salmon jam" takes place along Kenai Peninsula riverbanks when the fish head upriver to spawn. Anglers line the banks so closely that area hospitals remove at least a hook a day from people snagged by someone else's line.

Kenai, on the shore of Cook Inlet, is the peninsula's oldest and largest city. Founded in 1791 as a Russian fur-trading post, it's now a center for the oil and gas industries. For the visitor, Kenai makes a good base for canoe trips, flightseeing, fishing, and clamming.

Clam Gulch, about 18 miles from Soldotna, is an accessible beach along Cook Inlet where you can dig for clams during low tide. Clamming shovels can be rented in Kenai.

In the Old Town section stands the oldest Russian Orthodox church in Alaska, Church of the Assumption of the Virgin Mary, dating from around 1896. A log barracks in restored Fort Kenay, a 19th-century U.S. military post, contains an historical museum.

Four active volcanoes, part of the Pacific "ring of fire," and Lake Clark National Park are visible from Kenai across Cook Inlet.

Ninilchik's photogenic Russian church and neat cemetery (both still in use), located on the crest of the hills behind town, face Cook Inlet; on a clear day you can see the Chigmit Mountains across the bay. Several quaint fishing shacks and log cabins still survive in Ninilchik Village, the original town.

This is gently rolling forestland, interspersed with open meadows and active trout streams. Several rivers— Ninilchik, Deep Creek, and Anchor —have open periods for king salmon fishing.

Anchor Point, a small community, is located as far west as you can drive on the North American continent. Captain Cook, searching for the famed Northwest Passage, anchored here. The campground may be crowded during salmon season.

One of Alaska's most respected artists, Norman Lowell, paints in a studio on a side road off Mile 160.9. You're welcome to visit the Alaska Homestead Museum and Gardens and Lowell's large gallery.

Homer, an artist's delight

The early Russians who visited the Cook Inlet side of the lower Kenai Peninsula called this region Summerland, and for good reason. Protected from the storms of the Gulf of Alaska by the towering, ice-capped Kenai Range, this area enjoys a mild climate year-round and an average rainfall of 25 inches.

In summer the wildflowers—lupine and fireweed predominating— are a particular delight on hills and fields around town. And in autumn, after the first frosts have come, the fireweed turns red and the birches, poplars, and aspens glimmer with gold, a reminder of Indian summer.

Homer, often called Alaska's Cape Cod, lies at the end of the Sterling Highway on the shore of Kachemak Bay. Homesteads border the town on the land side. Those on a bluff overlooking the bay command a fine view of the Kenai Range. Moose and bear are frequent visitors.

A half-dozen glaciers that spill down from the Harding Icefield across the bay flank the horizon to the east. You see them as you approach town, but you get an even better view from East Road. It was just such vistas that attracted the numerous artists who live and work here.

In the early days, it was easy to live off the land. There were moose and mountain sheep, a profusion of wild berries, clams on the beach, and king crab, halibut, and salmon in Kachemak Bay. After a storm, coal accumulated on the beaches. A few settlers recognized the agricultural possibilities and took up farming, but it wasn't until a road was punched through that a real wave of homesteaders arrived.

Activities around town. The Pratt Museum (3779 Bartlett St.) features Russian, Indian, and Aleut artifacts, plus several aquatic exhibits focusing on Kachemak Bay's marine life.

At Alaska Wild Berry Products, you can sample some of the tasty jams, jellies, and candies made from berries. Each year, the plant processes Alaskan wild berries picked by local people throughout the state for gift packages sent all over the world.

Some of the local artists, including wildflower painter Toby Tyler, maintain studios downtown. Diana Tillion, another noted artist, paints with octopus ink; to visit her studio across the bay at Halibut Cove, take the Kachemak Bay ferry sightseeing trip from Homer Spit (see at right).

Noted for its midsummer halibut derby, Homer also hosts several other annual festivals. A celebration of the harvest takes place at the local fair in August. In February, residents hold a winter carnival.

Two of Homer's best restaurants are bakeries—the Fresh Sourdough Express and Wallaces Bake Shop. The city has a number of hotels, motels, and bed-and-breakfasts. You'll need to reserve in advance during the busy summer months.

Homer Tours offers daily sightseeing. For information, write to P.O. Box 1264, Homer, AK 99603.

Kachemak Bay. *Kachemak* in Aleut means "smoky bay"; the name probably is derived from the smoldering coal seams that long ago smoked along the shores of the bay. The erosion of these bluffs (particularly near Anchor Point) results in a plentiful supply of winter fuel for residents.

The magnificent deep-water bay reaches inland from Cook Inlet for 30 miles, averaging 7 miles in width.

Several air and boat charters offer opportunities for flightseeing, sportfishing, hunting, camping, clam digging, or photography. You can fly to the McNeil River State Game Sanctuary to watch brown bears fish or to Iliamna Lake, on the Alaska Peninsula, to angle for rainbow trout.

Some of the best scenic excursions are cruises around Kachemak Bay. A long gravel bar at Grewingk Glacier in Kachemak Bay State Park makes a popular outing by boat or plane.

Seldovia. This colorful fishing village across the bay from Homer is accessible by ferry or by daily air flights (weather permitting). Though the 1964 earthquake severely damaged Seldovia's boardwalk, rebuilt sections are again lined with canneries, stores, restaurants, and waterfront houses.

Seldovia is home port for salmon and king crab fishing boats. St. Nicholas Orthodox Church is a reminder of the town's early history.

The Homer Spit

From the town of Homer on the Kenai Peninsula, a slim finger of land pokes out almost 5 miles into Kachemak Bay. The grass-covered, low-lying sandbar is called the Homer Spit.

A paved road leads out to its tip past gravel beaches, campgrounds, and wooden boardwalks that connect the collection of shops and eating places at Cannery Row and the Fishing Village. At the end of the spit, a busy harbor plays host to the Alaska State Ferry and hundreds of small commercial and pleasure boats.

Both tourists and halibut and salmon anglers patronize the historic Salty Dawg Saloon near the docks. This tower-topped log tavern started life as a cabin in the late 1890s; since that time, it has survived fire, earthquake, and relocation.

The Kachemak Bay Ferry leaves the harbor daily on excursions to Halibut Cove, a picturesque artists' community across the bay that is accessible only by boat or plane. The ride allows views of Gull Island, home to a host of pelagic birds.

Other seagoing excursions include cruises in a glass-bottomed boat, guided kayak trips, and scheduled runs to Seldovia across the bay. Charters offer full- or half-day fishing, sightseeing, or sailing trips.

In addition to a resort at the tip of the spit, a variety of lodging is available in Homer, one of Alaska's most charming cities.

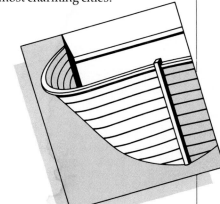

Southwest Alaska

*S*outhwest of Anchorage lies a 40,000-square-mile region with a population of about 6,000. This is the Bristol Bay country, laced with five important rivers that together produce the greatest red salmon run in the world. The names of the rivers read like a series of sneezes—Kvichak, Nushagak, Naknek, Ugashik, and Egegik.

At one time 24 canneries operated around the bay. Rex Beach worked in one of them in the early 1900s, gathering material for his novel *The Silver Horde*. Many canneries still rumble busily, and visitors are welcome.

Southwest Alaska also encompasses the Alaska Peninsula, which juts 550 miles into the sea. At its head is Lake Clark National Park and Preserve, a magnificent wilderness filled with lakes and braided rivers noted for trophy rainbow trout. Along its length are two more vast preserves: Katmai National Park and Preserve, with its Valley of Ten Thousand Smokes, and Aniakchak National Monument and Preserve.

Also a part of far-flung southwestern Alaska are the Aleutian Islands, the Pribilof Islands, Kodiak Island (noted for its large brown bears), isolated St. Matthew Island, Nunivak Island (a grazing range for musk oxen), and the vast bird nesting regions in the deltas of the Kuskokwim and Yukon rivers.

You won't find crowds here or big cities, but you will discover a region of breathtaking natural beauty with miles of untracked valleys and unnamed rivers. Streams flash with silvery trout. At prime fishing spots, bears often outnumber people.

A visit to the islands in the Bering Sea offers bird-watchers and wildlife photographers unusual opportunities. Here, rocky cliffs support some of the world's largest seabird and fur seal populations.

Except for small hotels in such towns as Kodiak, Dillingham, Bethel, Dutch Harbor, and Cold Bay, your accommodations will be limited to fly-in fishing lodges offering hearty, home-cooked (and home-caught) fare.

Getting there

Since no roads connect this region, the best way to get around Southwest Alaska is by air. Many destinations can be easily reached by scheduled or charter flights from Anchorage. Interstate airlines include ERA Aviation, MarkAir, Reeve Aleutian, and Ryan. Air taxi, charter, and commuter service to more remote areas is also available from Bethel, Dillingham, Dutch Harbor, Iliamna, King Salmon, Kodiak, and Naknek.

State ferries provide year-round service to Kodiak from Seward and Homer. Ferries also make scheduled summer runs to the Aleutians.

What to wear

The Southwest's mainland area receives little rain or snow along its coastal regions; the Alaska Peninsula and the Bering Sea islands receive more precipitation. Weather in the Aleutians can be very damp and cold. The best time to visit is from late spring to early autumn.

For all these areas it's wise to dress in layers to accommodate weather that can change almost hourly.

Lone kayaker on Naknek Lake, in the heart of beautiful, unspoiled Katmai National Park and Preserve, heads back to camp.

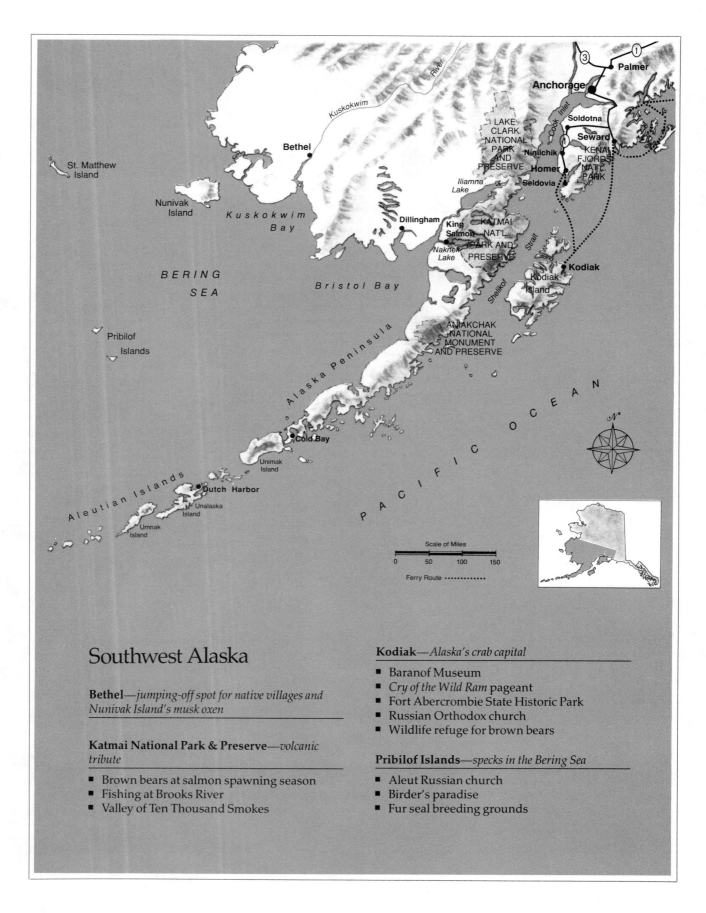

Southwest Alaska

Bethel—*jumping-off spot for native villages and Nunivak Island's musk oxen*

Katmai National Park & Preserve—*volcanic tribute*

- Brown bears at salmon spawning season
- Fishing at Brooks River
- Valley of Ten Thousand Smokes

Kodiak—*Alaska's crab capital*

- Baranof Museum
- *Cry of the Wild Ram* pageant
- Fort Abercrombie State Historic Park
- Russian Orthodox church
- Wildlife refuge for brown bears

Pribilof Islands—*specks in the Bering Sea*

- Aleut Russian church
- Birder's paradise
- Fur seal breeding grounds

Kodiak Island

Anchored in the Gulf of Alaska off the tip of the Kenai Peninsula, Kodiak, Alaska's largest island, is a part of the state that many travelers overlook. Known for its Russian heritage, its gigantic king crabs, and its bears—the largest species in the world—Kodiak has been until recently just a little too far out of the way for most visitors. Yet a tour of the island and the town that shares its name is well worth the extra effort.

The town of Kodiak, largest of the eight communities on the island, nestles around an island-dotted bay. This lush green island experiences about 60 inches of rain yearly. On a clear day, however, your eye can feast on mountains, valleys, and coastline in a panorama rivaling few other Alaskan sites in scenic beauty.

Mid-May through late September is the best time to visit; July and August are the warmest months. But even sunny, warm days can turn rainy and chilly by evening.

A Russian capital

Kodiak's name comes from the native word *kikhatah*, meaning "island." As time passed, the word was pared down to Kadiak and finally Kodiak. Discovered by a Russian explorer in 1673, it's the home of the oldest permanent European settlement in Alaska.

Russian fur traders and hunters established their first North American colony at Three Saints Bay on the south side of the island in 1784, but Alexander Baranof, who took over leadership of the colony, moved it in 1792 to the site of the present-day town of Kodiak. It was the capital of Russian America until Sitka took over that position in 1804.

Woody Island, 2 miles east of Kodiak, was a boat-building center and a port from which the Russians shipped ice to the California coast in the early and middle 1800s. Supposedly, Alaska's first horses were brought to Woody Island. Certainly, the first road in Alaska was built around the island. The settlement diminished as the population drifted to Kodiak.

The sea is Kodiak's front yard. In the small harbor, Alaska's largest fishing fleet is sometimes moored three boats deep. Boats supply the canneries on Marine Way and Shelikof Street with crab (Dungeness, king, and tanner), salmon, shrimp, halibut, bottomfish, and herring. Call ahead for an informal cannery tour.

The Baranof Museum, on Center Street just above the ferry terminal, makes a good first stop on an easy walking tour of downtown Kodiak. Treasures from Kodiak's rich Aleut and Russian past are housed in Alaska's oldest building, a fur warehouse built in the 1790s. Its gift shop sells Russian crafts, in addition to maps, brochures, and books on Kodiak. The museum, open daily year-round, charges a small admission fee.

The Russian Orthodox church, across the street from the museum, continues to serve Alaska's oldest parish. It's a picturesque building with traditional onion-shaped cupolas. Visitors are invited to attend a service (Saturday at 6:30 P.M., Sunday at 9 A.M.), followed by a tour of the ornate interior. Ask about St. Herman, America's first Russian Orthodox saint, who lived in Kodiak. Up the hill is a photogenic site—a neglected Russian cemetery.

Exploring the island

Guided tours of the island are offered by Custom Tours of Kodiak and Island Terrific Tours. Or you can rent a car to drive around the island's 83 miles of paved and graveled roads. For the best views of the city and offshore islands, drive to the top of Pillar Mountain, a misnomer for the 1,300-foot hill behind town.

Fort Abercrombie State Historic Park, a 4½-mile drive northeast of Kodiak, has some grim reminders of World War II defenses; fourteen campsites, each with a pit toilet, are scattered throughout the spruce forest.

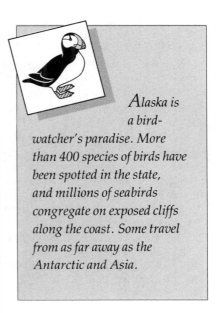

Alaska is a bird-watcher's paradise. More than 400 species of birds have been spotted in the state, and millions of seabirds congregate on exposed cliffs along the coast. Some travel from as far away as the Antarctic and Asia.

Cape Chiniak Road, which crosses the Buskin River 5 miles south of town, follows almost 50 miles of wild coastline, passing by many beach campsites; you'll find excellent clam digging (at low tide) wherever the road crosses a river mouth. Anton Larsen Bay Road leads north to wilderness hiking and high-lakes angling.

Hiking is the best way to see some of the island's more than 100 bird species, including nesting bald eagles (near rivers) and seabird rookeries along the rugged coast.

The refuge's giant bears

For a true wilderness experience and a glimpse of the famed half-ton Kodiak brown bears, explore the 2,780-square-mile Kodiak National Wildlife Refuge, which occupies almost 80 percent of the island.

Established in 1941 to preserve the natural habitat of the Kodiak bear, the refuge is also home to the red fox, river otter, short-tailed weasel, little brown bat, and tundra vole. Other wildlife inhabiting the refuge include the black-tailed deer, reindeer, mountain goat, beaver, muskrat, mink, snowshoe hare, red squirrel, and marten, all transplanted to Kodiak in the 1930s. Also look for Dall sheep and moose, more recent introductions.

Of course, most visitors are curious about the Kodiak bears. Approximately 2,400 of these tremendous animals inhabit the island. Males weigh up to 1,200 pounds.

Ferocious and dangerous, the bears generally avoid confrontation, lumbering away hurriedly as soon as they identify a human being. However, rare instances of unpredictable behavior do occur; always be sure to keep a respectable distance away from these large, powerful animals. Summer, when the salmon swarm upstream, and early autumn, when the berries are ripe, are the best times to catch sight of bears.

A limited number of backcountry cabins are available for fishing, hunting, and wildlife-viewing opportunities. Access is mostly by charter plane. For information, contact the refuge center at 1390 Buskin River Rd., Kodiak, AK 99615.

Fishing & hunting

Charter boats listed in the Yellow Pages take anglers offshore for salmon or giant halibut that can top 100 pounds. Stream fishing begins with Dolly Varden trout in the Buskin River and nearby streams in May and June; lake fishing for grayling picks up in June. Red salmon (sockeye) move into the rivers in early June, pink salmon in mid-July; salmon fishing peaks with the silver (coho) run in September.

Around the end of May, Kodiak holds its annual Crab Festival with seafood tasting, Russian dancing, art and ethnic crafts, and boat parades. King crabs can weigh up to 30 pounds and attain a span of 6 feet.

Remote Afognak Island, 30 miles northwest of Kodiak, offers good hunting and fishing. Accommodations are available at the Afognak Wilderness Lodge (Seal Bay, AK 99697), or you can check with the U.S. Forest Service in Kodiak to reserve one of the limited number of cabins sprinkled around the island.

For complete information on fishing and hunting, write to the Alaska Department of Fish and Game, P.O. Box 3-2000, Juneau, AK 99802. To obtain a list of registered guides, send $5 to the Department of Commerce and Economic Development, Division of Occupational Licensing, P.O. Box 110806, Juneau, AK 99811-0806.

Nonresident fishing permits are sold in local sport shops, where you can also pick up a free copy of the *Kodiak Area Sport Fishing Guide* to check on the best angling spots.

Accommodations

The two largest hotels, Buskin River Inn and Westmark Kodiak, offer restaurants and lounges. Other accommodations include the Northland Ranch Resort (10 rooms), several bed-and-breakfasts, and a few wilderness lodges scattered around the island. Make advance reservations in summer.

Restaurants, which feature specialties ranging from Chinese cuisine to local seafood, are plentiful.

Campgrounds are located at Fort Abercrombie State Park, north of town, and at Middle Bay, south of town. You'll find lots of other free scenic camping sites along the roads and beaches.

For additional information, write to the Kodiak Island Convention and Visitors Bureau, 100 Marine Way, Suite 100, Kodiak, AK 99615.

Kodiak's Russian past

Anchored in the Gulf of Alaska off the tip of the Kenai Peninsula, Kodiak Island is a wild parcel of the state that many travelers hear about but few visit.

Kodiak was the first Russian settlement in Alaska. Drawn to the land in their search for sea otters, Russian explorers founded a colony on the island in 1784. The site of the present city of Kodiak was chosen by Alexander Baranof in 1792.

Artifacts and diaries of early Russian settlers can be viewed at the Baranof Museum, just above the ferry terminal. Across the street are the beautiful, bulb-shaped cupolas of the Russian Orthodox church, which continues to serve Alaska's oldest parish.

On the first three weekends in August, residents recall their Russian heritage with performances of an ambitious pageant. *Cry of the Wild Ram* reenacts Kodiak's conquest by Russian fur traders. Theatergoers watch ferocious battles played out under the setting sun in Alaska's only outdoor theater.

The play, written by an Alaskan, Frank Brink, and performed by local residents, is a tale of Baranof's efforts to turn a wilderness into a community. Seating in the amphitheater is plentiful. August nights are cool, so dress warmly. Most viewers bring along hot coffee and sandwiches.

For more information, write to the *Cry of the Wild Ram* Pageant, P.O. Box 1792 (summer) or Box 481 (winter), Kodiak, AK 99615.

Tiny village on Atka Island is only a blink in the vastness of the far-flung Aleutians. The Aleuts who live on the often fog-blanketed isle subsist largely on fish, sea mammals, reindeer, and birds.

Giant crabs from the waters around Kodiak Island weigh in at about 400 pounds per load.

Katmai National Park

Famed for its Valley of Ten Thousand Smokes, Katmai National Park and Preserve covers more than 4 million acres. One of the largest units in the nation's park system, it's among North America's greatest wilderness recreation areas. Once remote and largely undiscovered by visitors, today it's readily accessible from Anchorage by air.

Established as a monument in 1918 and upgraded to park status in 1980, the area encompasses over a hundred miles of ocean bays, fjords, and lagoons set against a backdrop of glacier-covered peaks and volcanic crater lakes. Beyond the peaks lies a "wilderness within a wilderness" —forests, long lake chains, and the Valley of Ten Thousand Smokes.

History of an eruption

In June, 1912, Novarupta Volcano, then just a vent 6 miles east of Mt. Katmai, literally blew its top with a terrific explosion.

Before the eruption, the Katmai region was a land of tall grasses, groves of trees, and scattered lakes. A trail, used by trappers crossing from the Pacific Ocean to Bristol Bay, climbed Katmai Pass and wound through the valley.

The series of events that transformed the heart of the region into a scene of barren desolation began with a number of earthquakes, which caused the local natives to abandon their villages. Then the floor of the peaceful basin of the Ukak and Lethe rivers split into fissures at Novarupta; incandescent sand welling up on a cushion of escaping gases flowed swiftly for 15 miles, covering everything in its path to depths as great as 300 feet.

Next, the top of Mt. Katmai itself collapsed, perhaps from a subterranean outpouring of magma that emerged through Novarupta. The sound of the explosion was heard as far away as Juneau.

Volcanic ash from the eruption covered thousands of square miles. The resulting dust cloud spread around the world, blocking some of the sun's heat and thereby lowering temperatures over the entire Northern Hemisphere that year. When scientists arrived to study the area a few years later, "ten thousand smokes" curled up from the valley to the west of the ragged stump of Mt. Katmai. Steam from the fumaroles was still hot enough to fry bacon.

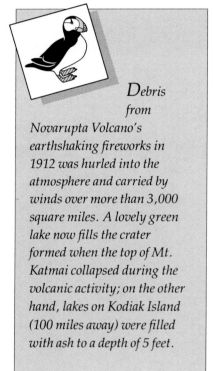

Debris from Novarupta Volcano's earthshaking fireworks in 1912 was hurled into the atmosphere and carried by winds over more than 3,000 square miles. A lovely green lake now fills the crater formed when the top of Mt. Katmai collapsed during the volcanic activity; on the other hand, lakes on Kodiak Island (100 miles away) were filled with ash to a depth of 5 feet.

Later, deposits of ash and sand consolidated into tuff, a type of rock. (You can still see small pieces floating in the park's lakes.) There are only a few wisps of smoke in the valley today, but the volcanoes around it still puff and rumble. During the past several decades, Mt. Trident has erupted four times, most recently in 1969.

Since the 1912 eruption, the turbulent Ukak River has cut deep, narrow, polished gorges through the ash. Plant life is slowly returning. But this is a dynamic region—an eruption could occur at any time, bringing with it dramatic changes to the landscape.

Valley of Ten Thousand Smokes

A high point for first-time visitors to Katmai is an excursion into the Valley of Ten Thousand Smokes.

Your scenic bus tour begins from Brooks Camp early in the morning and takes you 23 miles to the valley's edge, stopping along the way for short walks or wildlife observation. After fording three streams, you reach Overlook Cabin.

From the overlook, you gaze down upon some 40 square miles of valley, buried under 700 feet of volcanic debris, and across to snow-capped mountains. Pumice cliffs rise starkly from the valley floor along the meandering river.

Rangers lead hikes—about 2½ miles on a switchback trail—or you can hike through the valley independently. The climb back up is fairly steep; if you're not used to hiking, it's better to remain at the top.

Tickets for the full-day excursion (a box lunch is included) are available at Brooks River Lodge.

Wildlife in the park

More than 30 species of land mammals have been observed at Katmai; the Alaska brown bear, in evidence from early spring until late autumn, is the most prominent. You may catch a glimpse of these bears feasting on wild berries or fishing the streams for spawning salmon.

When you arrive at Katmai, a ranger meets you to explain precautions to take in the backcountry. A viewing platform at Brooks River Lodge allows you to watch the bears from a safe distance as they feed.

Moose inhabit the coastal and lake regions, nibbling on willows, water plants, and grasses. Smaller animals you may see in the park include the red fox, Arctic fox, lynx, and wolverine.

Waterfowl are abundant in the lakes region, and some 40 species of songbirds can be observed during summer months. Even the rare bald eagle makes an occasional appearance. Sea lions and hair seals frequent rock outcroppings along the coast.

Activities

Fishing is probably the reason most people come to Katmai. Erudite anglers claim that the Brooks River has some of the best salmon fishing in the world—and they would like to keep it a secret!

Each summer, nearly a million salmon return to the Naknek River system to spawn after spending several years in ocean waters. You'll often share fishing space along the river with bears.

Fishing is also good for rainbow trout, lake trout, Dolly Varden trout, grayling, whitefish, and northern pike. Silver, king, and humpback salmon are occasionally taken from the streams. You'll need an Alaska fishing license to cast your line in park waters.

At Brooks River Lodge, ranger-naturalists lead walks and hikes and present evening programs to acquaint visitors with the park. One of the easiest walks follows a trail along the Brooks River, where you'll get a good look at salmon jumping the falls on their way upstream to spawn.

Backcountry hikes

Hikers and backpackers find that Katmai offers some of the most exciting and rewarding wilderness experiences to be found anywhere. Though it's a rough and, at times, inhospitable country, it can give you the hiking trip of a lifetime, if you take reasonable precautions.

Late summer is the best time for hiking. The pesky mosquito is less bothersome, and the terrain is more stable. During bad weather, hikers are warned about the trail at the head of the Valley of Ten Thousand Smokes. The exchange of air between the Bering Sea and the Gulf of Alaska can produce winds of over 100 miles an hour there—enough to blow hikers off their feet.

The National Park Service provides plenty of information on hiking in the park.

Getting to the park

MarkAir and Reeve Aleutian airlines offer regularly scheduled service to the Alaska Peninsula, where you transfer to a floatplane that splashes down at a lodge's front door. Package tours from Anchorage, including accommodations at Brooks River Lodge, are available during the summer.

You can also charter a floatplane from Katmai Air Service in King Salmon for transportation to the park or for flightseeing or sportfishing in the surrounding area.

Accommodations

Located on Naknek Lake, Brooks River Lodge provides seasonal accommodations (June 1 to September 17) in a modern building or in cabins equipped with bathrooms. Hearty, family-style meals are available in the lodge. The Trading Post sells fishing tackle and souvenirs.

Facilities at Grosvenor Lodge (open from May 30 to September 30) include a dining room and cabins with outdoor plumbing. You can rent fishing equipment and boats (with or without a guide) at both locations. Kulik Lodge, one of the state's premier fly-out sportfishing camps, offers lodging, meals, boat and guide service, and fishing gear. The lodge operates from June 9 to October 2.

For information on these camps, write to Katmailand, Inc., 4700 Aircraft Dr., Anchorage, AK 99502.

Two more lodges in the area, Battle River Wilderness Retreat (8076 Caribbean Way, Sacramento, CA 95826) and Katmai Lodge (2825 90th S.E., Everett, WA 98208), offer trophy fishing and other activities.

Camping facilities

The National Park Service maintains a campground at Brooks River with tables, water, wood, fire pits, shelters, and a food cache. For information, write to the Superintendent, Katmai National Park and Preserve, P.O. Box 7, King Salmon, AK 99613.

You may also camp in the park's backcountry. Fire permits, required for camping, are issued at Brooks River Ranger Station or at the King Salmon headquarters.

Wild fruits and berries abound in amazing variety in Alaska. Two favorites of backcountry hikers are highbush cranberry, tasty even when frozen, and rose hip, a few of which provide as much vitamin C as an orange.

Bring your own camping supplies and groceries. Tents and stoves can usually be rented; fuel and some food are available at Brooks River Lodge.

Weather

Come prepared for some sunshine and some stormy weather. Strong winds and sudden rainstorms, known as "williwaws," frequently sweep through the area. Summer temperatures at Brooks River Lodge hover around 60°F.

Bring comfortable clothing—a warm sweater or windbreaker, walking shoes or hiking boots, wool socks, and rain gear. You'll need insect repellent if you're planning to spend time near the water.

Horned puffin breeds on the rocky cliffs along the state's coastal waters, but winters far offshore.

Richly gilded icons and ornate hangings adorning the interior of the small Russian Orthodox church on St. Paul Island amaze visitors to the remote Pribilofs.

Out to the Aleutians

The Alaska Peninsula extends in a southwest crescent to form the 1,200-mile chain of islands known as the Aleutians. This chain marks the dividing line between the North Pacific and the Bering Sea.

Called the "Land of the Smoky Sea" by the natives, it's a treeless region of fog and wind, the birthplace of storms where cold air from the north meets the warmth of the Japanese current.

The area includes about a dozen small, sparsely populated villages on seven islands. The region's meager economy is based on fishing, as well as some sheep and cattle raising.

At its farthest point, the Aleutian chain is only an hour (by air) from Siberia and 2 hours from Japan. It's surprisingly close to Hawaii—closer than any point on the California coast.

The semivolcanic archipelago of about 200 large islands and hundreds of smaller ones stretches from Unimak Island (closest to the Alaska mainland) to Attu Island, the most distant.

The island chain acts as a living textbook for vulcanologists. Most of the state's active or recently active volcanoes are strung out along the Alaskan Peninsula to the western tip of the Aleutians.

One of the islands on the Bering Sea side has amazed—and amused—the experts for two centuries. It has, in turn, risen from the sea, subsided, shifted its location, blown up, and reappeared. Currently, the mile-long island is home to colonies of birds and sea lions.

Aleut history

Native Aleuts dominate the population of the area. Skillful fishermen, in earlier times they often ventured far from shore in lightweight skin boats, searching for otters, seals, sea lions, and an occasional whale.

Early contacts with the Russian fur traders were stormy. Aleuts were often killed or taken hostage, families were divided, and entire communities were relocated.

After the United States purchased Alaska, the Aleuts were ignored. It took the bombing of Dutch Harbor in 1942 by the Japanese and their subsequent invasion of Attu and Kiska islands before attention turned to these remote reaches. American military bases were built in Dutch Harbor and on Adak Island, but it wasn't until 1943 that the costly battle to retake the islands was won.

Attu and Kiska islands at the end of the Aleutian chain were invaded by the Japanese during World War II. It was almost a year before the islands were regained. The area's weather was so bad that pilots bombed the Pribilof Islands, thinking they were attacking the Japanese fleet in the Aleutians.

Natives of Attu were interned in Japan throughout the war. On their return, they were settled on Atka Island because the Navy felt their village was too far away to defend.

Today, a Coast Guard station is the sole structure on Attu. The U.S. military maintains extensive facilities on Adak and Shemya islands; visitors need clearance.

Most of the 2,000 Aleuts fish commercially. Others travel all the way to Bristol Bay each summer to work in canneries.

What you'll see

Izembek National Wildlife Refuge, a 320,000-acre waterfowl reserve near the tip of the Alaska Peninsula, attracts over 100 species of birds. Established to benefit the black brant, Izembek Lagoon has the world's largest eelgrass beds, the feeding grounds of many of North America's brants during their spring and autumn migrations.

Hunting for waterfowl and caribou is excellent. Some watery trails lead into the refuge from Cold Bay, but most of the area is accessible only by foot. For more information, contact the Refuge Manager, Pouch 2, Cold Bay, AK 99571.

Adak Island's small community museum contains World War II memorabilia, wildlife displays, and native artifacts.

The tour companies listed below operate out of Dutch Harbor and offer a chance to view military reminders from "The Forgotten War," explore Aleut culture, or go flightseeing and bird-watching.

Aleutian Experience Tours
3400 Kvichak Circle
Anchorage, AK 99515

Aleutian Island Tours
320 Dock Street
Ketchikan, AK 99901

Unalaska Island
Box 248
Unalaska, AK 99685

Getting there

Reeve Aleutian Airways provides scheduled service between Anchorage and the Aleutians. The largest hotel in the Aleutians, Grand Aleutian, adds 112 rooms to Dutch Harbor on Unalaska Island.

The Pribilof Islands

Several tiny dots of land lie in the Bering Sea 200 miles north of the Aleutians, some 300 miles west of the Alaskan mainland. These are the Pribilofs, the "Galapagos Islands of the North," a once-in-a-lifetime experience for visitors.

Over 1½ million Pacific northern fur seals breed on St. George and St. Paul islands. The fur seal herd annually swims over 5,000 miles between Southern California, northern Japan, and the Pribilofs, though it's never been established why this migration occurs.

The two main islands and a few offshore rocks also support over 100 million birds, one of the most extraordinary collections of wildlife in the world. Even if you were not a birdwatcher before you arrived, you'll end up eagerly comparing notes with other members of your group on what exotic birds were sighted or photographed.

Brilliantly colored flowers, ferns, and foliage make St. Paul a horticulturist's heaven, as well as a good hiding place for many a small bird.

A Russian discovery

During the era of Catherine the Great of Russia, history-making Russian explorers ventured farther and farther north from Siberia, conquering new lands for the Czarina. Many returned from their voyages with tales of incredible sights. Among the early mariners was Georg Wilhelm Steller, who brought word of magnificently furred water animals who swam the northern seas. He was referring to seals.

Later, seafarers told of seeing huge herds of fur seals swimming northward through the passes of the Aleutian Islands and then simply disappearing into the fog of the Bering Sea. These springtime sightings lent substance to the ancient Aleut legend of a mysterious group of islands far to the north of the Aleutian chain where millions of fur seals gathered each year.

Looking for an island to name? Alaska has several thousand unnamed islands, located primarily in the Panhandle and in the Aleutian Islands chain.

These misty, fog-bound islands were discovered by Russian explorer G. Pribylov in 1786. He had located the breeding grounds of the largest fur seal herd in the world. During the first year, zealous hunters took some 40,000 seal skins, 2,000 sea otter skins, and 14,400 pounds of walrus ivory. The big fur rush was on. It proved to be the beginning of a stormy international battle for conservation of one of the most beautiful and courageous animals known to man.

At one time, indiscriminate killing of seals for their valuable fur decimated the herds, but good management has rebuilt their population. The Pribilofs are home for sea otters, too, also once hunted almost to the point of extinction.

Getting to the Pribilofs

Three-day (or longer) tours are offered from Anchorage via Cold Bay in the Aleutians to the island of St. Paul in the Pribilofs. The basic tour, offered only during the summer, includes round-trip air fare, transfers, accommodations, guided motor coach sightseeing to bird rookeries and seal breeding grounds, and other entertainment.

Guided naturalist tours of smaller St. George Island are also offered every summer. For information, write to St. George Tanaq Corporation, 4000 Old Seward Hwy., Suite 302, Anchorage, AK 99503.

Touring St. Paul Island

Headquarters for most travelers is the Aleut-operated hotel on St. Paul, the largest of the five Pribilof islands. Rooms are simple and clean; bathrooms are "down the hall."

The dining room is a few blocks away on the main street of this small town. Everyone eats together. Menu selection is fairly limited, but the food is well cooked—and quite expensive.

Prices in the community store are about the lowest in Alaska. Souvenirs include native crafts and "Pribilof" sweatshirts.

The small Russian church in town is probably the most fascinating in Alaska. Built in the early part of the century, it has a traditional design, but its onion-shaped dome is made from gold-painted metal, and the cross above the gate is constructed from sections of pipe. The interior of the church is one of the richest and most colorful in Alaska. Services are held in Slavonic, Aleut, and English.

St. Paul Island is about 13½ miles long and 8 miles wide. It has roughly 45 miles of shoreline, composed of alternating stretches of sand and broken rock. Cliffs often rise as high as 400 feet above the water. No trees break the rolling, grassy plains.

From atop one of the cinder cones sprinkled around the island, you get fine views of the village, of several freshwater lakes, and of the island's small reindeer herd.

Weather

Warm, clear weather is rare; wet and windy is the usual forecast. Bring warm, rainproof clothing and comfortable walking shoes. A waterproof parka with a hood is a good choice.

Other Western Destinations

Several small towns along the Bering Sea make fine jumping-off spots for exploring the far-flung western area. Flights from Bethel, the region's largest town, take you into the vast Yukon Delta National Wildlife Refuge, out to Nunivak to view reindeer herds and the shaggy musk oxen, or to outlying native villages.

Exploring Bethel

A major deep-water port and commercial fishing center at the mouth of the Kuskokwim River, Bethel is reached by scheduled air service from Anchorage. Originally an Eskimo village and trading post, it's a place to talk to the natives and buy arts and crafts, including delicate, handwoven baskets from the Yukon and Kuskokwim deltas. For a look at the past, visit the Yugtarvik Regional Museum.

Trips from Bethel

Several air taxi services offer flightseeing tours and fishing and hunting excursions. By plane or riverboat, a visitor can reach out-of-the-way villages unknown to most tourists.

Yukon Delta National Wildlife Refuge. Bethel lies in the center of Alaska's largest wildlife refuge, over 19½ million acres of some of the most extensive waterfowl breeding grounds in the world. Moose, caribou, grizzly and black bears, and wolves inhabit the northern hills and eastern mountains. The refuge also encompasses 36 Eskimo villages. For information, contact the Refuge Manager, P.O. Box 346, Bethel, AK 99559.

Nunivak Island. A flight to the native village of Mekoryuk on Nunivak Island, 160 miles to the west, offers a look at a commercially managed reindeer herd, the economic core of the town. Gentle musk oxen are cultivated for their *qiviut*, the cashmere-soft wool used in garments.

Some of the finest ivory carving in the world is done here. Villagers also make unique wooden masks. Tourist accommodations are limited.

Galapagos of the North

The Pribilof Islands' enormous fur seal herd and huge bird population, including some rarely seen species, draw visitors and scientists from all over the world to this remote area.

Life in a harem. The vanguard of the great fur seal herd, the breeding bulls (or "beach-masters," as they're popularly known), reach the rookeries early in May. These massive bulls are tremendously powerful animals, measuring 6 to 7 feet long and weighing between 450 and 600 pounds—about five times as much as the females.

The bull must reach at least 7 years of age before he can acquire a harem; once he has collected his cows (the average harem numbers 30 to 40), he dares not leave even to eat or drink for fear of losing them. He sleeps very little and, during the breeding season, is a vicious, restless, uncompromising lord and master over his "wives."

The battle for harems begins when the females arrive in June to give birth and breed again. A scene of wild confusion ensues, accompanied by the cacophony of seal sounds. The unattached or idle bulls form a solid fringe outside the breeding rookeries, maintaining a constant vigil for a stray wife or two to start their own families.

After their arrival on the islands, the cows give birth within a few days. Each breeding cow bears one pup a year. Pups weigh between 10 and 12 pounds at birth. The females have an uncanny instinct for recognizing their own young and will nurse no other.

Harems begin breaking up in early August. The herd leaves as gradually as it arrived, reaching a peak in November. By the end of the year, the beaches are usually deserted.

Because the seals are easily disturbed, blinds have been erected so visitors can observe the seals' antics without inhibiting them.

For the birds. The Pribilofs are one of the largest bird sanctuaries in the world. Over 180 species can be sighted here; some, like the Mongolian wheatear, are extremely rare. It's also virtually the only place in the world to see the red-legged kittiwake.

The Pribilofs are one of the few places where other species appear in such large numbers. Hundreds of bird rookeries dot the coastline.

Bring binoculars and a camera equipped with a telephoto lens. A bird identification book is also very handy.

Some people enjoy tramping through the lush, grassy terrain and along the rocky cliffs to record a bird sighting. Others find a comfortable viewing spot on the tundra and don't budge from it. Either approach can lead to success.

The Far North

Visitors to the Far North have an opportunity to enjoy one of the most unusual regions of the United States. A fascinating land, the Arctic adds high adventure to any Alaskan trip.

Regularly scheduled flights reach the Arctic's few cities; bush pilots make runs to more remote sections of "Eskimoland." Comfortable, though not necessarily luxurious, hotels await guests.

Alaska's 200,000-square-mile Arctic territory comprises the northern third of the state. For the most part, the area is separated from the Interior by the far-flung Brooks Range, which extends 600 miles westward from the Canadian border.

Here you'll find some of America's finest wilderness parks: Noatak National Preserve, Kobuk Valley National Park, and Gates of the Arctic National Park and Preserve. Though few services are available, fishing for arctic grayling, backpacking (on your own or with a guide), and floating down unspoiled rivers are premier wilderness experiences.

The Arctic's scant population of a little more than 18,000 would be lost in Pasadena's Rose Bowl. During winter, a continuous icy sheet weds land and sea, melting only in late spring. Temperatures remain low in winter, but much of the land receives no more precipitation than Phoenix, Arizona.

Permafrost may be only a few feet deep in some places; in others, it reaches down several thousand feet. It's overlaid with a treeless mat known as tundra, a springy layer of mosses, sedges, and dwarf willow and spruce.

In summer, the offshore ice melts, permitting oceangoing vessels to pass. On land, a bright carpet of wildflowers flares into brief bloom; summer temperatures soar up to 70°F.

At Barrow, the sun does not set from May 10 to August 2; in Kotzebue, the sun is above the horizon for 36 days between June 2 and July 8. The late spring visitor may have the thrill of seeing the ice "go out" (usually between June 5 and 15) or of spotting a polar bear from the air.

The Arctic's economy is based on tourism and exploration for natural resources. The North Slope oil discoveries stimulated accelerating industrialization here where the military Distant Early Warning Line is strung out along the top of the world.

Even though their age-old fishing and hunting economy is rapidly changing, some sturdy Eskimos still cling to that way of life. A few old traders and a sprinkling of trappers remain, though in many places snowmobiles have replaced dog teams for winter transportation.

Excitement runs high during whaling and hunting seasons. Fish are an important food staple, and Eskimo women still make beautiful fur garments, following patterns designed by their ancestors. Men carve ivory from walrus tusks into figurines and jewelry.

Getting there

Most visitors come by air. A network of scheduled and bush routes reaches into nearly 100 scattered settlements. Travelers who cross the Arctic Circle on any of the air tours receive impressive certificates stating that they've been to the Far North. In this land of aurora borealis and midnight sun, a summer visitor can fly in continuous daylight.

Anchorage and Fairbanks are gateway cities to Nome, Kotzebue, Barrow, and Prudhoe Bay. In addition to scheduled jet service on Alaska Airlines and Markair, air taxi operators provide service to practically any point in this region.

What to wear

Despite high summer temperatures, be sure to take along a warm sweater and comfortable walking shoes. For a winter trip, wear thermal underwear, boots, mittens or gloves, a hat, and a woolen or down coat.

Under brooding skies, Dalton Highway travelers take a lunch break on their 2-day trek to Prudhoe Bay. In the background stretches a portion of the 800-mile-long oil pipeline that bisects the state.

The Arctic

Barrow—*top of the continent*

- Blanket tosses
- Eskimo dancing
- Naval Arctic Research Laboratory
- Rogers-Post Monument
- Tundra tour

Fort Yukon—*Athabascan Indian village features beadwork, fish, and furs*

Kotzebue—*colorful Eskimo village*

- Eskimo dances
- Jade factory
- NANA Museum of the Arctic
- Reindeer camp
- Tundra tour

Nome—*former gold camp*

- Gold panning
- Museums
- Dog sled exhibition

Prudhoe Bay—*pipeline terminus*

- Bird-watching
- Community center tour
- Geological film

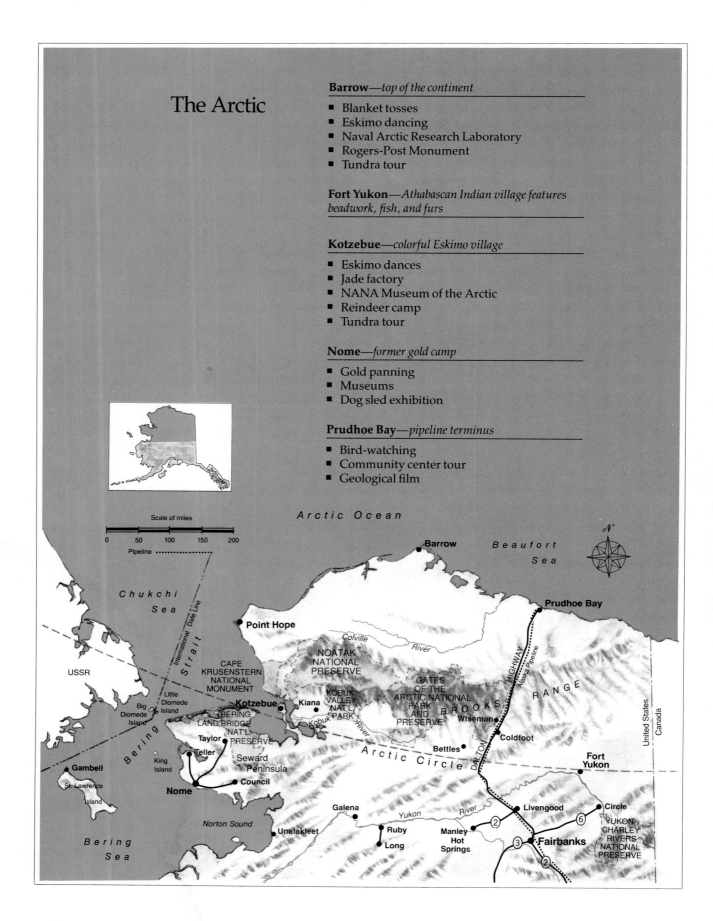

Nome & the Far West

Though it's considered a part of the Arctic, Nome is technically 30 miles south of the Arctic Circle. Situated in the southeast corner of the Seward Peninsula, it faces the Bering Sea.

You'll have to look indoors for the local color in this deceptively drab-appearing city. Houses and commercial buildings lean unevenly, reflecting their tentative footing on the permafrost. Some are kept level with house jacks; others are mounted on skids ready to be moved when the permafrost melts.

A number of modern structures, including hotels, restaurants, museums, gift shops, and the Nome Convention and Visitors Bureau, stand on the west side of the main street—the only strip of land that is not permafrost. A massive breakwater now shields them from the fury of winter storms that have devastated the city in the past.

Nome was spawned by the discovery of gold in nearby Anvil Creek in 1898 by three men known as the "lucky Swedes." When grains of gold were discovered on the beach itself the following year, the gold rush was on. Nome once boasted 40,000 residents.

Though the gold rush passed with the decline of mining, an aura of those glamorous days lingers on. Several small mining operations are located in the area, a massive dredge operates offshore, and fortune seekers still sift the sands in front of the town. Today's city, a far cry from the tent community of those former years, numbers 3,700, 60 percent of which are Eskimos.

Highlights

Most package tours include visits to both Nome and Kotzebue, with an overnight stop in one town or the other. Nome has the better accommodations, restaurants, shops, and activities. Two hotels (Nome Nugget Inn and Polaris Hotel), two bed-and-breakfast inns, and rental suites offer a range of accommodations.

During the summer season, daily sightseeing trips with knowledgeable driver-guides are offered. Visitors are often surprised to find more than 300 varieties of wildflowers carpeting the Seward Peninsula.

The tour visits abandoned gold-mining sites and gives you a look at a working mine. A slide show provides peeks into Nome's colorful past. You may even find your own "color"; an old-timer will show you how to wield a gold pan.

How did Nome get its name? One story is that in the 1850s, an officer on a British ship off the coast of Alaska noted that a prominent point on the map was not identified. He wrote "Name" next to the point. When the map was copied later, a draftsman read the "a" as an "o," and Nome was born.

Others believe that the word was derived from the Eskimo phrase "kn-no-me" meaning "I don't know," which was probably an Eskimo's reply when asked the name of the area.

Howard Farley, one of the founders of the Iditarod Trail Sled Dog Race, raises and races dogs. At his summer beach camp, he exercises the dogs on the sand, demonstrating how they respond to the musher.

Nome is the best place in the Arctic to buy gold nugget and jade jewelry. Gift shops also feature examples of fine native crafts; note particularly the carved walrus ivory and soapstone. Some furs, mukluks, and a few parkas can be found around town.

Special events

Nome marks the finish line of the annual Iditarod Trail Sled Dog Race that begins in Anchorage. In March, Nome hosts the month-long "Iditarod Daze" celebration. (For a description of the race, see page 68.)

Another major annual event is the Midnight Sun Festival in June. Highlights include a midnight baseball game, footraces, and raft races on the Nome River. Old-timers and new-comers alike dress in costumes to celebrate continuous daylight.

Fourth of July is an old-fashioned celebration in Nome, as in most Arctic towns.

King Island Eskimos, master ivory carvers who once paddled walrus-hide boats 80 miles to reach Nome from their former home in the Bering Sea, occasionally perform dances for visiting groups.

For more information on Nome celebrations, write to the Nome Convention and Visitors Bureau, P.O. Box 251, Nome, AK 99762.

Side trips from Nome

Since Nome is the aerial center for this part of Alaska, you can arrange for a bush pilot to fly you to such remote Eskimo villages as Unalakleet, Shishmaref, Wales, Teller, Little Diomede Island (2½ miles from Siberian Big Diomede Island), and Golovin.

Gambell. One of the Arctic villages travelers can visit easily on a 1-day tour is Gambell, located on St. Lawrence Island within sight of Siberia's Chukotsky Peninsula. Archaeologi-

Young native adds his catch to the curtain of drying fish. Many Eskimos spend their summers at fish camps, catching, cleaning, and curing the food that they—and their dogs—will depend on throughout the long winter.

A sea of remarkably smug-looking ivory walruses, intricately carved by native craftspeople, await buyers in a Nome store.

cal evidence indicates that it was inhabited 2,400 years ago; whalers lived there in the 1800s.

Gambell is a friendly community. You'll see villagers curing hides and meat, foraging the tundra fields for bird eggs and bitter berries, and setting out in skin boats to hunt walruses, whales, seals, and sea lions. Life on the ocean is serious and basic for Gambell residents.

Bird-watchers will enjoy exploring Gambell Mountain, the rolling tundra, and beaches near the village. Arctic terns, gulls, sea parrots, auklets, jaegers, murres, puffins, and cormorants are just a few of the island's feathered summer residents.

Unalakleet. Located about an hour's flying time southeast of Nome on the eastern edge of Norton Sound, the Eskimo village of Unalakleet is noted for its fine salmon fishing. The river that cuts right through the town has a large run of king salmon in late June, and, unlike many other areas, the limit can be as high as six fish a day.

Silvertip on the Unalakleet, a private fishing lodge 8 miles upriver from the village, can arrange accommodations for anglers trying for salmon, arctic char, or grayling.

Bering Land Bridge National Preserve. On the northern shores of the Seward Peninsula, almost 2½ million acres have been set aside to preserve the region believed to be where the earliest inhabitants settled when they crossed the land bridge that once linked Asia and North America. Access information is available at Nome's visitors bureau.

Roads from Nome

Roads connect Nome with three tiny villages on the Seward Peninsula. Along the way you'll pass old mining cabins and good fishing rivers. No accommodations, gas stations, restaurants, or major towns are found along these routes. Adventurous travelers should take along food, camping gear, adequate clothing, and mosquito repellent.

For a short drive (4 to 5 miles one-way), take a trip to the top of Anvil Mountain. From here, you can look over the city, the Bering Sea, Sledge Island, and a vast expanse of tundra. Nome's visitors bureau can provide directions.

Nome-Council Road. The road follows the coast for about 30 miles before heading inland to the village of Council (30 to 40 people), 72 miles from Nome. You'll enjoy expansive views of the Bering Sea shoreline. About 34 miles from Nome is Solomon, once a prosperous community, now home for five families.

A river crosses the highway just before Council; residents wade across or cross in boats (you may be able to get a ride), depending on the water level.

Nome-Taylor Road. You pass through some of the original mining claims on this popular, 85-mile fishing route. Some evidence remains of an old railroad. Several summer camps are located on the road about 8 miles from Nome. At Mile 38, there's a campground adjacent to beautiful Salmon Lake. Watch for moose, reindeer, fox, and even bears along the road.

Nome-Teller Road. A 2-hour, 71-mile trip leads to the community of Teller, population 200. Here you'll find a small gift shop and a town store.

Panning for profit

Three "lucky Swedes" spawned the 1898 gold rush that brought thousands of fortune seekers to the wind- and wave-battered Seward Peninsula. Though the boom lasted for only a little more than a dozen years, sporadic mining attempts continue up to the present time.

In 1901, a miner unearthed a gold nugget weighing 107.2 ounces and measuring 7 inches long, 4 inches wide, and 2 inches thick. Though its fantastic size has never been equaled, over the years other would-be miners have picked up fairly sizable nuggets from the beach in front of town.

Word of these "strikes" is enough to inspire gold miners to head for Nome much as they did in 1898, hauling gold pans, sluice boxes, and other ore-retrieving inventions to the long stretch of sand fronting the Bering Sea.

The Nome waterfront is one of the few places in Alaska where you don't need a permit to search for gold. In other areas, recreational mining is allowed on some public lands. Before you can dip a pan or start a sluice, you'll need to know whether or not it's legal for you to prospect. The U.S. Bureau of Land Management and the Alaska Department of Natural Resources can tell you who owns the property and whether it's open for recreational mining. You will then have to check with the agency that manages the property for any specific land use restrictions.

Before you do any recreational mining, consider the impact of the activity on the land. Mining can adversely affect plant and animal life in the area; for example, silt washed into streams and rivers during the process of separating soil and minerals can threaten fish.

If you're planning to use a dredge or any other earth-moving equipment, you must obtain a permit. Contact the Alaska Department of Fish and Game's Habitat Division (P.O. Box 3-2000, Juneau, AK 99802) for information.

Kotzebue, an Eskimo Village

Named for Otto von Kotzebue, a navigator who discovered the village in 1816, this rapidly growing Eskimo settlement thrives 30 miles north of the Arctic Circle. The air route to it from Nome passes within 150 miles of East Cape, Siberia.

Beginning on June 2 and lasting for 36 days, the sun never falls below the horizon. Each day it swings in a huge circle in the sky. A great photo subject each "night" during this period is the midnight sun. You can shoot it from here at 20-minute intervals as it dips toward the northern horizon and rises again without ever going out of sight.

Kotzebue has no sidewalks. The colorful main street runs along the beach. Here you'll find the Nullagvik Hotel, which has glass-enclosed observation lounges on the second and third floors where you can watch the midnight sun. The hotel's dining room serves reindeer and sheefish, two local favorites.

Kotzebue's other streets ramble among houses and other buildings in no apparent pattern. Wooden prefab houses have virtually replaced traditional sod and driftwood dwellings in all but the most remote areas.

In many yards, dogs are chained to houses. Though these dogs may look docile, they're usually unfriendly to strangers, so don't venture too close.

The natives live with one foot in the modern era and the other in their old way of life. Though they'll eat corn flakes, they prefer *muktuk* (whale blubber).

After the ice goes out, the beluga (white) whales migrate. Much excitement is generated as the whalers put out to sea for these highly prized mammals, which attain 12 to 17 feet in length and average about 100 pounds to the foot. During June and July, you may see these whales being cut up, their meat hung on racks along the street to dry for winter food.

Boats manned by today's Eskimos are similar in style to those made by their ancestors, but in most cases materials have changed. The *oomiak*, an oval-shaped vessel originally made of walrus skin, and the familiar kayak are occasionally used.

Highlights

One of the best ways to explore Kotzebue is to take a guided tour. Packages include air fare, accommodations, and sightseeing. Outfitted with colorful parkas, visitors are offered an introduction to Eskimo life on a tour of the town's 9 miles of roads. You'll see an authentic sod igloo, discover the multitude of plants that grow in the spongy tundra, and visit a fish camp to learn how Eskimos catch, clean, and cure this food staple.

*N*otice *in the* **Kotzebue's newspaper,** The Arctic Sounder—"*Our last sunset was June 1, 2:21* A.M. *Next sunrise will be July 9 at* 2:34 A.M."

Situated well north of the tree line, Kotzebue boasts only one tree in its "National Forest," a dubious specimen that is nevertheless proudly pointed out to visitors.

The highlight of any Kotzebue tour is the chance to meet some of the natives at the NANA Museum of the Arctic. Tourists enjoy dramatic presentations of Inupiat Eskimo history and culture, as well as lifelike dioramas that interpret wildlife in the Arctic environment. After the show, an informal crafts fair is offered.

Villagers participate in lively native dances done to chants and the beat of skin drums. The dances tell stories of the hunt and other activities central to Eskimo life. You'll also have an opportunity to take part in the ancient practice of blanket tossing, where a hunter is flung aloft from a walrus skin.

Next to the museum, the Jade Products factory offers a look at items made by natives from the local gemstone.

If it's open, stop by the excellent city museum nearby. On display at Ootukakuktuvik, meaning the "place of old things," are a raincoat made from walrus intestine and a coat fashioned from bird feathers, among other objects from the past.

Side trips

From Kotzebue you can take a bush pilot tour to small Eskimo villages seldom seen by visitors. Kotzebue is also the jumping-off point for wilderness adventure in Cape Krusenstern National Monument, Noatak National Preserve, and Kobuk Valley National Park. Check with the park headquarters office in Kotzebue for backpacking and camping information.

Kobuk River. The Kobuk River country, one of the Arctic's most scenic areas, contains a dozen or so Eskimo villages. Kiana is one of the more modern, with a lodge where you can stay overnight. Nearby lie the Kobuk Sand Dunes, about 25 square miles of desert, incredible as it may seem in the Arctic.

Sheefishing is popular in Kiana. The sheefish, unique to Alaska, is a good fighting fish not known to many anglers. Though it has a number of small bones, the white fish has an excellent taste.

Point Hope. At this very remote Eskimo village, you get the true feeling of the rugged, timeless, isolated—yet friendly—Arctic. A popular whaling and hunting site, the village has been continuously occupied for more than 1,000 years.

As a tour destination, Point Hope is a real adventure, but it's not for everyone. Limited overnight accommodations are available. You can buy food to fix your own meals, or you can eat at local restaurants.

On a guided walking tour, you visit the old sod igloo village, the underground natural deep-freeze meat storage, the whale-feasting grounds, a mission church, and a cemetery completely fenced with whale jawbones.

Cape Krusenstern. Recent archaeological finds on this spit in northwestern Alaska (now a national monument) establish the fact that people have lived in this area for over 4,000 years. The discovery of flints, pottery

It's hard to keep a permanent address in the Arctic. Building heat often causes the permafrost (perennially frozen ground) to thaw, so with time, buildings begin to tilt and sag. Some houses are built on skids so they can be moved easily; one Nome home has been relocated seven times.

shards, ivory and whalebone harpoons, and even burial sites has allowed archaeologists to learn about the culture of the prehistoric relatives of today's Inupiat Eskimos.

About 10 miles across the sound from Kotzebue, Cape Krusenstern is easily accessible by plane or boat. Adventurers will have to bring in their own tents, bedding, stoves, food, and water; no facilities are available.

The economy of the two small native villages of Kivalina, north of the monument along the Chukchi Sea, and Noatak, to the east across the Mulgrave Hills, revolves around subsistence hunting and fishing. Both communities have airstrips.

Several families live year-round at Sheshalik, a meeting place near the southern tip of the cape for seal and beluga whale hunters.

"Bird men" of Alaska

As any resident will tell you, you haven't really seen Alaska until you leave the highways and take to the air.

More people have pilot's licenses in Alaska than in any other state in the country. The reason is purely practical: distances are great and some settlements can be reached only by light plane.

Air travel to almost anywhere is easy to arrange. Several airlines provide scheduled service to various points around the state. In addition, numerous air taxis (operated by bush pilots) travel to outlying areas. Fishing enthusiasts use them to fly to remote lakes and rivers. Hunters travel to where the big game is.

Why are such pilots called bush pilots? The answer is fairly obvious. They fly to remote areas in the backcountry where no scheduled service, or even an airstrip, exists.

Because of their daring feats, great legends have embellished the

reputation of Alaska's "bird men." But for all their romance, bush pilots are a variable lot.

Don't call the first name you see advertised in the Yellow Pages. Instead, shop around; rates vary—and so does experience. In some areas, you'll find only one flight service; such large population centers as Anchorage and Fairbanks give you a wider choice.

Planes also come in various shapes and sizes. You could find yourself in a turbo jet or a prop plane; the craft might have wheels for conventional landing strips, pontoons for watery landings, or skis for icefields.

In some cases, you'll discover that chartering a plane can be no more expensive than taking a commercial flight, and even more convenient.

A good way to cut costs is to plan your trip to coincide with a drop or pickup the pilot is already scheduled to make. You pay only for your

additional stop, and you may have the opportunity to fly a scenic route. Naturally, the more people there are to share a charter, the less expensive it is for each person.

Some of the most scenic areas for charter flights are among the richly forested islands in southeastern Alaska, over Southwest Alaska's lake-studded wilderness, through the glacier country of Prince William Sound and Kenai Fjords National Park, around Mt. McKinley, and up to the remote regions of the Arctic.

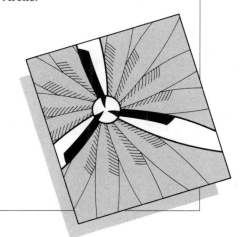

Barrow & the North Slope

Sir John Barrow's name is preserved at Point Barrow, the northernmost point in the United States. This man helped finance many polar expeditions, including that of Sir John Franklin and Sir William Parry.

The town of Barrow, with a population of close to 3,000, shares honors with Kotzebue as the largest of the Inupiat Eskimo villages. Its jerry-built shacks and shanties contrast sharply with the town's ultramodern school, shopping mall, and corporate offices for the North Slope Regional Corporation, one of the Alaska native cooperatives.

Most people come on a brief tour that gives them the opportunity to observe an ancient culture and to stand on the windswept beach that marks the edge of the North American continent. Often, such tours are combined with a day trip to the oil fields of Prudhoe Bay.

The ancestors of many of today's most prominent families were whalers and traders who began following the big bowhead whale into the Arctic Ocean more than a century ago. Barrow's most famous resident was Charlie Brower, who wrote *50 Years Before Zero*. Many of his descendants still live in the village.

Point Barrow made it into the news when humorist Will Rogers and pilot Wiley Post crashed near here in 1935 during an around-the-world flight. The Rogers-Post Monument is located 12 miles southwest of the village. The airfield near the village is also named for the famed duo.

Touring Barrow

Barrow probably has the starkest appearance of any city in the Arctic. Much of the year the Arctic Ocean is frozen solid from Barrow to the North Pole, 1,200 miles away.

The village is randomly clustered along a barren strand of beach fronting the ocean. There are no sidewalks and no water or sewer systems. Water must be transported from a small lake 4 miles inland; during winter, drinking water is melted ice. The city starts "spring housecleaning" by mid-June, probably the best time to visit.

The modern Top of the World Hotel may surprise you; it has 40 rooms, a gift shop, a coffee shop, and a restaurant. You'll find several other restaurants in town.

Four miles north of Barrow, the Naval Arctic Research Laboratory, open to group tours, contains a museum featuring native handicrafts and scientific specimens.

Both bus and walking tours are conducted by knowledgeable guides. You'll watch Eskimo dances (join in, if you like) and blanket tossing. Following the festivities, a "flea market" of local handicrafts is held. You bargain directly with the Eskimos.

If you're curious, you can dig down to the permafrost, the frozen subsoil that never thaws. In summer, even though the top layer of earth is tufted with wildflowers and grasses, the ground is still frozen underneath.

Whaling remains an important activity for the Eskimos. You'll also see other evidence of the Eskimos' dependence on the sea. Fishing boats and drying racks dot the coastline.

Special events. If the whale hunts are successful in early spring, a colorful whale feast and celebration may be held in June or July.

As in many other Eskimo villages, the Fourth of July always calls for a big festival that features dancing, kayak races, high jumping, muktuk eating, choosing of a queen, and many other interesting Eskimo games.

Prudhoe Bay

Deadhorse is where you land when you take a 1-day tour of Prudhoe Bay, the northern terminus of the Alaska pipeline. It's also possible to reach the area on a bus tour up the Dalton Highway (the pipeline haul road) from Fairbanks. The town looks like something out of science fiction, but the attitude is strictly business for the people who live and work here.

The wages are high and housing and food are included at no cost to the employees of the oil companies. But, outside of their jobs, there's little for the workers to do.

Most people live and eat in large community centers. For entertainment, there are swimming pools, saunas, exercise rooms, game rooms, and movies. The food is generous and more than utilitarian—steak, lobster, ice cream, and pastries are almost always on the menu.

For several weeks at a stretch, employees put in 12-hour days, 7 days a week. Then they are flown out to their homes for a week or two of vacation.

Highlights. If you're lucky, you'll be met by a driver-guide who's a geology major with a minor in ornithology. Various structures devoted to oil and birds are about all there is to see.

Your first stop may be for lunch at one of the community cafeterias. The price, which may not be included in the cost of the tour, is high.

On your tour, you'll see the Prudhoe Bay National Forest, a lighthearted reference to a setting where the trees are metal and only oil tanks and other industrial structures break the horizon.

The main attraction is the pipeline, snaking its way over the tundra, across mountains and rivers never conquered until now, to waiting tankers 800 miles away in Valdez harbor. Environmentalists successfully battled for careful treatment of the tundra and crossings for caribou herds along the pipeline's route.

Though Prudhoe Bay is not a particularly attractive destination, it does give you an insight into the gargantuan task of laying the pipeline. (For a description of the construction of the pipeline and its effect on the state's economy, turn to page 72.)

Other Arctic Destinations

Several other fascinating areas of the Arctic are best reached from cities in the Interior. Among the most interesting destinations are Gates of the Arctic National Park, the ultimate wilderness, and Fort Yukon, the state's largest Athabascan Indian village.

Gates of the Arctic National Park & Preserve

About 200 miles south of Barrow and 200 miles north of Fairbanks, in the heart of northern Alaska, lies Gates of the Arctic National Park and Preserve. The park includes the scenic heartland of the Brooks Range, the northernmost extension of the Rocky Mountains and an area whose grandeur and austere beauty defy description.

The headwaters of both the Noatak and Kobuk rivers lie within the park's vast mountainous reaches. The Kobuk Valley National Park lies to the west.

Combined, the park and preserve are four times the size of Yellowstone National Park. Two different cultures are represented within its boundaries: the Athabascan Indians, who inhabit the taiga forestland, and the Nunamiut Eskimos, who hunt caribou in the high valleys.

Only some isolated trappers' cabins and a few remote villages intrude on the solitude of the vast landscape.

What to do. Among the most popular park excursions are backpacking trips to the north fork of the Koyukuk River and float trips down the Koyukuk to the Eskimo village of Noatak. Anglers seek Walker Lake in the southern part of the park. A lodge at the edge of the lake offers the park's only public lodging.

This pristine land is also an exceptional area for mountaineering, fishing, viewing birds and wildlife, and berry picking. Hunters try for geese, rabbits, ducks, moose, caribou, and bear. In winter, cross-country skiing and snowshoeing attract visitors.

Getting to the park. The remote wilderness is accessible by plane from Bettles or by foot along trails from the communities of Coldfoot and Wiseman on the Dalton Highway (the pipeline haul road). At Bettles, visitors will find outfitters, guides, and a lodge. Coldfoot, long a favorite spot with Prudhoe Bay truckers, has motel rooms and a family-style dining hall.

You'll need to prepare carefully for an excursion to this isolated backcountry. Fairbanks is the best place to assemble gear, buy supplies, and obtain topographical maps. For information, write to the Superintendent, Gates of the Arctic National Park and Preserve, P.O. Box 74680, Fairbanks, AK 99707.

Fort Yukon

Starting above Whitehorse in the Canadian Yukon, the great Yukon River flows in a 2,081-mile arc through the middle of Alaska to empty into the Bering Sea. At its northernmost bend, just above the Arctic Circle, it widens out to 3 miles. Here is the location of Fort Yukon, the largest Athabascan Indian village in Alaska.

Fort Yukon was the first English-speaking settlement in the territory. Established in 1847 by the Hudson's Bay Company, it operated as a fur trading post for 20 years. By 1873, the first gold prospectors had arrived.

The Yukon River has gradually eroded the old townsite, and newer log cabins have been built on higher ground among the lean spruce trees. But the village hasn't changed a great deal over the years, except for the addition of a few modern buildings that contrast sharply with the town's more primitive structures. Trading posts still deal in furs, thimbles, tractors, and general merchandise.

Instead of by the great stern-wheel river steamers that once plied the river between St. Michaels (near the river's mouth) and Dawson, today's traffic moves by air. Regularly scheduled service is available from Fairbanks. Charter flights offer half- or full-day tours. Gwitchyaa Zhee Lodge (open all year) has four nice log cabins and a restaurant.

Athabascan Indian women tan moose and caribou hides and do exceptionally artistic beadwork. Raw furs and beadwork moccasins are good buys. Look for outstanding examples of Indian beadwork on the altar cloths of the wooden Episcopal church. (The church's hymnals are printed in the Athabascan language.)

Along the river, fish wheels scoop up salmon during the annual migration. The Indians clean and hang the fish that, after drying, will provide winter food both for themselves and for their malemute dogs.

Eskimos didn't start blanket tosses for fun. It was a way to spot game at a distance. Under the right conditions, a hunter tossed up on a blanket could reach a height of 20 feet.

Old Fort Yukon has been reconstructed from original Hudson's Bay Company plans. The 1847-style fort includes a stockade, a trading post, and a small museum selling Indian beadwork.

Dinjii Zhuu Enjit Museum contains artifacts, books, maps, and photographs dealing with the history and culture of the people of the Yukon Flats area. Open year-round, the museum requests a $1 donation.

Alaska Recreation Directory

Outfitters & Guides

Backpacking, hunting, mountaineering, and wild river canoe trips—whatever your choice of activity, getting into Alaska's backcountry is most easily accomplished on an organized wilderness trip. Outfitters usually furnish transportation, lodging, meals, and equipment; you bring your personal gear.

The directory below lists the state agency that licenses outfitters and guides. In the next column are several associations of wilderness guides to whom you can write for more information.

STATE LICENSING AGENCY

Department of Commerce and Economic Development
Division of Occupational Licensing
Box 110806
Juneau, AK 99811
Send $5 for a list of registered guides/outfitters

WILDERNESS GUIDE ASSOCIATIONS

Alaska Professional Hunters
Box 91932
Anchorage, AK 99509-1932

Alaska Wilderness Guides
Box 141061
Anchorage, AK 99514

Master Guides–Registered Guides
Guide Board, Box D
Juneau, AK 99811
Send $5 for list

Registered Guides in the Yukon
Box 2703
Whitehorse, Yukon, Canada
Y1A 2C6

Yukon Assoc. of Wilderness Guides
Box 5405
Whitehorse, Yukon, Canada
Y1A 4Z2

STATEWIDE

ABEC
1304 Westwick Dr.
Fairbanks, AK 99712
Brooks Range, Denali, Lake Clark, Wrangell–St. Elias

Adventure Alaska
1231 Sundance Loop
Fairbanks, AK 99709
Brooks Range, Lake Clark, Wrangell–St. Elias, Yukon-Charley

Adventure North
1030 W. Fourth Ave.
Anchorage, AK 99501

Alaska Air Outfitters
Box 81897 (in summer)
Fairbanks, AK 99708
Box 270168 (in winter)
San Diego, CA 92128
Brooks and Alaska ranges

Alaska Fishing/Run Wild River Tours
1831 Kuskokwim St., Suite V
Anchorage, AK 99508

Alaska Guides and Outfitters
Box 1350
Palmer, AK 99645
Brooks Range, Talkeetna Mountains, Alaska Peninsula

Alaskan Wilderness Outfitting Company
Box 1516
Cordova, AK 99574
Brooks Range to Katmai

Alaska Sojourns Wilderness Guides
Box 87-1410
Wasilla, AK 99687

Alaska Treks N Voyages, Inc.
Seward Small Boat Harbor
Box 625
Seward, AK 99631
Brooks, Alaska, and Aleutian ranges; Chugach and Kenai mountains; wild scenic rivers

Alaska Wilderness, Inc.
Box 81267
Fairbanks, AK 99708
University-accredited tours

Alyeska Wilderness Guide
Box 111663
Anchorage, AK 99511

Chuck Wirschem's Hunting & Fishing
6608 Blackberry
Anchorage, AK 99502

Cross-Country Ski Adventure
1831 Kuskokwim St., Suite V
Anchorage, AK 99508

Denali Hunting Adventures
Box 295
Talkeetna, AK 99676
Alaska Range and Talkeetna Mountains

Hautanen Enterprises
3157 W. 64th Ave.
Anchorage, AK 99502

Hugh Glass Backpacking Co.
Box 110796
Anchorage, AK 99511

Kichatna Guide Service
Box 670790
Chugiak, AK 99567
Alaska Range, Kodiak

Mountain Travel of Alaska, Ltd.
1398 Solano Ave.
Albany, CA 94706

Mountain Trip
Box 91161
Anchorage, AK 99509
Guided climbs

North to Alaska
200 W. 34th Ave., Suite 300
Anchorage, AK 99503
Katmai, Chilkoot Trail, Chugach Mountains

Run Wild Tours
1831 Kuskokwim St.
Anchorage, AK 99508

Sound Adventures
Box 190146
Anchorage, AK 99519-0146

HUNTING

Hunters who plan to go after sheep and bear must be accompanied by a registered guide. All hunters need licenses for all game and nonresident game tags for big game: bear, bison, caribou, deer, elk, goat, moose, mountain sheep, musk oxen, wolf, and wolverine.

Winter Fun

Winter brings two of Alaska's biggest, and liveliest, celebrations—Anchorage's Fur Rendezvous in February and the Iditarod Trail Sled Dog Race from Anchorage to Nome in March.

It's also the time to catch the aurora borealis, the state's free light show, as it shimmers and shakes in a colorful midnight celebration of its own.

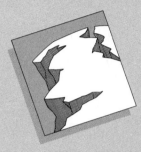

Alaska's winters aren't much different from winters in many other parts of the Lower 48. Anchorage temperatures compare to those in Minnesota, Vermont, or Montana.

SKI SITES

Alaska has world-class skiing, both Alpine and Nordic. Skiers enjoy powdery slopes that vie with the best of those in Colorado, Utah, and California. They have a choice of well-groomed tracks or natural wilderness trails reached only by helicopter.

Alyeska Resort and Ski Area
Box 249
Girdwood, AK 99587
Premier ski area in the state just outside Anchorage, with 5 lifts, ski school, equipment rental, resort hotel

Alpenglow at Arctic Valley
Box 92121
Anchorage, AK 99509-2121
Lifts, pony tows, snow boarding, ski school; open weekends

Eaglecrest Ski Area
155 S. Seward St.
Juneau, AK 99801-1332
12 miles northwest of town, lifts operate December to April

Hilltop Ski Area
7015 Abbott Rd.
Anchorage, AK 99516-6559
Chairlift, 3 runs, 2 jumps, cross-country trails

Sheep Mountain Lodge
Box 8490
Palmer, AK 99645-9460
Miles of groomed cross-country trails; overnight accommodations

DOG SLEDDING

Mushing, Alaska's official sport, gives visitors a taste of the wilderness. Sled dog tours whisk riders across the landscape for an hour —or several days. A sampling of companies offering mushing is listed below. Nome and Kotzebue summer tours also include sled dog demonstrations.

Or watch well-trained dogs and drivers show off in annual competitions. The Alaska Sled Dog Racing Association in Anchorage has sled dog team races at their track in Anchorage every weekend from January through March.

EVENTS

Dalton Trail 30 Dog Sled Race
Haines
Mid-January
For information, call (907) 766-2418

Iditarod Sled Dog Race
Anchorage to Nome
Early March
1,049 miles in 2 weeks
For information, call (907) 376-5155

North American Open Dog Sled Championship
Fairbanks
Mid-March
For information, call (907) 479-8166

World Championship Sled Dog Races
Anchorage
Mid-February during Fur Rendezvous
For information, call (907) 277-8615

Yukon Quest Sled Dog Race
Mid-February
Whitehorse to Fairbanks
For information, call (403) 668-4711 or (907) 452-7954

EXPEDITIONS

Alaska Budget Tours
Box 91795
Anchorage, AK 99509
Sets up back-country adventures including dog sled excursions

Alaska River Charters
Box 81516
Fairbanks, AK 99708
Includes Yukon Quest dog race and mushing in winter trips

Arctic Treks
Box 73452
Fairbanks, AK 99707
Arctic outfitter lists dog sledding under northern lights

Eagle Custom Tours of Alaska
329 F St., #206
Anchorage, AK 99501
Custom package tours include dog sledding

Fairbanks Floatplane Tours
Box 61661
Fairbanks, AK 99706
Winter dog sledding at historic Tolovana Lodge in the arctic

Outland Expeditions
Box 92401
Anchorage, AK 99509-2401
Variety of environmentally aware adventure packages such as mushing

Sourdough Outfitters
Box 90
Bettles, AK 99726
Wilderness guides in Brooks Range have dog sledding and snowmobiling among other arctic offerings

"Van Go" Custom Tours
Box 81914
Fairbanks, AK 99708
Winter tours include workshops with state's top mushers

Wilderness Lodges

From log cabins on trout-filled lakes to luxury lodges in remote reaches of Alaska's backcountry, wilderness hideaways are generally accessible only by air or water. Your accommodations are often part of a package trip that includes transportation, meals, boats, guides, and equipment.

STATEWIDE

Alaska Bush Camps
361 13th St., #1
Seal Beach, CA 90740

Alaska Sportfishing Lodge Association
500 Wall St., #422
Seattle, WA 98121

Alaska Sportfishing Packages, Inc.
15375 S.E. 30th Pl., #350
Bellevue, WA 98007

Alaska Wildland Adventures
Box 389
Girdwood, AK 99587

Great Alaska Safari
Box 218
Sterling, AK 99672

THE PANHANDLE

Admiralty Inn
Juneau, AK 99803
Wilderness retreat on Admiralty Island

Alaskan Home Fishing Lodge
11380 Alderwood St. N
Ketchikan, AK 99901
Secluded with ocean view

Anchor Point Lodge
1315 S. King St., #4
Honolulu, HI 96814-2341
Fishing from cabin cruisers

Baranof Warm Springs Lodge
9720 Trappers Ln.
Juneau, AK 99801
Mineral springs

Baranof Wilderness Lodge
Box 21022
Auke Bay, AK 99821
Individual cabins, hot springs, hot tubs

Clover Bay Floating Fishing Lodge
Box 8944
Ketchikan, AK 99901

Elfin Cove Lodge
Box 44 (in summer)
Elfin Cove, AK 99825
Box 4007 (in winter)
Renton, WA 98057
Fishing trips from Juneau

Glacier Bay Country Inn
Box 5 (in summer)
Gustavus, AK 99806
Box 2557 (in winter)
St. George, UT 84771
Secluded, good food, fishing, adventure

Glacier Bay Lodge
520 Pike St. #1610
Seattle, WA 98101
Lovely resort in magnificent setting

Green Rocks Lodge
Box 110
Petersburg, AK 99833
Rustic island comfort

Gustavus Inn at Glacier Bay
Box 60 (in summer)
Gustavus, AK 99826
7920 Outlook (in winter)
Prairie Village, KS 66208
Historic homeside, fresh food, nature walks, fishing

Misty Fjords Resort
1600 International Airport
Ketchikan, AK 99901
A-frame chalet on Humpback Lake

Prince of Wales Lodge
Box 72
Klawock, AK 99925
Lodge, hotel, restaurant

Rocky Point Resort
Box 1512
Petersburg, AK 99833
Cabins, motorboats

Shelter Lodge
Box 210064
Auke Bay, AK 99821-0064
Hot fishing area

Silverking Lodge
Box 8331
Ketchikan, AK 99901
Heated log cabins, home cooking

Taku Glacier Lodge
Number 2 Marine Way, #229
Juneau, AK 99801
On Taku River, daily salmon bake

Tenakee Inn
Box 54 (in summer)
Tenakee Springs, AK 99841
167 S. Franklin (in winter)
Juneau, AK 99801
Beachfront Victorian-style lodge

Thayer Lake Lodge
Box 211614 (in summer)
Auke Bay, AK 99821
Box 5416 (in winter)
Ketchikan, AK 99901
Fishing, hiking, canoeing

Thunderbird Lodge
Box 136
Hoonah, AK 99829
Rustic log cabin accommodates small groups

Waterfall Resort
Box 6440
Ketchikan, AK 99901
Luxury accommodations on remote island

Whale Pass Resort
Box 7975
Ketchikan, AK 99901
Fishing packages

Whaler's Cove Lodge
Box 101
Angoon, AK 99820
Sportfishing and wilderness recreation lodge

Whales Resort
1315 S. King St., #4
Honolulu, HI 96814-2341
Remote island setting

Yes Bay/Mink Bay Lodges
Box 8660
Ketchikan, AK 99901
Fly-in sportfishing lodges

ANCHORAGE AREA

Air Adventures
Box 22
Kenai, AK 99611
Tent camps to lodges

Alaskan Fishing Smorgasbord
Box 1516
Cordova, AK 99574
Saltwater and mountain fishing lodges

Angler's Lodge & Fish Camp
Box 508
Sterling, AK 99672
Fishing lodge on Kenai River

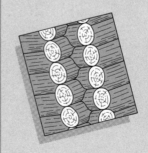

Chelatna Lake Lodge
3941 Float Plane Drive
Anchorage, AK 99502
Fly-in fishing, rafting, hiking; hot tub and sauna

Dersham's Outlook Lodge
Box 537
Anchor Point, AK 99556
Log lodge, fishing

Deshka Silver-King Lodge
Box 1037
Willow, AK 99688
Salmon fishing

Great Alaska Fish Camp
Box 218
Sterling, AK 99672
Good looking fishing lodge

Growler Island Wilderness Camp
Box 1297
Valdez, AK 99686
Fully staffed and heated tent camp

Ishmalof Island Lodge
Box 6430
Halibut Cove, AK 99603
On Kachemak Bay

Kachemak Bay Wilderness Lodge
Box 956
China Poot Bay
Homer, AK 99603
Log lodge, private cabins, fishing

Kenai Princess Lodge
2815 Second Ave., #400
Seattle, WA 98121
Nice lodge at Cooper Landing

Kenai Riverbank Resort
Box 1270
Soldotna, AK 99669
Rustic log building

Kenai River Retreat
360 W. Endicott
Soldotna, AK 99669
Riverfront lodging

Kenai River Sportfishing Lodge
Box 389
Girdwood, AK 99587
Full-service lodge

Kenai Wilderness Lodge
Box 2631 (in summer)
Soldotna, AK 99669
3117 Commercial Dr. (in winter)
Anchorage, AK 99501
Bunkhouse-stye fishing lodge

Kennicott Glacier Lodge
Box 103940
Anchorage, AK 99510
Rafting, historic tours, flightseeing

King Point Lodge
Box 241604
Anchorage, AK 99524
Creek fishing northwest of Anchorage

Lodge at Eagle River
Box 9014
Anchorage, AK 99509
Cedar home with grand views

Majestic Mountain Alaska Adventures
Box 879013
Wasilla, AK 99687
Remote fly-in lodge with fishing, riding, hiking

McCarthy Lodge
McCarthy, AK 99588
Hotel, restaurant, bunkhouse in Wrangell-St. Elias

Northwoods Lodge
Box 56
Skwentna, AK 99667
Fishing, rafting, sauna

Osprey Alaska
Box 504
Cooper Landing, AK 99572
Fishing, rafting

Point of View Lodge
Box 1706
Glennallen, AK 99588
Modern rooms with lake view

Ptarmigan Lake Lodge
1001 Lakeview Ter.
Fairbanks, AK 99701
Mountain lodge, cabins

Riversong Lodge
2463 Cottonwood St.
Anchorage, AK 99508
Fly-in fishing lodge noted for cuisine

Sheep Mountain Wilderness Cabins
Box 8490
Palmer, AK 99645
Overlooks Chugach and Talkeetna mountains, home-cooked meals

Skwentna Roadhouse
100 Happiness Ln.
Skwentna, AK 99667
In Yentna River Valley

Soaring Eagle Lodge
Box 1203
Soldotna, AK 99669
Cabins on Kenai River, hot tub

Stephan Lake Lodge
Box 770695
Eagle River, AK 99577
Sportfishing, hunting

Summit Lake Lodge
Box 7195
Delta Junction, AK 99737-9202
Modern lakeside cottage

Talaview Lodge
Box 49
Skwentna, AK 99667
Fly-in fishing lodge, cabins

Tutka Bay Lodge
Box 960
Homer, AK 99603
For nature lovers, anglers, photographers

Ultima Thule Outfitters
Box 109
Chitina, AK 99566
Fly-in lodge in Wrangell-St. Elias

Wilderness Lodge on Seldovia Bay
Harmony Point
Box 110-AK
Seldovia, AK 99663
Lodge, cabins, fresh seafood

Wilderness Place Lodge
Box 190711
Anchorage, AK 99519
Lodge and cabins on Lake Creek

INTERIOR

Anvik River Lodge
Box 500
Anvik, AK 99558
Open year-round for riverboat and fly-out fishing, big game hunts, dog sledding, ice fishing

Camp Denali
Box 67 (in summer)
Denali National Park, AK 99755
Box 369 (in winter)
Cornish, NH 03746
Nature center in Denali

Denali West Lodge
Box 40
Lake Minchumina, AK 99757
Fly-in log cabins, guides

Grandview Lodge
Box 882
Delta Junction, AK 99737
Fly-in cabins, family-style meals, west side of Denali

Great Alaska Safari
Box 218
Sterling, AK 99672
Deluxe and canvas lodge bases, fishing, wildlife viewing

Kantishna Roadhouse
Box 130
Denali National Park, AK 99755
Wilderness lodge deep in the park

North Face Lodge
Box 67 (in summer)
Denali National Park, AK 99755
Box 369 (in winter)
Cornish, NH 03746
Inn in the heart of Denali Park

Taste of Alaska Lodge
551 Eberhardt Rd.
Fairbanks, AK 99712
Log house with panoramic view of Alaska Range outside Fairbanks

...wilderness lodges

FAR NORTH

Alatna Lodge and Wilderness Cabins
Box 80424
Fairbanks, AK 99708
Inholdings in Gates of the Arctic National Park

Camp Bendeleben
Box 1045
Nome, AK 99762
Lodge and tent camp on the Niukluk River 75 miles from Nome

Iniakuk Lake Lodge
Box 80424
Fairbanks, AK 99708
Fine lodge, meals in Brooks Range

Peace of Selby Wilderness
Box 86
Manley Hot Springs, AK 99756
Wilderness lake log cabins within Gates of the Arctic National Park

SOUTHWEST

Afognak Wilderness Lodge
Seal Bay, AK 99697
Cabins on Afognak Island

Alaska's Wilderness Lodge
General Delivery (in summer)
Port Alsworth, AK 99653
Box 700 (in winter)
Sumner, WA 98390
On Lake Clark, gourmet food, sauna

Aniak Lodge
Box 83
Aniak, AK 99557
Near Kuskokwim River

Battle River Wilderness Retreat
8076 Caribbean Way
Sacramento, CA 95826
Outback of Katmai National Park

Big Mountain Lodge Inc.
14940 Longbow Dr.
Anchorage, AK 99516
Fly-out fishing, maid service

Bristol Bay Lodge
Box 1509 (in summer)
Dillingham, AK 99576
Box 580 (in winter)
Ellensburg, WA 98926
Old fishing lodge in Wood-Tikchik region

Brooks Lodge
4700 Aircraft Dr.
Anchorage, AK 99502
Fly-in lodge in Katmai, sportfishing, bear watching, hiking

Cannery at Zachar Bay
Box 2609
Kodiak, AK 99615
Converted cannery on wildlife refuge

Chenik Wilderness Camp
Box 956
Homer, AK 99603
Near brown bear refuge, fishing

Copper River Lodge
Box PVY (in summer)
Iliamna, AK 99606
Box 200831 (in winter)
Anchorage, AK 99520-0831
Fly fishing for rainbow trout, sauna, boats, guides

The Farm Lodge
Box 1
Port Alsworth, AK 99653
Fishing, hunting, boating, hiking

Grosvenor Lodge
4700 Aircraft Dr.
Anchorage, AK 99502
In Katmai; boats, guides, gear

Haeg's Wilderness Lodge
Box 338
Soldotna, AK 99669-0338
Fly in to join a bush family

Iliamna Lake Resort
Box 208 (in summer)
Iliamna, AK 99606
Box 103984 (in winter)
Anchorage, AK 99501
Luxury fishing and hunting lodge

Karluk Lodge
Box 3
Karluk, AK 99608
Fishing at mouth of Karluk River on Kodiak Island

Katmai Lodge
Box 421 (in summer)
King Salmon, AK 99613
2825 90th St. S.E. (in winter)
Everett, WA 98208
River fishing in Lake Iliamna-Bristol Bay area

King Salmon Lodge
3300 Providence Dr., #309
Anchorage, AK 99508
Lodge on Naknek River

Kodiak Nautical Discoveries
Box 95
Kodiak, AK 99615
Lodge with boat for island exploring

Kulik Lodge
4700 Aircraft Dr.
Anchorage, AK 99502
Fly-out sportfishing lodge

Northland Ranch Resort
Box 2376
Kodiak, AK 99615
Alaska dude ranch

Ole Creek Lodge
Igiugig via King Salmon,
AK 99613 (in summer)
506 Ketchikan St. (in winter)
Fairbanks, AK 99701
Food and meals on Lake Iliamna and Kvichak River

Saltery Lake Lodge
1516 Larch St., #1
Kodiak, AK 99615
Fishing, flightseeing, float trips

Silver Salmon Lodge
Box 378
Kodiak, AK 99615
Wilderness fishing and hunting lodge

Tikchik Narrows Lodge
Box 220248
Anchorage, AK 99522
In Wood-Tikchik region

Ugashik Narrows Lodge
Box 103984
Anchorage, AK 99510
Remote cabin on Alaska Peninsula, fly-out fishing

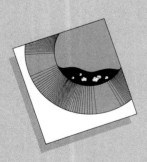

River Trips

Majestic scenery, undisturbed wildlife, and a marvelous sense of an untamed land—these are just a few benefits of taking a river trip in Alaska. Whether you yearn to get away on your own for a few days of paddling or want to join other adventurers in a guided float trip, you'll get ideas from this sampling of companies offering floating expeditions.

ABEC's Alaska Adventures
1550 Alpine Vista Ct.
Fairbanks, AK 99712
Guided river trips in the Far North

Admiralty Island/Glacier Bay Natural History Cruises
520 Pike St., #1610
Seattle, WA 98101
Sea kayaking from a cruising base camp

Alaska Discovery Expeditions
234 Gold St.
Juneau, AK 99801
Guided paddle raft trips in Arctic Wildlife Refuge

Alaska Rafting Adventures
Box 295
Talkeetna, AK 99676
Wilderness rafting, float trips

Alaska Rivers Company
Box 827
Cooper Landing, AK 99572
Scenic and whitewater rafting on Kenai Peninsula

Alaska Treks N Voyages
414 K St.
Anchorage, AK 99501
Coastal kayaking

Alaska Wildland Adventures
Box 389
Girdwood, AK 99587
Kenai River trips

Bettles Lodge Wilderness Trips
Box 82317
Fairbanks, AK 99708
Float trips in Brooks Range and Gates of the Arctic

Brooks Range Adventures
1231 Sundance Loop
Fairbanks, AK 99709
Paddle on rivers throughout the Arctic

Chillat Guides Ltd.
Box 170
Haines, AK 99827
Float trip through bald eagle preserve, back country rafting

Coastal Adventures of Alaska
211 W. Harvard Ave.
Anchorage, AK 99501
Sea kayaking off Shuyak Island

Denali Raft Adventures
Drawer 190
Denali National Park, AK 99755
Scenic and whitewater day trips on Nenana River

Gates of the Arctic Wilderness Adventures
Box 84060
Fairbanks, AK 99708
Guided rafting trips

Glacier Bay Kayaking
234 Gold St.
Juneau, AK 99801
Guided expeditions with tent camping

Mendenhall Glacier Float Trip
9085 Glacier Hwy., #204
Juneau, AK 99801
Whitewater trip down glacial river

Mountain Lake Canoe Adventure
9085 Glacier Hwy., #204
Juneau, AK 99801
Canoeing on alpine lake in Tongass National Forest

North Star
Box 1724
Flagstaff, AZ 86002
Wilderness rafting and canoeing

Osprey Expeditions
Box 209
Denali National Park, AK 99755
Scenic and whitewater rafting

Peace of Selby Wilderness
Box 86
Manley Hot Springs, AK 98756
Far North rafting and canoeing

Quest Expeditions
Box 671895
Chugiak, AK 99567
Float wilderness rivers around Mt. McKinley

Rifle Charter Company
Box 1928
Kodiak, AK 99601
Kayaking in Katmai and around Kodiak Island

Sea Kayak Rentals
369 S. Franklin St.
Juneau, AK 99801
Guided Inland Passage expeditions or on your own

Sourdough Outfitters
Box 90
Bettles, AK 99726
Canoeing and rafting on arctic rivers

Spirit Walker Expeditions
Box 240
Gustavus, AK 99826
Sea kayaking in Inland Passage

Takahula Lake Guide Service
Box 84908
Fairbanks, AK 99708-4908
Trips in Gates of the Arctic

Wavetamer Kayaking
Box 228
Kodiak, AK 99615
Sea kayaking day trips

Fishing

Renowned for its fine fishing waters, Alaska offers a variety of opportunities for any type of angler. All five species of salmon are present: king (chinook), red (sockeye), pink (humpback), silver (coho), and chum. The Bristol Bay area of Southwest Alaska is the red salmon capital of the world; the Kenai River in Southcentral is famous for record king salmon. Charter fishing boats, moored in Panhandle, Southcentral, and Southwest ports, make trips ranging from a half-day to several days. Full gear is usually provided.

Licenses are required for all nonresident anglers age 16 and above. Four types are available: 1-day, 3-day, 2-week, and full season. All can be purchased by mail.

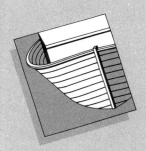

For complete information on sportfishing requirements and license fees see the addresses listed on page 114.

Wildlife Viewing

Alaska is home to some of the world's rarest wildlife. It's a place where you find bears, caribou, musk oxen, moose, Dall sheep, reindeer, wolves, and walrus. In glacier-lined bays, whales cavort as playfully as do their dolphin friends. And offshore islands are home to seals, sea lions, and exotic seabirds, like the colorful puffin.

It takes no special effort to view many species. Moose, for instance, are plentiful on the Kenai Peninsula and even spotted occasionally around Anchorage. But you may need to track down some of the more elusive creatures. The companies listed at right are among those who specialize in wildlife viewing.

FISH & WILDLIFE

If you're interested in fishing and/or wildlife viewing, the following agencies can be very helpful. You can get information on everything from where to pick up a fishing license to when the whales will be migrating.

Alaska Department of Fish & Game
Box 25526
Juneau, AK 99802-5526

U.S. Fish and Wildlife Service
1011 E. Tudor Rd.
Anchorage, AK 99503

Canada
Yukon Government Department of Renewable Resources
F & W Branch
Box 2703
Whitehorse, YT
Canada Y1A 2C6

BEAR

Taking the Tundra Tour through Denali National Park and Preserve is your best bet to see a grizzly, even from a distance. Kodiak National Wildlife Refuge, home to the famed Kodiak bruins, occupies 80 percent of the island; one program allows access. Plenty of brown bear live along the Inside Passage, particularly at Admiralty Island's Pack Creek Bear Preserve (you need a Forest Service permit to visit) and along Anan Creek near Petersburg (access by charter boat).

Here are three other sites where bear gather.

Kenai National Park and Preserve
Campgrounds:
Box 7
King Salmon, AK 99613
For permits and a copy of Bear Facts, the park's newspaper

Lodges:
Katmailand
4700 Aircraft Dr.
Anchorage, AK 99502
For information on float trips, lodging in camps at three locations, and meals

McNeil River Game Sanctuary
If you want to visit this enormously popular viewing area, you need a permit—but you have to win a lottery to get one. Each spring a drawing is held for 10 people a day to visit during July and August, peak salmon spawning period. Winners are responsible for their own arrangements for food, camping gear, and float plane transportation. Applications must be received by March 31.
For information and applications, write to:
Alaska Department of Fish & Game
Division of Wildlife Conservation
Attention McNeil River
333 Raspberry Rd.
Anchorage, AK 99516

Chenik Brown Bear Photography Camp
Box 956
Homer, AK 99603
Private wilderness lodge near the McNeil River

BIRDS

Southeast Alaska is home to thousands of bald eagles from October to December. The largest concentration is at a preserve near Haines. In the Interior, Creamer's Field Waterfowl Refuge, near Fairbanks, serves as a resting place for migratory birds. Birding treks are provided by many companies. The following list samples some offerings.

Alaska Horseback Vacations
58335 East End Rd.
Homer, AK 99603
Horseback riding to photograph eagles

Alaska Maritime Tours
Box 3098
Homer, AK 99603
Gull Island Rookery, Barren Islands trip

Alaska Nature Tours
Box 491
Haines, AK 99827
Explore Chilkat Bald Eagle Preserve

Alaskan Wilderness Sailing Safaris
Box 1313
Valdez, AK 99686
Bird watching in Prince William Sound

Alaska River Charters
Box 81516
Fairbanks, AK 99708
Birding along wilderness rivers

Amos Services
General Delivery
Mekoryuk, AK 99630
Nunivak Island tour includes sea birds

Coastal Adventures of Alaska
211 W. Harvard Ave.
Anchorage, AK 99501
Individually guided bird watching from tent camp base

Iniakuk Lake Lodge
Box 80424
Fairbanks, AK 99708
Bird life in the Brooks Range

Kachemak Bay Adventures Boat Tours
Box 1196
Homer, AK 99603
Birding on Kachemak Bay

Kenai Fjord Tours, Inc.
Box 1889
Seward, AK 99664
Cruise coast of park, wildlife

Kodiak Tours
Box 3831
Kodiak, AK 99615
Watch shore birds and marine mammals

Major Marine Scenic Wildlife Dinner Cruises
509 W. Third Ave.
Anchorage, AK 99501
Kenai Fjords cruise to see puffin, eagles

Marine Exploration
9085 Glacier Hwy., #204
Juneau, AK 99801
Bird rookeries around Sitka

North Star
Box 1724
Flagstaff, AZ 86002
Birding in Arctic National Wildlife Refuge

Polar Tours
Box 80488
Fairbanks, AK 99708
Follow the pipeline through the migratory bird-inhabited tundra

Tour Arctic
1001 E. Benson Blvd.
Anchorage, AK 99508
Guided expeditions in the Arctic

CARIBOU

Caribou outnumber people in Alaska, and you'll see them throughout the state. One of 13 distinct herds, the Nelchina migration crosses the Copper River in April in Southcentral Alaska. Several companies offer in-depth looks at Arctic herd migrations across the North Slope.

ABEC's Alaska Adventures
1550 Alpine Vista Ct.
Fairbanks, AK 99712
Arctic caribou viewing

Alatna Lodge and Wilderness Cabins
Box 80424
Fairbanks, AK 99708
Herds in Gates of the Arctic

North Star
Box 1724
Flagstaff, AZ 86002
Caribou migrations in Arctic National Wildlife Refuge

MUSK OXEN

Most tourists get their first look at the shaggy musk ox on tours at the University of Alaska's research station. And products made from their soft hair are sold at the Oomingmak Musk Ox Producers Co-op in Anchorage.

Musk Ox Farm
Box 587
Palmer, AK 99645
Domestic musk ox farm in Matanuska Valley

REINDEER

Another member of the caribou family, reindeer are found in the Arctic. Herds are raised by Natives.

Amos Services
General Delivery
Mekoryuk, AK 99630
Reindeer roundups and musk oxen viewing on Nunivak Island tour

WHALES

In evidence throughout the Inside Passage in summer, whales feed at Point Adolphus outside Glacier Bay. Some of the companies who specialize in watching include the following:

Glacier Bay Tours & Cruises
520 Pike St., #1610
Seattle, WA 98101
Go where whales feed and play

Whales!
Box 5 (in summer)
Gustavus, AK 99826
Box 2557 (in winter)
St. George, UT 84771
Half- or full-day trips into Icy Straits/ Pt. Adolphus feeding grounds

Whale Watching Natural History Excursion
Box 34098
Juneau, AK 99803
Fly and cruise to whale feeding grounds

Backpacking

Many repeat visitors to this grand land prefer to get away from the usual tourist spots by heading into the countryside for a few days. Some may simply yearn to follow in the footsteps of the gold miners by climbing the Chilkoot Trail. Others want to wander even farther off the beaten path.

For information on visiting the Chilkoot Trail, contact the National Park Service, Klondike Historical Park, Box 517, Skagway, AK 99840; and the Canadian Park Service (Yukon National Historic Sites), Box 5540, Whitehorse, YT, Canada Y1A 5H4.

Some of the organizations that traipse through the tundra in the Far North or the forests in the Panhandle are listed below.

ABEC's Alaska Adventures
1550 Alpine Vista Ct.
Fairbanks, AK 99712
Guided trips in Gates of the Arctic, Arctic Refuge, or Arrigetch Peaks

Alaska Rainforest Treks
369 S. Franklin St., #200
Juneau, AK 99801
Chilkoot Trail tours, back country expeditions

Arctic Treks
Box 73452
Fairbanks, AK 99702
Outfitter specializes in trips into the Far North

Bettles Lodge Wilderness Trips
Box 82317
Fairbanks, AK 99708
Trips into Gates of the Arctic or Brooks Range

Brooks Range Adventures
1231 Sundance Loop
Fairbanks, AK 99709
Guided trips in arctic mountains

Denali West Lodge
Box 40
Lake Minchumina, AK 99757
Guided packing into Mystic Pass from Scotty Lake base camp

Gates of the Arctic Wilderness Adventures
Box 84060
Fairbanks, AK 99708
Backpack through a national park in the Far North

Hugh Glass Backpacking Co.
Box 110796
Anchorage, AK 99511
Small groups for statewide treks

North Star
Box 1724
Flagstaff, AZ 86002
Guided naturalist tours in Arctic National Wildlife Refuge and Brooks Range

Sourdough Outfitters
Box 82317
Fairbanks, AK 99708
Gates of the Arctic and Brooks Range treks

Wolf's Alaska Tours, Inc.
712 Monastery St.
Sitka, AK 99840
Widerness camping in Tongass

Mountain Climbs

Ascending Alaska's tall peaks is a goal for many mountaineers. And the state has companies that arrange ascents for both the experienced and the novice climber.

Alaska Alpine School
Box 111241
Anchorage, AK 99511
Mountaineering and first-ascent courses

Mountain Trip
Box 91161
Anchorage, AK 99509
Guided climbs on Mt. McKinley, Mt. Sanford, and other peaks

St. Elias Alpine Guides
Box 11241
Anchorage, AK 99511
First ascent and high-altitude climbs in Wrangell-St. Elias

Glacier Walks

Slipping around on the top of an ancient glacial icefield is one of the great adventures offered in Alaska. Many flightseeing companies outfit you with the proper equipment and drop you off on a glacier for a short stroll.

ERA Helicopters
Box 21468
Juneau, AK 99802
Walk on Norris Glacier in Juneau Icefield

K2 Aviation
Box 545
Talkeetna, AK 99676
Glacier landings in Mt. McKinley area

Mt. McKinley Flight Tours
Box 42
Talkeetna, AK 99676
Glacier landings on Mt. McKinley

St. Elias Apine Guides
Box 111241
Anchorage, AK 99511
Glacier trekking in Wrangell-St. Elias

TEMESCO Helicopter Glacier Tours
1650 Maplesden Way
Juneau, AK 99801
Step onto a glacier in the Juneau Icefield

Parklands

The roster below is a complete listing of Alaska's national parklands. A few of these parks encourage camping; others have no facilities for visitors. For further information, write directly to the park.

GENERAL INFORMATION

Alaska Public Lands Information Centers
605 W. 4th Ave. #105
Anchorage, AK 99501-5162

220 Cushman St. #1A
Fairbanks, AK 99701

Box 359
Tok, AK 99780-0359

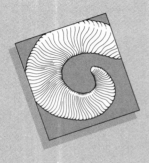

Alaska State Park Information
Box 107001
Anchorage, AK 7001

USDA Forest Service Information Center
101 Egan Dr.
Juneau, AK 99801

Canada
Yukon National Historic Sites
Box 5540
Whitehorse, YT
Canada U1A 5H4

Kluane National Park
Box 5495
Haines Junction, YT
Canada Y0B 1L0

NATIONAL PARKS, PRESERVES & MONUMENTS

Aniakchak National Monument and Preserve
Box 7
King Salmon, AK 99613

Bering Land Bridge National Preserve
Box 220
Nome, AK 99762

Cape Krustenstern National Monument
Box 287
Kotzebue, AK 99752

Denali National Park and Preserve
Box 9
McKinley Park, AK 99755

Gates of the Arctic National Park and Preserve
Box 74680
Fairbanks, AK 99707

Glacier Bay National Park and Preserve
Gustavus, AK 99826

Katmai National Park and Preserve
Box 7
King Salmon, AK 99613

Kenai Fjords National Park
Box 1727
Seward, AK 99664

Klondike Gold Rush National Historical Park
Box 517
Skagway, AK 99840

Kobuk Valley National Park
Box 287
Kotzebue, AK 99752

Lake Clark National Park and Preserve
Box 61
Anchorage, AK 99513

Noatak National Preserve
Box 287
Kotzebue, AK 99752

Sitka National Historical Park
Box 738
Sitka, AK 99835

Wrangell–St. Elias National Park and Preserve
Box 29
Glennallen, AK 99588

Yukon–Charley Rivers National Preserve
Box 64
Eagle, AK 99738

Camping Areas & RV Parks

The campground roster below includes both public and private camping facilities. No reservations are required for state or federal campgrounds, and the state charges no fee for camping.

THE PANHANDLE

PRIVATE

Auke Bay RV Park
Box 210215
Auke Bay, AK 99821
Member Alaska Campground Owners Association

Eagle Camper Park
Box 28
Haines, AK 99827
Electrical hookups, propane, showers, dump stations, toilets

Haines Hitch-up RV Park
Box 383
Haines, AK 99827
Full hookups, showers, laundry

Hoover's Chevron RV Park
Box 304
Skagway, AK 99840
Full hookups, showers, propane, dump stations, seasonal

Klawock Camper/Trailer Court
Box 113
Klawock, AK 99925
Water, dump stations, year-round

Oceanside RV Park
Box 149
Haines, AK 99827
Electrical hookups, showers, laundry, seasonal

Port Chilkoot Camper Park
Box 473, Mudbay Rd.
Haines, AK 99827
Electrical hookups, showers, laundry, seasonal

Sealing Cove
304 Lake St.
Sitka, AK 99835
Water, garbage, dump station, year-round

Ten Mile Camping Park
Box 865
Haines, AK 99827
Electrical hookups, showers, steakhouse, year-round

Tides Camper Park
5000 Glacier Hwy., Suite 1
Juneau, AK 99801
Electricity, showers, laundry, restaurant, year-round

Twin Creek RV Park
Box 90
Petersburg, AK 99833
Electricity, showers, dump stations, toilets, year-round

Van's RV Park
Box 763
Petersburg, AK 99833
Hookups, showers, laundry, toilets, year-round

PUBLIC

Auke Village Campground
U.S. Forest Service
Box 21628
Juneau, AK 99802-8863
Fireplaces, tables, water, pit toilets, seasonal

Chilkat State Park
400 Willoughby
Juneau, AK 99801
Water, picnic area, boat launch

Chilkoot Lake Mosquito Lake, Portage Cove Campground
Box 518
Haines, AK 99827
State-maintained campsites

Glacier Bay National Park and Preserve
Gustavus, AK 99826
Tent sites, grills, seasonal

Hanousek Park
Box 304
Skagway, AK 99840
City-owned campground, toilets, dump stations

Mendenhall Lake Campground
U.S. Forest Service
Box 21628
Juneau, AK 99802-8863
Water, fireplaces, pit toilets, dump station, trailers to 22 feet

ANCHORAGE AREA

PRIVATE

Bing Brown's Sportsman's Service
Box 235
Sterling, AK 99672
Hookups, showers, laundry, dump station, seasonal

Chandalar RV Park
Star Route A, Box 408
Willow, AK 99688
Full or partial hookups, showers, dump station, laundry, supplies

Eklutna Lodge
Star Route 2-8156 Eklutna Lake Rd.
Chugiak, AK 99567
Restaurant, lounge, laundry, year-round

Golden Nugget RV Park
4100 Debarr Rd.
Anchorage, AK 99504
Full hookups, showers, laundry, year-round

Green Belt RV Park
5550 Old Seward Hwy.
Anchorage, AK 99518
Full hookups, laundry, showers, toilets, year-round

Green Ridge Camper Park
1130 Vicky Way
Wasilla, AK 99687
Full hookups, showers, laundry, seasonal

Hillside RV Park
2150 Gambell
Anchorage, AK 99503
Full hookups, showers, laundry, toilets

Homer Spit Campground
Box 1196
Homer, AK 99603
Electrical hookups, showers, dump station, toilets, seasonal

Kamping Resorts of Alaska
Star Route C, Box 8795
Palmer, AK 99645
Full hookups, cabins, lodge, laundry, year-round

King's Recreational Properties
Mile One, Big Eddy Rd.
(in summer)
Soldotna, AK 99669
2230 Paxson Dr. (in winter)
Anchorage, AK 99504

Matanuska Lake Park
Star Route A, Box 6155 (in summer)
Palmer, AK 99645
3122 Mapu Place (in winter)
Kihei, HI 96753
Seasonal

Nancy Lake Marina
Box 114
Willow, AK 99688
Camping spaces, year-round

Olson's Salmon Creek Trailer and RV Park
Box 1858
Seward, AK 99664
Full hookups, showers, laundry, year-round

Rainbow Acres
Box 520109
Big Lake, AK 99652
Full hookups, laundry, propane, seasonal

Sea Otter RV Park
Box 947
Valdez, AK 99686
Full or partial hookups, showers, laundry, dump station, seasonal

Tolsona Wilderness Campground
Mile 173 Glenn Hwy.
Glennallen, AK 99588
Electrical hookups, tent sites, showers, toilets, dump station, seasonal

PUBLIC

Captain Cook State Park
Nikishka Chamber of Commerce
Box 8053
Nikishka, AK 99635
Campsites, tent sites, water, fireplaces, toilets

Centennial Camper Park
Box 19-6650
Anchorage, AK 99519
Showers, toilets, firewood, seasonal

Kenai Municipal Park
Box 580
Kenai, AK 99611
Campsites, water, fireplaces, toilets, year-round

Lion's Camper Park
Box 19-6650
Anchorage, AK 99519
Campsites and tent sites in Russian Jack Springs Park, showers, toilets, seasonal

USDA Forest Service Campgrounds
Huffman Business Park, Bldg. C
(in summer)
Anchorage, AK 99511
334 Fourth Ave. (in winter)
Seward, AK 99664
16 campgrounds, cabins, fire grates, water, toilets

INTERIOR & FAR NORTH

PRIVATE

Bergstad's Traveland Trailer Park
Box 273
Delta Junction, AK 99737
Full hookups, tent sites, year-round

Chena Hot Springs
Drawer 25, 1919 Lathrop St.
Fairbanks, AK 99701
Unlimited spaces, water, showers, toilets, laundry

Denali Campground
Box 323
Healy, AK 99743
Hookups, showers, dump station, seasonal

Denali Grizzly Bear Cabins & Campground
Box 7 (in summer)
Denali National Park, AK 99755
5845 Old Valdez Trail (in winter)
Salcha, AK 99714
RV sites, tent cabins, showers, laundry, store

Golden Bear Camper Park
Box 276
Tok, AK 99780
Trailer hookups, bath house, seasonal

Lynx Creek Campground
825 W. Eighth Ave.
Anchorage, AK 99501
Electrical hookups, showers, dump station, seasonal

Manley Hot Springs Resort
Old Manley Hwy. & Spring Dr.
Manley Hot Springs, AK 99756
Year-round

McKinley KOA Kampground
Box 34
Healy, AK 99743
Hookups, tent sites, showers, seasonal

Monson Motel Campgrounds
1321 Karen Way
Fairbanks, AK 99701
Hookups, tent sites, showers, laundry, year-round

Norlite Campground
1660 Peger Rd.
Fairbanks, AK 99709
Full hookups, tent sites, showers, toilets, store, seasonal

North Ranch
1470 Chena Hot Springs Rd.
Fairbanks, AK 99712
RV spaces, campsites, food, seasonal

Roads End RV Park
1463 Wescott Lane
North Pole, AK 99705
Full hookups, showers, seasonal

Santa Claus House
Santa Land
North Pole, AK 99705
Tables, water, year-round

Sourdough Campground
Box 47
Tok, AK 99780
RV spaces, campsites, showers, meals, seasonal

Summer Shades Campground
Mile 290 Parks Hwy. (in summer)
Nenana, AK 99743
Box 2 (in winter)
Healy, AK 99743
Hookups, dump station, showers, cabins, seasonal

Tanana Valley Campground
Box 188
Fairbanks, AK 99707
Laundry, fireplaces, showers, seasonal

Tok RV Village
Box 741 (in summer)
Tok, AK 99780
2506 Glenkerry Dr. (in winter)
Anchorage, AK 99504
Full hookups, showers, dump station, seasonal

Tundra Lodge-KOA Campground
Box 336, 1315 Alaska Hwy.
(in summer)
Tok, AK 99780
300 Elliot Ave. W. (in winter)
Seattle, WA 98119
Trailer and RV hookups, tent sites, showers, laundry, seasonal

Yukon Trading Post
18 Front St.
Circle, AK 99733
Campground, store, seasonal

PUBLIC

Byers Lake Campground
Denali State Park
Box 182
Palmer, AK 99701
In park, year-round

Chena River State Recreation Area
4418 Airport Way
Fairbanks, AK 99709
Picnic tables, toilets, year-round

Denali National Park and Preserve
Box 9
Denali National Park, AK 99775
Campgrounds, RV spaces, year-round

Harding Lake Recreation Area
4418 Airport Way
Fairbanks, AK 99709
Campsites, beach, toilets, dump station, seasonal

Upper Chatanika Campground
4418 Airport Way
Fairbanks, AK 99709
Water, fireplaces, tables, toilets, seasonal

SOUTHWEST

PUBLIC

Abercrombie State Historic Park
Star Route, Box 3800
Kodiak, AK 99615
Tent sites, water, latrines, year-round

Brooks River Campground
Box 7
King Salmon, AK 99613
Year-round

Buskin State Recreation Site
Box 3800
Alaska State Parks
Kodiak, AK 99615
RV spaces, dump station, latrines, year-round

Tour Services

Explore the scenic Inside Passage by luxurious cruise ship or friendly state ferry. Some cruise itineraries include magnificent Glacier Bay National Park and Preserve; others add ports in the southcentral part of the state. Alaska's ferry system even allows you to put your vehicle aboard. During the summer season, British Columbia ferries (Vancouver Island to Prince Rupert) connect with Alaska's ferry system.

The following ideas are just the tip of the iceberg when it comes to tours to and around Alaska, but they will give you an idea of what's available. Check with your travel agent for excursions to fit your budget and interests.

CRUISES

Alaska Discount Cruise Guide
242 N.W. Market St., #367
Seattle, WA 98107
Compares itineraries and discount fares for cruises

Alaska Sightseeing/Cruise West
Fourth & Battery Building, #700
Seattle, WA 98121
Weekly cruises between Seattle and Juneau

Bendixen Yacht Cruises
818 W. Argand
Seattle, WA 98119
Week-long cruises by yacht

Cunard
555 Fifth Ave.
New York, NY 10017
Cruises between Vancouver and Prince William Sound

Glacier Bay Tours & Cruises
520 Pike St., #1610
Seattle, WA 98101
Inside Passage cruises of varying lengths

Holland America Line-Westours, Inc.
300 Elliott Ave. W
Seattle, WA 98119
Round-trip Inside Passage and Southcentral cruises

Princess Cruises
2815 Second Ave., #400
Seattle, WA 98121
Round-trip cruises of varying lengths as far as Southcentral

Regency Cruises
260 Madison Ave.
New York, NY 10016
Cruises from Vancouver

Special Expeditions
720 Fifth Ave.
New York, NY 10019
Coastline Alaska luxury wilderness adventures

World Explorer Cruises
555 Montgomery St., #1400
San Francisco, CA 94111-2544
14-day cruise adventures through the Inside Passage to Seward

FERRIES

Alaska Marine Highway System
Box 25535
Juneau, AK 99802-5535
Passenger and vehicle transport between Southeast Alaska and Prince Rupert, B.C., and Bellingham, WA; Southcentral service connects ports on Kenai Peninsula with Kodiak, Port Lions, Cordova, Valdez, and Whittier

British Columbia Ferry
1112 Fort St.
Victoria, B.C., Canada V8V 4V2
Passenger and vehicle transport between Port Hardy on Vancouver Island and Prince Rupert, B.C.

TRAINS

Alaska Railroad Corp.
Passenger Service Dept.
Box 107500
Anchorage, AK 99510-7500
Service between Anchorage and Fairbanks, stop at Denali National Park; daily service in summer to Seward

McKinley Explorer
300 Elliott Ave. W
Seattle, WA 98119
Westours parlor car on Anchorage/Denali/Fairbanks runs

Midnight Sun Express
2815 Second Ave., #400
Seattle, WA 98121
Princess Tours parlor car on Anchorage/Denali/Fairbanks run

White Pass & Yukon Route
Box 435
Skagway, AK 99840
Daily summer excursions from Skagway to White Pass summit

PACKAGE TOURS

American & Pacific Tours, Inc.
Box 101068
Anchorage, AK 99517

Air Adventures
Box 22
Kenai, AK 99611-0022

Alaska Budget Tours
Box 91795
Anchorage, AK 99509

Akaska Photographic & Adventure Tours
1831 Kuskokwim Street, #13
Anchorage, AK 99508

Alaska Travel Bureau
15375 S.E. 30th P., #350
Bellevue, WA 98007

Alaska Wildland Adventures
Box 389
Girdwood, AK 99587

Alaska World Tours
206 W. 34th Ave.
Anchorage, AK 99503

All Alaska Tours Inc.
Box 10-0036
Anchorage, AK 99510

Gray Line of Alaska
300 Elliott Ave. W
Seattle, WA 98119

Mt. McKinley Alaska Glacier Tours, Inc.
405 L St.
Anchorage, AK 99501-1945

Osprey Alaska
Box 504
Cooper Landing, AK 99572

Princess Tours
2815 Second Ave., #400
Seattle, WA 98121

Visitor Services

When you're ready to start planning your northern adventure, you can write to the addresses below for information on activities and accommodations in specific areas.

GENERAL INFORMATION

Alaska State Division of Tourism
Box 110801
Juneau, AK 99811-0801
(907) 465-2010

Klondike Visitors Association
Box 389
Dawson City, YT
Canada YOB 1G0
(403) 993-5575

Tourism Yukon
Box 2703
Whitehorse, YT
Canada Y1A 2C6
(403) 667-5340

DISABLED VISITORS INFORMATION

Access Alaska
3710 Woodland Park, Suite 900
Anchorage, AK 99517
(907) 248-4777

Challenge Alaska
Box 110065
Anchorage, AK 99511
(907) 563-2658

VISITOR INFORMATION CENTERS

Anchorage Visitor Information Center
546 W. Fourth Ave.
Anchorage, AK 99501
(907) 274-3531, 276-3200

Bethel Visitor Center
Box 388
Bethel, AK 99559
(907) 543-2098

Cordova Visitor Center
Box 391
Cordova, AK 99574
(907) 424-7443

Delta Junction Visitor Information Center
Box 987
Delta Junction, AK 99737
(907) 895-5068

Denali Visitor Information Center
Box 7
Cantwell, AK 99729
(907) 768-2420

Fairbanks Convention and Visitors Bureau
550 First Ave.
Fairbanks, AK 99701
(907) 456-5774

Haines Visitor Information Center
Box 518
Haines, AK 99827
(800) 458-3579

Homer Visitor Information Center
Box 541
Homer, AK 99603
(907) 235-5300

Juneau Visitor Information Center
134 Third St.
Juneau, AK 99801
(907) 586-2201

Kenai Peninsula Visitor Information Center
Box 236
Soldotna, AK 99669
(907) 262-1337

Ketchikan Visitors Bureau
131 Front St.
Ketchikan, AK 99901
(907) 225-6166

Kodiak Island Convention and Visitors Bureau
100 Marine Way
Kodiak, AK 99615
(907) 486-4782

Nome Convention and Visitors Bureau
Box 251
Nome, AK 99762
(907) 443-5535

Petersburg Visitor Information
Box 649
Petersburg, AK 99833
(907) 772-3646

Prince Rupert Convention and Visitors Bureau
Box 669
Prince Rupert, B.C., Canada
V8J 3S1
(604) 624-5637

Seldovia Chamber of Commerce
Drawer F
Seldovia, AK 99663
(907) 234-7816

Seward Information Cache
Box 749
Seward, AK 99664
(907) 224-3094 (in summer)
(907) 224-8051 (in winter)

Sitka Convention and Visitors Bureau
Box 1226
Sitka, AK 99835
(907) 747-5940

Skagway Convention and Visitors Center
Box 415
Skagway, AK 99840-0415

Southeast Alaska Tourism Council
3695 Franklin St., #205
Juneau, AK 99801
(907) 586-4777

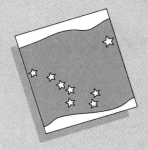

Tok Chamber of Commerce
Box 389
Mile 1314 Alaska Highway
Tok, AK 99780

Valdez Convention and Visitors Bureau
Box 1603
Valdez, AK 99686
(907) 835-2984, 835-INFO

Wasilla Chamber of Commerce
Box 871826
Wasilla, AK 99687
(907) 376-1299

Whittier Visitor Center
Box 747
Whittier, AK 99693
(907) 472-2379, 472-2327

Wrangell Visitors Bureau
Box 1078
Wrangell, AK 99929
(907) 874-3779

Index